THE COLLECTOR'S ILLUSTRATED GUIDE TO FIREARMS

THE COLLECTOR'S ILLUSTRATED GUIDE TO
FIREARMS

MARTIN MILLER

MAYFLOWER BOOKS

Contents

Acknowledgements

The greatest thanks are due to Messrs. Wallis and Wallis Ltd. of Lewes, Sussex, who have given invaluable assistance with both text and pictures. All the illustrations are from photographs they have provided, and all items shown have been offered at auction by Wallis and Wallis over the past few years.

Mr. Roy Butler, of Wallis and Wallis, is Series Editor, and this volume has been compiled and edited by Martin Miller and Judith Cairns M.A.

Preface

The Collector's Illustrated Guide to Firearms is the first in a two volume series of illustrated reference works to be published covering firearms and weapons. The second title is *The Collector's Illustrated Guide to Edged Weapons.*

The series has been developed to provide a comprehensive visual reference work which will prove invaluable in aiding the identification of pieces. Each book contains many hundreds of photographic illustrations – the only means of obtaining positive identification.

The weapons in these volumes have largely been confined to pieces that a collector or dealer would be most likely to come across. We have tended therefore to concentrate on the middle range of the market and have deliberately avoided museum pieces. These it was felt are adequately dealt with in numerous publications which illustrate such unique and priceless weapons. Although the historical significance of these weapons is undeniable, they are, on the whole, beyond the means of the private collector. The closest he would normally get to such pieces is on the other side of a display cabinet. Similar pieces to virtually all the articles included in these books are available for examination and purchase in shops and at auctions.

The photographs are fully captioned and the volumes have been subdivided in such a way as to make identification as easy as possible. The description of each piece is concise yet comprehensive, ensuring that the reader is given the best possible information. Each section of the book has a short introduction which gives a brief description of the mechanism, weapon or range of pieces and places it within its general context. A comprehensive index, bibliography, glossary and table of abbreviations used in catalogues completes each book.

These volumes will provide both the private collector and the dealer with an invaluable visual reference set. Each volume with its hundreds of photographs will do great justice to these fascinating fields. Collectively they will be the most comprehensive work on weapons available and with their wealth of pictorial and descriptive material, they will be an indispensable reference work for anyone involved in the buying and selling of Firearms and Edged Weapons.

Introduction

To defeat his enemies and protect himself have been Man's main preoccupations since his history began. One of the most effective implements of his aggression has been the firearm, and Man has constantly been involved in its invention, refinement and improvement.

Most collectors view firearms, not as lethal weapons, but as works of art in their own right, for Man has expressed in these weapons his desire to make his artifacts decorative. He has used his decorative talents to the full: chiselling, engraving, inlaying and etching. This is one of the fundamental joys for the collector, mechanical ingenuity linked to aesthetic appeal. For the collector there is also the excitement of possessing a unique piece of history. Prior to 1825 all firearms were hand-made and close study will reveal that even a pair of holster pistols have many slight differences.

The main problem encountered by the would-be collector of firearms is availability. Since the Second World War, demand has increased in all areas of collecting. Before this the main demand had been from Royalty and museums with the demand concentrated on high quality, rare pieces. Many monarchs, like Emperor Maximilian, even prided themselves in large and decorative armour. Collectors such as Maximilian were however only a small minority, for the majority of powerful collectors viewed firearms from a purely functional viewpoint.

Participation in the two World Wars has meant that people have become familiar with firearms, and have taken a collector's interest in pieces. Demand for firearms has thus increased. As is normal in the field of antiques this increased demand caused dealers to search wider and carry a larger stock of firearms. The demand has continued leading to a steep rise in prices. Consequently there is very little room in this field for uninformed amateurs. Mistakes can be very expensive for this market is well-stocked with fakes and forgeries. Many of these fakes are quite interesting in their own right but certainly cannot be placed in the same price bracket as the genuine article. Knowledge of the subject is vital. The would-be collector must make every effort to read up his subject, and to visit museums where he may actually persuade the curator to allow him to handle firearms. There is a certain 'feel' to a genuine antique firearm – a quality, a balance. This is the knowledge that can only be slowly developed through experience. But collectors can still be informed.

The obvious place to find antique firearms is in antique shops and auctions. One must approach both with some amount of caution. In the high street antique shop it is more than likely that the dealer is not a specialist in firearms, and may himself be wrongly informed. Scant information can work in the favour of the collector or against him. The dealer may miss some feature of the weapon which makes it extremely valuable, but it is just as likely that he will overvalue a quite common piece. Specialist dealers, however, have their reputations to consider, and although mistakes can still occur their valuations are backed by intricate knowledge of the field.

Auctions are possibly the best guide to the 'value' of a piece. Value is always a difficult topic – the value of an antique is simply what someone is willing to pay for it, and this can vary tremendously in different parts of the world. A collector should compare prices in various auction rooms, bearing in mind that if several dealers are bidding against each other the price could well rise above normal value. It is always wise to compare good auction catalogues with full descriptions and price lists as this will give as accurate an estimate as one is likely to find.

The Collector's Illustrated Guide to Firearms is a visual reference work, designed to assist the collector in the identification of pieces he will come across and wish to collect. The book deliberately places emphasis on the firearms the active collector can readily obtain at auction. Study it well before investing.

JAPANESE 32-BORE MATCHLOCK PISTOL 19in. Flat-topped round barrel 11½in, with signature beneath breech, hinged brass pan-cover, all brass lock and mounts, single copper barrel band, plain dark wood full stocked with impressed inscription on butt.

The Matchlock

The matchlock musket, crude as it may appear, remained the main military firearm for two centuries. It was developed at the end of the 14th century and replaced the even more cumbersome method of igniting hand-guns by glowing embers.

The main developments associated with the matchlock are, firstly, the cord, which was dipped in saltpetre, allowed to dry and which burned very slowly. And, secondly, a simple mechanical system known as the serpentine. The serpentine was simply a double curved arm pivoted at the centre and fastened to the side of the stock. The method was, basically, that the glowing end of the match was fitted into the top arm and when pressure was applied to the lower section the glowing end of the match made contact with the touch hole. The reason for its success was that the matchlock was extremely inexpensive to produce and easy to maintain. Unfortunately, it was incredibly inaccurate in its aim. However when used in battle conditions by a large number of troops, who pointed vaguely in the direction of the opposing army, it was reasonably effective.

It was found that this accuracy improved if a long barrel was used – thus the matchlock musket was born. The wooden body was also lengthened and shaped to allow the weapon to rest against the shoulder. Now that the firer could make some form of aim, sights were soon added.

As the musket developed more complicated firing mechanisms evolved. The ramrod was developed to drive the powder and the ball down into the breech and since muskets were heavy, a musketeer would carry a rest, a stick of ash with a U-shaped metal arm. The drill involved in the preparation and firing of the matchlock musket was extremely complicated and the musketeer had to perform some twenty or more movements to fire his weapon. This was not a firearm for speed.

Although many good Japanese and Indian matchlock muskets can be found, good, verified European matchlocks are extremely rare.

Matchlocks

JAPANESE

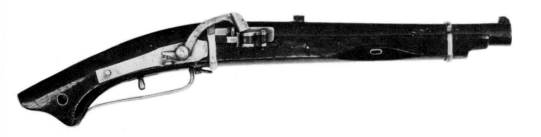

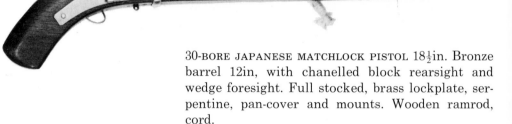

30-BORE JAPANESE MATCHLOCK PISTOL 18½in. Bronze barrel 12in, with chanelled block rearsight and wedge foresight. Full stocked, brass lockplate, serpentine, pan-cover and mounts. Wooden ramrod, cord.

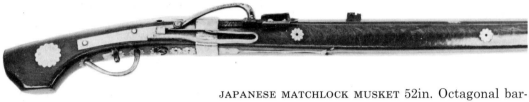

JAPANESE MATCHLOCK MUSKET 52in. Octagonal barrel, 39½in, chiselled with inscription, dragon, monster, etc, overlaid with silver. Full stocked brass mounts, brass lockplate mechanism, serpentine and swivel pan-cover, breech band engraved with kabuto and mask.

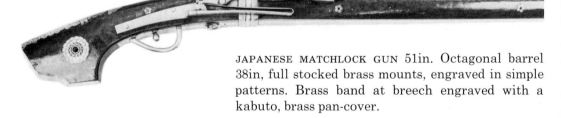

JAPANESE MATCHLOCK GUN 51in. Octagonal barrel 38in, full stocked brass mounts, engraved in simple patterns. Brass band at breech engraved with a kabuto, brass pan-cover.

18-BORE JAPANESE MATCHLOCK PISTOL 18½in. Octagonal iron barrel 11in, damascened with a silver dragon, details inlaid with copper and brass, block rearsight, turned muzzle. Full stocked, back-action brass lock, pillar mounted serpent, hinged pan-cover. Brass trigger and breech band, brass tipped iron ramrod.

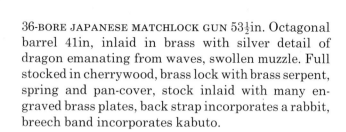

36-BORE JAPANESE MATCHLOCK GUN 53½in. Octagonal barrel 41in, inlaid in brass with silver detail of dragon emanating from waves, swollen muzzle. Full stocked in cherrywood, brass lock with brass serpent, spring and pan-cover, stock inlaid with many engraved brass plates, back strap incorporates a rabbit, breech band incorporates kabuto.

JAPANESE 29-BORE RIFLE 53in. Slightly fluted octagonal barrel 41½in, sighted, muzzle of bulbous silvered lotus bud form. Breech profusely inlaid in brass, silver and copper with dragon and clouds above waves, signed. Full stocked in typical Japanese style with brass tang engraved with stylised warrior, the other engraved mounts depicting doves, trees, shishi etc. Plain brass lock with hinged pan-cover.

HEAVY JAPANESE 12-BORE MATCHLOCK RIFLE 37in. 25in twist barrel of Persian origin, with silver bands and damascus decoration at muzzle, the pan crudely welded to the barrel at breech. Plain full stock with inlaid brass rosettes, all brass back-action lock with external brass mainspring. Butt also inlaid with brass rosettes.

30-BORE JAPANESE MATCHLOCK GUN 54in. Octagonal barrel 41½in inlaid with silver and brass flower designs and two silver storks, signed beneath breech, all brass lock with external mainspring. Full stocked with single barrel band, engraved brass mounts.

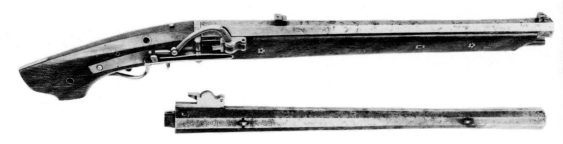

JAPANESE 40-BORE MATCHLOCK CARBINE $27\frac{1}{2}$in. Heavy plain octagonal barrel 18in, with hinged brass pan-cover and long signature beneath block. Plain brass lock, serpent and external mainspring, maple full stock with plain brass mounts and inlaid brass rosettes.

JAPANESE 20-BORE MATCHLOCK GUN $49\frac{1}{2}$in. Barrel 37in, with swollen muzzle and silver damascus but-terflies, leaves, and tendrils, signed 'Masatoshi Saku'. Brass back-action lock with internal mech-anism, plain butt and full stock, brass trigger and trigger plate.

JAPANESE 32-BORE MATCHLOCK PISTOL OR SHORT GUN 23in. Round cornered octagonal barrel $14\frac{1}{2}$in with circular section at muzzle and raised ring, inlaid with silver and brass flowers, foliage and inscription. Brass lock with internal spring and iron match-holder, brass mounts, plain polished full stock.

HEAVY 12-BORE JAPANESE MATCHLOCK WALL OR SWIVEL GUN $42\frac{1}{2}$in. Substantial steel barrel, octag-onal at bulbous muzzle $27\frac{1}{4}$in, inlaid with silver character and gold character montage signed under-neath Masayoshi. Plainly full stocked in typical Jap-anese style, plain brass lock with steel serpent.

28-BORE JAPANESE MATCHLOCK GUN 48in. Octagonal barrel 36in, with raised band at muzzle and decorated with silver damascus birds, engraved with foliage, a jelly-fish, etc. Plain full stock inlaid with small plain brass plaques. Plain all brass lock with external mainspring and impressed with maker's mark.

VAST JAPANESE MATCHLOCK WOODEN-BARRELLED WALL GUN 41in. Barrel 25in, bore $2\frac{1}{4}$in, 5 large iron barrel bands, large iron front and rearsights, brass sideplate, curving butt pierced with hole. The mechanism has side lever trigger for attachment of firing lanyard.

JAPANESE 34-BORE PILL LOCK GUN $46\frac{1}{2}$in. Ribbed octagonal barrel 35in, with swollen muzzle, bearing signature and description of method of forging beneath breech 'Sesshu No Ju Aiya Gonyemon Naka Maki' (middle roll), full stock with inlaid brass rosettes, rabbit, etc. All brass back-action lock with external mainspring, the match-holder fitted with round-nosed iron striker which is a close fit in the small pan, with hinged brass pan-cover.

28-BORE JAPANESE MATCHLOCK GUN 53in. Octagonal barrel $41\frac{1}{2}$in, with swollen overlaid octagonal muzzle, and inlaid with silver and brass dragon, waves, etc, with signature and description of method of forging beneath breech, 'Sesshu No Ju Shioya Gonyemon Saku Hankencho' (half-roll spread). Dark wood butt and full stock inlaid with engraved brass rosettes, long strip on lower side, cloud designs, branches, etc. Plain back-action lock with external mainspring.

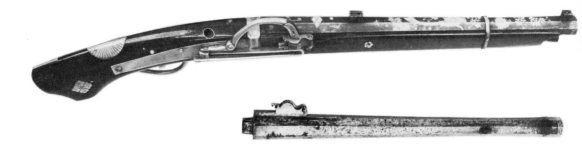

JAPANESE 28-BORE MATCHLOCK CARBINE 26½in. Heavy octagonal barrel 15½in, silver overlaid with bird of paradise amid foliage beneath moon, key design, etc. Signed beneath breech, dark wood full stock, plain brass lock, serpent and mainspring, brass mounts, including inlaid rosettes and large flower on top of butt.

24-BORE JAPANESE MATCHLOCK LONG GUN 47½in. Heavy octagonal barrel 33½in, with quartered block rear and foresights. Sliding brass pan-covers, cocking exterior brass action. Full stocked with wooden ramrod.

9-BORE MATCHLOCK ARQUEBUS, circa 1600, 67in. Half octagonal barrel 53in, tubular rearsight with fern finial, ball foresight, maker's mark 'AM' within shield. Rectangular lockplate, traces of serpent engraving to serpent with heart shaped screw. Particularly wide hooped and spurred trigger guard (to facilitate firing whilst wearing gauntlet). Distinct fishtail butt with steel butt plate, carved to receive thumb at foot of comb.

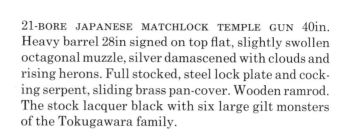

21-BORE JAPANESE MATCHLOCK TEMPLE GUN 40in. Heavy barrel 28in signed on top flat, slightly swollen octagonal muzzle, silver damascened with clouds and rising herons. Full stocked, steel lock plate and cocking serpent, sliding brass pan-cover. Wooden ramrod. The stock lacquer black with six large gilt monsters of the Tokugawara family.

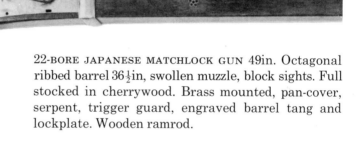

22-BORE JAPANESE MATCHLOCK GUN 49in. Octagonal ribbed barrel 36½in, swollen muzzle, block sights. Full stocked in cherrywood. Brass mounted, pan-cover, serpent, trigger guard, engraved barrel tang and lockplate. Wooden ramrod.

18-BORE JAPANESE MATCHLOCK GUN 38in. Barrel 28in with chiselled characters, carp and waterfall, block sights. Full stocked in cherrywood, brass mounted. Iron trigger guard and serpent inlaid with brass foliage at tendrils.

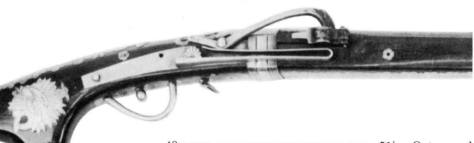

40-BORE JAPANESE MATCHLOCK GUN 51in. Octagonal barrel 39in, swollen muzzle, silver inlaid with dog of Fo amid landscape of trees, etc. Block sights. Full stocked in cherrywood, extensively overlain with engraved brass plaques and strips depicting dragon, mouse in the clouds, kabuto and chrysanthemums.

BURMESE MATCHLOCK GUN 55in. Octagonal barrel 44in, full stocked, brass lockplate and hammer, brass trigger guard, pierced brass mounts. Screw-in retaining bolts, embossed brass band to rear of breech, two brass mounts on chains.

INDIAN SUPER IMPOSED LOAD MATCHLOCK GUN TORADOR 66in. Barrel 45in full stocked, steel sideplates, swivel pan-covers, large silver bands to rear of stock the two hammers operated by single trigger.

INDIAN MATCHLOCK GUN TORADOR 67in. Octagonal barrel 50in, finely decorated at muzzle and breech and along edges with gold damascened foliate patterns. Full stocked, five barrel bands, steel sideplates with simulated gold damascened decoration. The action housing of three ivory panels, swivel pan-cover.

INDIAN MATCHLOCK GUN TORADOR 68in. Barrel 49in, the tang inlaid in gold with Indian inscription, gold damascened decoration to pan, full stocked, one brass and two Eastern silver barrel bands. Sideplates and mounts of plain polished Eastern silver, hammer with gold decoration, one silver sling swivel.

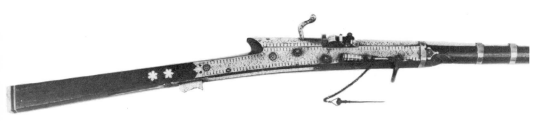

32-BORE INDIAN MATCHLOCK GUN TORADOR 69in. Barrel 48½in, silver damascened overall with a diaper repeat pattern, the muzzle of breech gold damascened with floral patterns. Full stocked, the lock sides, trigger, serpent and match cup similarly silver damascened overall with gold details. Brass barrel bands, damascened steel ramrod.

QUALITY INDIAN RAJPUT MATCHLOCK GUN TORADOR 64in. Octagonal Persian barrel 44in of watered steel, thickly gold and silver damascened overall with regular floral and foliate patterns. Full stocked, breech butting of floral carved ivory, stock overlaid with many intricately pierced steel strips and discs.

The Wheellock

The wheellocks, as a group, are without doubt the most aesthetically pleasing of all weapons. The wheellock system, which came into prominence early in the 16th century, was essentially an alternative system of ignition, using mechanical means instead of combustion. The earliest examples of this mechanism date from 1510 and for the following century it remained the most commonly used form of ignition.

At the centre of the wheellock mechanism was quite naturally a metal wheel. This had a grooved edge traversed by a series of cross cuts. The wheel was attached by a short, strong chain to a large and powerful V spring. The wheel also had a protruding square shank onto which fitted a key which served a dual purpose; it turned the wheel and compressed the mainspring. This activated the sear, which pressed forward and fitted into a notch on the inside edge of the wheel. The outside edge of the wheel projected into the lower edge of the priming pan. Set at the front of the priming pan was the dogshead or cock, which pushed the pyrites into contact with the wheel.

The mechanism was activated by pressing the trigger, which pulled back the sear and compressed the mainspring which caused the wheel to rotate rapidly. The system worked due to the fact that friction caused sparks to be produced when steel was rotated against the common mineral pyrites and these sparks fired the charge.

The powder was poured into the breech and then the lead ball placed on top. Once this was done the weapon could be left quite safely for any length of time. When it was needed only two actions were needed; firstly the dogshead had to be swung forward to place the pyrites on the wheel and, secondly, simply pull on the trigger. This made the wheellock a much more deadly weapon than the matchlock as it could be prepared ready for use.

Wheellocks could be made in any size but it was an extremely complex mechanism requiring great skill from the gunmaker. This made them expensive weapons and mainly bought by the rich, which is no doubt the reason that 16th century wheellocks are highly decorative and elaborate. It became a mode for a gentleman to show his true nobility and status.

Wheellocks were mainly made in Germany but were also popular in France and Italy. There had been very few matchlock pistols but with the introduction of the wheellock pistols gunmakers used their skills to design smaller weapons which could be stuck in the belt or in a holster – the day of the pistol had dawned.

Most of the late 16th and early 17th century wheellocks were highly decorated with a variety of materials inlaid in the stock, often mother-of-pearl, ivory, bone, steel and precious metals. As the 17th century progressed, however, the gunsmiths tended towards a plainer style which cut the costs of production slightly and a greater number were produced, particularly for some military purposes.

Wheellock hunting weapons were extremely popular with the rich, sporting class and continued to be produced long after the wheellock pistol had been replaced. The wheellock rifles were exceptionally expensive but of such exquisite craftsmanship, each individual part executed by a specialist, that they were indeed worthy of a rich nobleman. The barrels of these rifles were often chiselled or inlaid with some precious metal and were usually very heavy. One reason for this was that the weapon was held against the cheek and the heavy barrel tended to reduce recoil.

These weapons normally had hair triggers, which needed only a touch to operate the mechanism and preserved the aim.

These weapons were still in great demand long after the mechanism itself had been surpassed and this is perhaps due to the exquisite craftsmanship and decoration.

Wheellocks

GERMAN AND AUSTRIAN

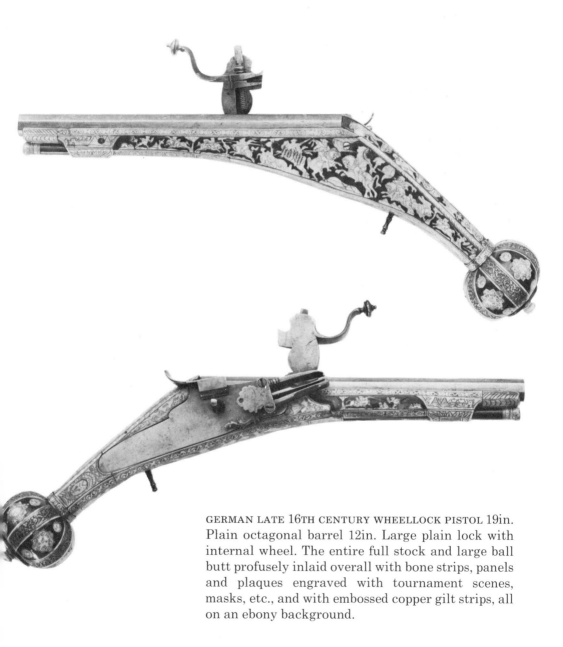

GERMAN LATE 16TH CENTURY WHEELLOCK PISTOL 19in. Plain octagonal barrel 12in. Large plain lock with internal wheel. The entire full stock and large ball butt profusely inlaid overall with bone strips, panels and plaques engraved with tournament scenes, masks, etc., and with embossed copper gilt strips, all on an ebony background.

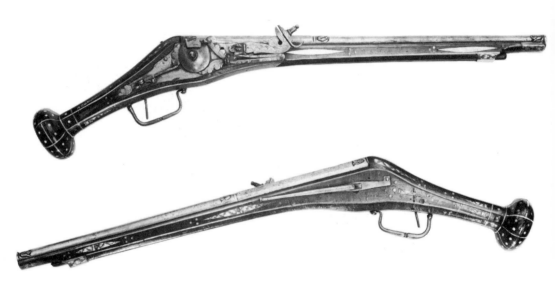

SOUTH GERMAN 16TH CENTURY WHEELLOCK PISTOL
24in. Barrel 14½in, with octagonal breech bearing
Augsburg mark. The unusually long lockplate bears
maker's mark of a barrel and three arrows, and with
engraved foliate overlay behind wheel-cover; secured by three screws, two of which secure the backplate which originally had a belt hook. The entire full
stock inlaid with bone leaves and tendrils, dogs'
heads on each side of barrel tang, and grotesque mask
on ramrod throat pipe. The large ball butt contemporary but probably an early replacement, as is
the pierced steel Brescian-type trigger guard.

PAIR OF GERMAN LATE 16TH CENTURY WHEELLOCK PIS-
TOLS 28in. 19½in barrels having octagonal breeches
with maker's marks and bands of chiselled acanthus
leaves at breech, muzzle and end of octagonal section. Flat locks with engraved foliate overlay round
wheel-covers; the flat cocks engraved with monster
heads, inside of the locks also engraved. Full stocks
and flattened ball butts inlaid with staghorn strips,
dots and engraved panels; fore-end caps and ramrod pipes also of engraved staghorn; the flattened
butts originally inlaid with large circular plaques.
Rounded iron trigger guards and flat sideplates.

UNUSUALLY SMALL GERMAN LATE 16TH CENTURY
WHEELLOCK PISTOL 15in. 8½in barrel of small bore
with raised muzzle ring and band of chiselled acanthus leaves, the breech deeply fluted and with raised
ridges. The flat lockplate engraved with roped border
and with open-work protector to external wheel. The
full stock and 'fishtail' butt inlaid with bone flowers
and tendrils, and the figure of a soldier on horseback.
Plain iron trigger guard.

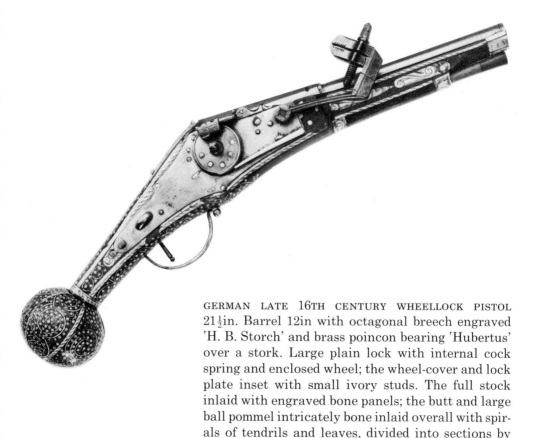

GERMAN LATE 16TH CENTURY WHEELLOCK PISTOL
21½in. Barrel 12in with octagonal breech engraved
'H. B. Storch' and brass poincon bearing 'Hubertus'
over a stork. Large plain lock with internal cock
spring and enclosed wheel; the wheel-cover and lock
plate inset with small ivory studs. The full stock
inlaid with engraved bone panels; the butt and large
ball pommel intricately bone inlaid overall with spir-
als of tendrils and leaves, divided into sections by
engraved bone strips. Plain iron trigger guard.

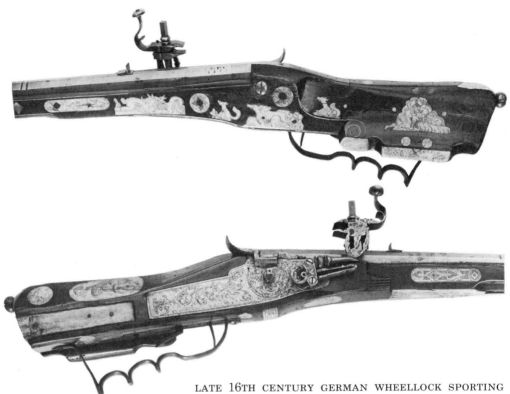

LATE 16TH CENTURY GERMAN WHEELLOCK SPORTING
GUN 51in. Octagonal barrel 39in, dated 1591 with two
leaf brass rearsight stamped 1677 at breech. The lockplate engraved with many scrolls and a grotesque
dog's head, internal wheel, cock spring bridle in form
of pierced and engraved dolphin. Full stocked, steel
mounts, scrolled fingered trigger guard to double set
triggers. Stock inlaid with many bone plaques engraved with hounds, boar, ladies in Elizabethan cos-
tume, and two embracing lovers. Sliding one piece
bone patch box cover.

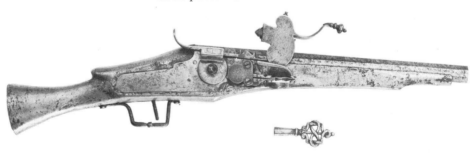

GERMAN ALL METAL MILITARY TYPE WHEELLOCK PISTOL
24in. Octagonal barrel 14in, with traces of engraving
at breech. Large plain lock, probably originally from
a rifle. The full stock and rounded 'fishtail' type butt
of hammered sheet iron; rounded trigger guard.

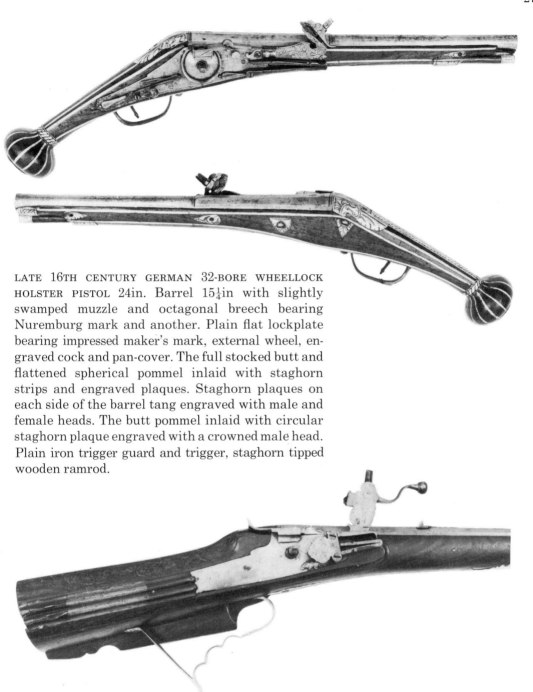

LATE 16TH CENTURY GERMAN 32-BORE WHEELLOCK
HOLSTER PISTOL 24in. Barrel 15¼in with slightly
swamped muzzle and octagonal breech bearing
Nuremburg mark and another. Plain flat lockplate
bearing impressed maker's mark, external wheel, engraved cock and pan-cover. The full stocked butt and
flattened spherical pommel inlaid with staghorn
strips and engraved plaques. Staghorn plaques on
each side of the barrel tang engraved with male and
female heads. The butt pommel inlaid with circular
staghorn plaque engraved with a crowned male head.
Plain iron trigger guard and trigger, staghorn tipped
wooden ramrod.

20-BORE BOHEMIAN WHEELLOCK SPORTING RIFLE 44in.
Octagonal rifled barrel, 31in, full stocked, enclosed
wheel, bridled cock and spring, longspur enclosed
cock head, sliding pan-cover, engraved brass mounts,
sideplate engraved with dog and stag amidst profuse
scrolls, scroll carved above three-piece horn and
wood sliding patch box cover.

32-BORE EARLY 17TH CENTURY GERMAN MILITARY
WHEELLOCK HOLSTER PISTOL. Overall length 23½in,
half octagonal barrel 16in, struck at breech with Suhl
proof marks. Full stocked, lockplate with external
wheel, sliding pan-cover, bridled cock. Plain steel
furniture, ovoid buttcap, sprung trigger, steel tipped
wooden ramrod.

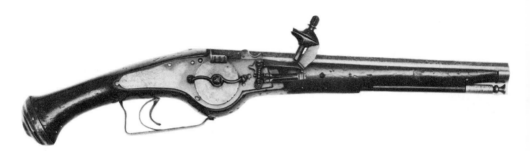

26-BORE EARLY 17TH CENTURY GERMAN MILITARY
WHEELLOCK HOLSTER PISTOL. Overall length 20½in,
octagonal barrel 12½in, struck at breech with 'H'
within crowned circle. Full stocked, lockplate with
external wheel, sliding pan-cover, bridled cock. Plain
steel furniture, octagonal faceted buttcap, rosette
sidenail plates, sprung trigger, sheet steel forecap,
baluster turned ramrod.

32-BORE MID-17TH CENTURY MILITARY WHEELLOCK PIS-
TOL 22½in. Octagonal barrel 14in full stocked, sliding
pan-cover, iron mounts, steel tipped wooden ramrod,
stock stamped with large '3' on left.

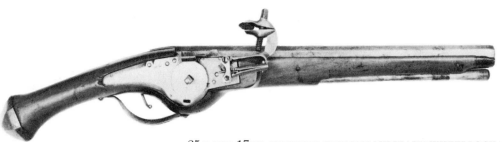

25-BORE 17TH CENTURY GERMAN MILITARY WHEELLOCK
HOLSTER PISTOL 21in. Octagonal barrel, 13½in, struck
at breech with crowned proof mark, full stocked,
sliding pan-cover, exposed wheel, bridled cock, steel
furniture, slightly boat-shaped trigger guard, octagonal faceted domed buttcap, wooden ramrod, stock
carved with letter 'F'.

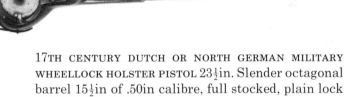

17TH CENTURY DUTCH OR NORTH GERMAN MILITARY
WHEELLOCK HOLSTER PISTOL 23½in. Slender octagonal
barrel 15½in of .50in calibre, full stocked, plain lock
and plain iron mounts, including rounded buttcap.

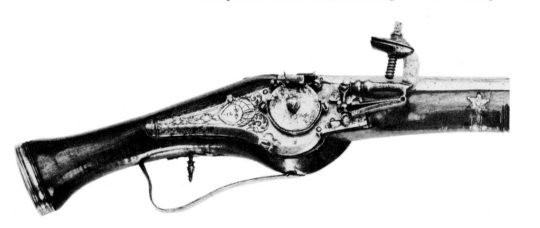

GERMAN MID-17TH CENTURY WHEELLOCK HOLSTER PIS-
TOL 25in. Octagonal barrel 17¼in with traces of floral
engraving, with the Nuremburg Guild mark at the
breech. The large lock is deeply engraved with a
human face and scrollwork, also bears the Nuremburg mark. Plain walnut stock with short flared butt
and plain iron mounts.

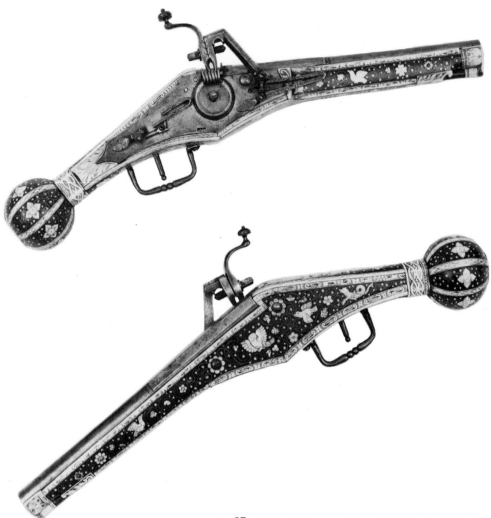

PAIR OF 27-BORE GERMAN BALL BUTTED WHEELLOCK
HOLSTER PISTOLS circa 1580/90 22½in. Slightly flared
half octagonal barrels 13in with roped steps, struck
with the maker's mark 'I.F.' above fleur-de-lys within
shield (Stockel No. a.3294) and a Gothic letter 'S'
within lozenge. Full stocked in fruitwood, some
simple, engraving to locks, fluted pans, sliding pan-
covers button released, swivel safety catches with
external springs fully enclosed wheels (covers integral with lockplates), baluster bridled cocks with
turned spurs. The stock profusely inlaid overall with
engraved staghorn borders, plaques, scrolls and pellets depicting grotesque and classical masks, squir-
rels, owls, birds, serpent-tailed griffons. Foliate tendrils with flower heads; borders mostly engraved
with fruit, geometric straps and scrolls. Bone tipped
wooden ramrods, baluster trigger guards.

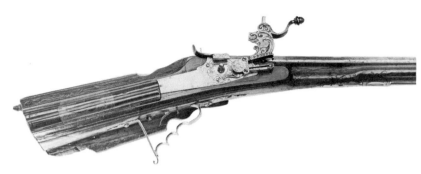

EARLY 18TH CENTURY SOUTH GERMAN OR AUSTRIAN
WHEELLOCK RIFLE 43in. Octagonal barrel 30in with
rear and foresight. Enclosed wheel, lockplate engraved with entwined marine monsters and foliage.
Cock profusely scroll engraved with form of a monster head. Bridle engraved with single flower. Full
stocked with much scroll and acanthus carving overall particularly around the cheek piece which is inlaid with a large finely engraved bone plaque bearing
the Habsburg Arms. Cheek piece also bone and horn
inlaid one edge. Horn tipped wooden ramrod. Gilt
brass furniture. Scroll engraved and finialed scrolled
brass trigger guard to set double triggers, scroll
edged piece sideplate, inset thumb piece and mount.
Horn sectioned sliding butt trap.

LATE 18TH CENTURY AUSTRIAN WHEELLOCK HUNTING
RIFLE with left hand lock, the barrel signed Wolf-
gang Leithner in Ischl 43in. Octagonal rifled barrel
30in, with exceptionally proficient adjustable peepsight lining up with back and scroll engraved rearsight. Full stocked in walnut. Scroll engraved lock
with interior wheel. Scroll engraved brass furniture, scrolled trigger guard to double set trigger
brass sideplate chiselled with hunters and deer. The
lock retained by 'butterfly folding winged' bolts. Sliding patch box cover well carved cheek piece, much
scroll and floral carving around furniture and finials.
Brass tipped wooden ramrod.

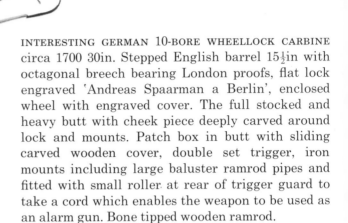

INTERESTING GERMAN 10-BORE WHEELLOCK CARBINE circa 1700 30in. Stepped English barrel 15½in with octagonal breech bearing London proofs, flat lock engraved 'Andreas Spaarman a Berlin', enclosed wheel with engraved cover. The full stocked and heavy butt with cheek piece deeply carved around lock and mounts. Patch box in butt with sliding carved wooden cover, double set trigger, iron mounts including large baluster ramrod pipes and fitted with small roller at rear of trigger guard to take a cord which enables the weapon to be used as an alarm gun. Bone tipped wooden ramrod.

ITALIAN

NORTH ITALIAN MID-17TH CENTURY WHEELLOCK HOLSTER PISTOL 23in. Octagonal barrel 15½in of .56in calibre. The plain lock of pleasing form with chiselled surround to wheel and elegant cock. Full stocked with flattened octagonal butt and plain iron mounts.

ITALIAN MID-17TH CENTURY WHEELLOCK BELT PISTOL 14in. Barrel 8¼in with octagonal breech, the lock with scroll engraved external wheel bearing inside the initials 'C.P.' over three stars. Full stocked, 'fishtail' butt, pierced steel foliate mounts.

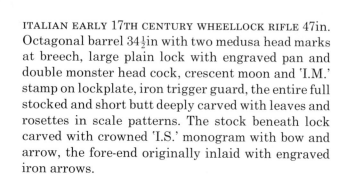

ITALIAN EARLY 17TH CENTURY WHEELLOCK RIFLE 47in. Octagonal barrel 34½in with two medusa head marks at breech, large plain lock with engraved pan and double monster head cock, crescent moon and 'I.M.' stamp on lockplate, iron trigger guard, the entire full stocked and short butt deeply carved with leaves and rosettes in scale patterns. The stock beneath lock carved with crowned 'I.S.' monogram with bow and arrow, the fore-end originally inlaid with engraved iron arrows.

MID-17TH CENTURY ITALIAN WHEELLOCK CARBINE OF GOOD FORM 40in. Half octagonal barrel 28½in stamped with maker's initials 'H.R.V.' Full stocked, exterior wheel, elegant cock baluster stemmed with foliate neck. Fern tip engraved buttband with shell worked buttcap, leaves engraved on trigger guard. Wooden ramrod.

25-BORE ITALIAN MILITARY WHEELLOCK HOLSTER PISTOL circa 1620 21in. Half octagonal barrel 13¾in. Full stocked, foliate finialed lockplate, scrolled wheel bridle, foliate chiselled cock, sliding pan-cover. Plain steel mounts, geometric sidenail plates, steel buttband with inset rosette boss. Wooden ramrod, baluster trigger.

34

MID-17TH CENTURY 22-BORE ITALIAN WHEELLOCK PIS-
TOL 21½in. Half octagonal barrel 13½in chiselled with
grotesque mask inlaid with much silver in flutes and
panels, partly engraved, ribbed muzzle. Full stocked.
The lock of classic Italian form, baluster cock and
wheel bridle. Part acanthus decorated, part baluster
turned trigger guard, baluster trigger, engraved crescent cupped buttcap, ball finial. Star sidenail plates,
baluster ramrod pipe, ramrod tip with worm behind
barrel tang, flute fore of stock.

MID-17TH CENTURY WHEELLOCK HOLSTER PISTOL 20in.
Italian barrel 13in, with fluted breech impressed 'Gio
Batt. Francino', the front 7½in of the barrel of round
section decorated with fluted herringbone design,
narrow raised bands at breech and muzzle, large
plain flat lock, the inside of the plate impressed with
'AR' maker's mark. Full stocked, in dark hardwood,
octagonal iron buttcap and fluted ramrod pipe, steel
tipped wooden ramrod.

ITALIAN MID-17TH CENTURY 26-BORE WHEELLOCK HOL-
STER PISTOL 22½in. Half octagonal barrel 15½in with
illegible mark at breech, good quality plain flat lock
with delicate tendril wheel-guard, rectangular pan,
and elegant cock, the inside of the plate impressed
with maker's circular mark of 'DB' and spray of
leaves. Plain walnut full stock with plain iron
mounts and rosette sidenail plates.

OTHER COUNTRIES OF ORIGIN

SAXON DOUBLE BARRELLED SIDE BY SIDE 34-BORE MILI-
TARY WHEELLOCK HOLSTER PISTOL 22in. Half octagonal barrels 12½in with long breech tangs extending
to butt, large plain flat locks with raised wheel-
covers, external hinged safety catches and sliding
pan-covers. Blackened full stock and ball butt with
lightly carved borders and chequered panels, iron
mounts including roped band round fore-end and
seven roped bands round ball butt (originally eight).
Slender trigger guard over double triggers, two iron
ramrods with internally threaded ends to take cleaning tools.

32-BORE SAXON WHEELLOCK RIFLE circa 1620/40 41½in.
Octagonal barrel 31in with deep six groove rifling
struck twice at breech with makers mark of a pike-
man between initials 'I.V.' The mark recurs on the
lock. Channel and leaf rearsight. Full stocked in
engraved bone inlaid fruitwood. Sprung pan-cover,
bridled wheel, exterior cock. Double set trigger,
scrolled trigger guard. Carved cheek piece with
family coat of arms incorporating four lions, the
shoulder engraved 'H.L.G.Z.N.C.' and 'L.S.' behind
barrel tang. Other inlaid plaques incorporate marine
monsters, equestro-gorgon, bust portraits, rose
heads, etc, all amid profuse bone line inlaid scrolls
and leaves, some parallel lines demarking stock
borders. Horn tipped wooden ramrod, sliding patch
box cover.

48-BORE WHEELLOCK SPORTING GUN PROBABLY FROM SAXONY circa 1620 45½in. Octagonal sighted barrel 34½in, full stocked, baluster-pieced cock, bridled spring, sprung pan-cover with long fence. Double set triggers, scrolled trigger guard, fluted forestock, carved cheek piece inlaid with engraved staghorn plaques including lion, hound, hare and rosettes. Sliding butt trap.

LATE 16TH CENTURY SAXON WHEELLOCK MILITARY HOLSTER PISTOL 22in. Half octagonal blued barrel 12½in with a coat of arms at breech between the initials 'H.R.', and the date '1590'. Plain blued lock with enclosed wheel and external hinged safety catch. The full stock and ball butt are stamped over-all to simulate natural staghorn, and are inlaid with scroll and scale engraved bone plaques. The butt inlaid with bone roundel engraved with the arms of Saxony. Bone tipped wooden ramrod.

MID-17TH CENTURY SAXON WHEELLOCK SPORTING RIFLE 42in. Octagonal sighted barrel with two leaf rear-sight 30½in dated 'ano 1663'. Top three facets inlaid with brass in a geometric looping design. Pierced cover of enclosed wheel, baluster cock bridle and throat hole cock. Full stocked in fruitwood, carved cheek piece with neat scrolled end. The stock neatly inlaid with horn discs, horn buttcap and mounts to sliding butt trap. Steel slightly scrolled trigger guard to set trigger. Bone tipped wooden ramrod.

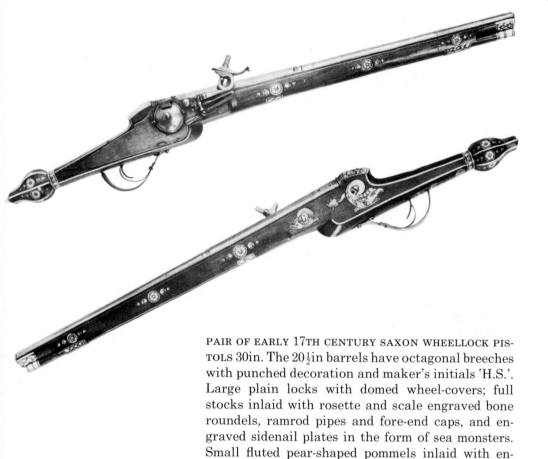

PAIR OF EARLY 17TH CENTURY SAXON WHEELLOCK PIS-
TOLS 30in. The 20½in barrels have octagonal breeches
with punched decoration and maker's initials 'H.S.'.
Large plain locks with domed wheel-covers; full
stocks inlaid with rosette and scale engraved bone
roundels, ramrod pipes and fore-end caps, and engraved sidenail plates in the form of sea monsters.
Small fluted pear-shaped pommels inlaid with engraved bone plaques and bands. Bone-tipped wooden
ramrods with threaded iron caps.

LATE 16TH CENTURY WHEELLOCK HOLSTER PISTOL 22in.
Half octagonal barrel 14in with traces of maker's
mark. Large plain lock with fretted wheel-cover; the
entire full stock and butt overlaid with polished
ebony and inlaid with entwined strapwork, engraved
bone strips and panels, male heads, and horseman
hunting a deer with dog. Flared wooden buttcap with
iron band.

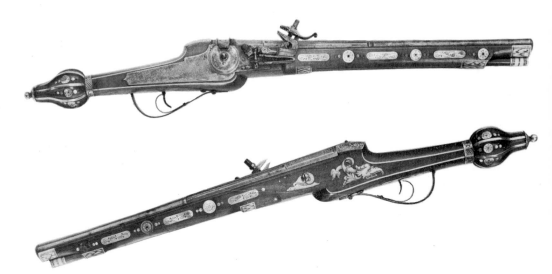

PAIR OF EARLY 17TH CENTURY SAXON WHEELLOCK PIS-
TOLS 30in. The 18½in barrels have octagonal breeches
dated 1610 and bear the poincons and initials of
Georg Gessler. Large plain locks with engraved gilt
brass wheel-covers; full stocks inlaid with mother of
pearl and staghorn plaques, the latter in the form of
snails and sea monsters. The inlay round barrel tangs
engraved with the arms of Saxony, the Deutsches
Ritter Order and the stockmaker's initials 'F.F.'.
Fluted pear-shaped pommels overlaid with silver gilt
bands and inset small mother of pearl plaques. These
pistols are from the State Guard of the Electoral
Prince, Christian II of Saxony (1591–1611).

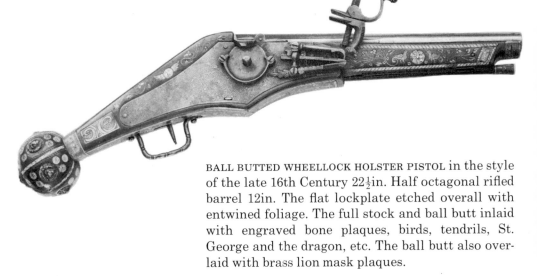

BALL BUTTED WHEELLOCK HOLSTER PISTOL in the style
of the late 16th Century 22½in. Half octagonal rifled
barrel 12in. The flat lockplate etched overall with
entwined foliage. The full stock and ball butt inlaid
with engraved bone plaques, birds, tendrils, St.
George and the dragon, etc. The ball butt also overlaid with brass lion mask plaques.

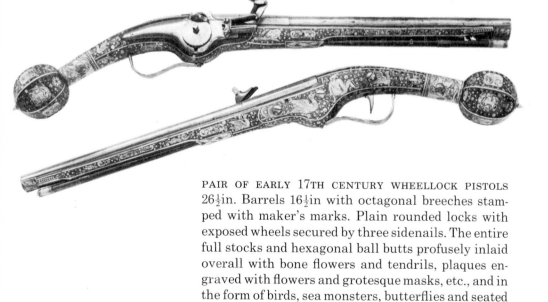

BRESCIAN 17TH CENTURY WHEELLOCK PISTOL 24in. The 16½in barrel of .58in calibre with octagonal breech. Large plain lock. The full stock, which terminates in a flared flat-ended butt, has simple overlaid open-work iron mounts and stout round section trigger guard.

MID-17TH CENTURY MILITARY WHEELLOCK HOLSTER PISTOL 24½in. The slender 16¾in barrel of .50in calibre, having two armourer's marks on the octagonal breech. The plain lock bears the maker's mark 'E.M.' on the inside. Natural wood full stock with plain iron mounts.

PAIR OF EARLY 17TH CENTURY WHEELLOCK PISTOLS 26½in. Barrels 16½in with octagonal breeches stamped with maker's marks. Plain rounded locks with exposed wheels secured by three sidenails. The entire full stocks and hexagonal ball butts profusely inlaid overall with bone flowers and tendrils, plaques engraved with flowers and grotesque masks, etc., and in the form of birds, sea monsters, butterflies and seated ram's headed figures. Plain iron trigger guards and ramrod pipes. Bone tipped wooden ramrods.

COMPOSITE 24-BORE LATE 16TH CENTURY WHEELLOCK MUSKET 50in. Barrel 33½in octagonal and polygonal at breech. Full stocked, Italian lock with foliate engraved cock, automatic pan-cover, scroll engraved bridled wheel and light fence, struck internally with maker's mark. Stock inlaid with engraved mother of pearl, bone and ivory, in foliate and floral scrolls with pellets, roundels and beasts, including lions supporting crowned emperor's bust, mythical beasts supporting female bust, long-eared caryatid, humanesque dragons, etc. Linear engraved borders.

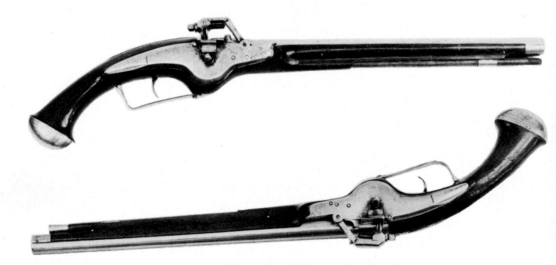

BRACE OF 16-BORE MID-17TH CENTURY SWEDISH MILITARY WHEELLOCK PISTOLS 24½in and 25in overall. Barrels 16½in with full length top rib for sighting stamped with 'P' at breech. Full stocked, enclosed wheellocks, automatically opening pan-covers, cocks sit on rear of plates, retained by three sidenail bolts. Crescent shaped concave buttcaps, sprung triggers, L-shaped trigger guards. Fluted stocks, steel fore-ends, pipes and tipped wooden ramrods.

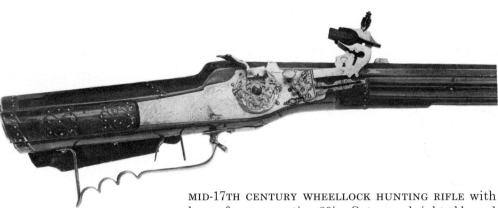

MID-17TH CENTURY WHEELLOCK HUNTING RIFLE with bore of square section 39in. Octagonal sighted barrel 28in, with faint fleur-de-lys at breech. Lockplate engraved with hounds chasing stag, pierced gilt wheelcover with two lions rampant supporting a crown over a lion passant. Gilt cock, spring bridle in form of lion rampant. Full stocked in fruitwood, fluted fore of stock; slightly scrolled carved cheek piece on butt with semi-circular gadrooning enriched with brass pique work. Florally engraved bone sidenail plates, forecap, ramrod pipe and butt plate, set trigger, scrolled trigger guard, floral and scroll carved sliding butt trap with brass pique work. Well restored bone capped wooden ramrod. The Danish gunmaker, Andreas Neidhart of Elsinore, specialised in making wheellock guns with barrels of peculiar section.

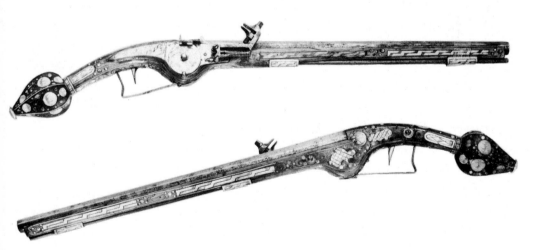

PAIR OF MID-17TH CENTURY WHEELLOCK HOLSTER PISTOLS 27½in. One octagonal barrel 18in, the other 18½in. Plain military style locks; the full stocks and hexagonal pear-shaped butts inlaid with engraved staghorn plaques.

17TH CENTURY 30-BORE MILITARY WHEELLOCK HOLSTER PISTOL, probably used by Sir Thomas Otley during the Civil War, 23¾in overall. Plain octagonal barrel 15½in, plain lock with external wheel and bearing an impressed maker's mark on the inside. Plain full stocked with iron ramrod pipe, the butt of unusual shape, being almost straight with a slightly down-turned swollen finial, sprung trigger with no provision for trigger guard, original wooden ramrod. Probably dates from the second quarter of the 17th century. The form of the stock around the ramrod throathole and the absence of a trigger guard are characteristic of a small group of early 17th century English pistols, suggesting that the original stock was damaged at a very early date and that the pistol was restocked by an English gunsmith. The pistol was purchased from the family home of Sir Thomas Otley, who fought in the Civil War.

COMPOSITE INLAID WHEELLOCK PISTOL 'PUFFER' 19½in. Barrel 9in stamped at breech with Spanish maker's marks, including the stamp of Santos, retaining some original gilt overlay. Barrel engraved in gilt with fine large upstanding Roman warrior. Full stocked, German military 17th century wheellock lock. Stock inlaid with engraved staghorn plaques depicting Roman military horn blower, 17th and 18th century infantrymen, musketeer, Orpheus, cherubs, stag and flowers, etc.

The Snaphaunce

The wheellock mechanism had many limitations. It was liable to jam, expensive to produce and any damage could only be repaired by an experienced armourer. Gunmakers all over Europe sought a cheaper and easier mechanism. It was the Dutch who came up with the Snaphaunce.

The name derived from the Dutch words 'snap hann' meaning 'snapping hen', probably from the pecking movement of the cock.

The snaphaunce overcame many of the difficulties of the wheellock, it used a durable flint, it was very cheap to produce and could be repaired more easily. The complex wheellock mechanism was replaced by a V spring and a metal arm. The cock, in this new mechanism, was a curved arm fitted at one end of the lock, with the flint held in a pair of jaws. The cock, actuated by the V spring, was bent back by the thumb until it engaged with a horizontal sear. When this was released by the trigger, the flint slid down the face of the steel to produce the sparks. The sparks fell into the priming pan and ignited the main charge via the touch hole.

The Snaphaunce appeared around 1540–50 and could be produced in quantity for use in pistols and longarms. The mechanism quickly spread over Northern Europe but was not introduced all over Europe due to the parallel development of the simpler mechanism – the flintlock.

The snaphaunce, however, remained popular in Northern Italy, Spain and North Africa long after it had been discarded in other countries. The Italian craftsmen were well-known for their superb decoration and chiselling on the snaphaunce pistols.

Often if the snaphaunce lock is removed, a date will be found inscribed on the inside of the lockplate.

Interesting to collectors, and even rarer than the genuine European variety, are the Scottish snaphaunce pistols made until the end of the 17th century. The snaphaunce pistol was almost the first really fine weapon made in the country. In general, genuine snaphaunces, whether pistols or longarms, are the scarcest of all the antique firearms and are extremely collectable.

CONTINENTAL & EASTERN

32-BORE MID-17TH CENTURY GERMAN SNAPHAUNCE HUNTING RIFLE 33½in. Octagonal barrel 19½in, twin line pellet engraved breech with maker's mark 'H.R.' Fixed brass sights, full stocked, lock with automatically opening pan-cover, adjustable set hair trigger, steel trigger guard, buttplate and ramrod tip, wooden ramrod, butt carved with cheek piece and sliding trap.

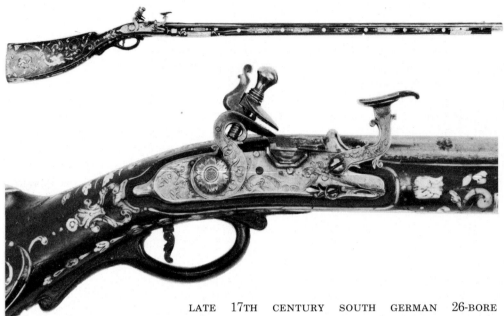

LATE 17TH CENTURY SOUTH GERMAN 26-BORE SNAPHAUNCE GUN 48½in. Plain round barrel 35½in with engraved tang and single engraved spray at breech, flat lock engraved with scrolls and serpent head, the plate bearing the initials 'F.M.' on the inside. Full stock and sweeping butt of fruitwood with wooden trigger guard, the entire stock inlaid with engraved staghorn tendrils, mythical beasts and plaques with female figures, also a few pieces of mother of pearl inlay.

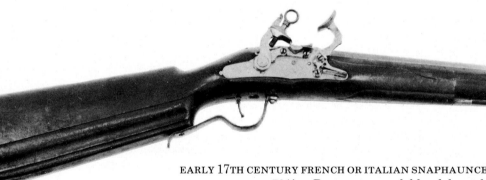

EARLY 17TH CENTURY FRENCH OR ITALIAN SNAPHAUNCE SPORTING GUN 70½in. Part octagonal blued barrel, 56¼in with brass sights and channel rearsight stamped 'ZZO', with four tri-pellet stamps Cominazzo. Full stocked in walnut, fine quality lock with automatically opening pan-cover, bridled battery, curved cock, sharply down-falling fluted club butt of regular cross section, simple trigger guard. Brass tipped, wooden ramrod.

PAIR OF 36-BORE ITALIAN SNAPHAUNCE PISTOLS BY BAS-
TIANO GIUSTI circa 1740 10¼in. Half octagonal barrels
5¾in bearing brass poincons of the barrel maker
being crowned 'XICOI' and with a horse. Full stocked
in walnut. Slightly banana-shaped lockplates linear
engraved with floral teats, reclining youths and
maker's name. Scrolled and scroll engraved with
'Steels' also engraved throat hole cocks. The cock
bolts well engraved with large flower heads. Automatic sliding pan-covers. Scroll engraved brass furniture. Sideplates and escutcheons with male busts.
Longspur buttcaps engraved with flowers, grotesque
mask bosses in relief, original brass tipped wood ramrods.

MID-18TH CENTURY 36-BORE ITALIAN SNAPHAUNCE PIS-
TOL 9¾in. Half octagonal barrel, 5in engraved 'A Tor-
tiglione'. Full stocked, engraved lockplate, cock and
steel with grotesque mask, serpent and bird; automatically opening pan-cover. Brass furniture, longspur buttcap engraved with flowers, chiselled with
foliage, the boss chiselled as a grotesque mask. Scroll
engraved sideplate, crowned escutcheon and barrel
tang surround. Finialed trigger guard and throat
pipe.

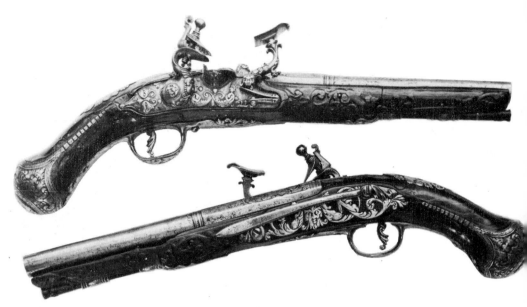

PAIR OF 32-BORE TUSCAN OR BRESCIAN SNAPHAUNCE
BELT PISTOLS circa 1700 14in. Half octagonal barrels
8½in chiselled at breech with large classical helmeted
busts in relief surrounded by scrolls. Full stocked
in carved walnut, the locks of fine workmanship,
slightly banana-shaped lockplates chiselled in relief
with grotesque masks at teat ends, opposing busts
joined by scrolls in centres. Automatic sliding pan-
covers, human and grotesque masks on cocks, cock
bolts, pans, and frizzen shanks. Pierced steel sideplates with females, mask and serpent head, chiselled
steel furniture, incorporating masks, pierced trigger
guard finials and escutcheons with opposing nude
female busts as supporters. Scrolled triggers, wood
ramrods, with screw and worm tips. Steel belt hooks.

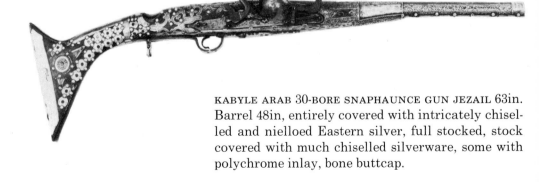

KABYLE ARAB 30-BORE SNAPHAUNCE GUN JEZAIL 63in.
Barrel 48in, entirely covered with intricately chiselled and nielloed Eastern silver, full stocked, stock
covered with much chiselled silverware, some with
polychrome inlay, bone buttcap.

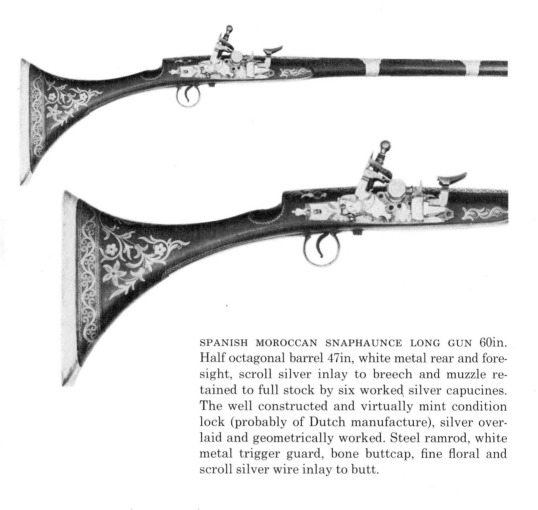

SPANISH MOROCCAN SNAPHAUNCE LONG GUN 60in.
Half octagonal barrel 47in, white metal rear and foresight, scroll silver inlay to breech and muzzle retained to full stock by six worked silver capucines.
The well constructed and virtually mint condition
lock (probably of Dutch manufacture), silver overlaid and geometrically worked. Steel ramrod, white
metal trigger guard, bone buttcap, fine floral and
scroll silver wire inlay to butt.

SPANISH MOROCCAN SNAPHAUNCE LONG GUN 62in.
Half octagonal barrel 48in, scroll silver inlay to barrel overall, gold poincons at breech, retained to full
stock by five worked silver capucines. The well constructed and virtually mint condition lock, silver
overlaid and geometrically worked. Wooden ramrod,
brass trigger guard, bone buttcaps, fine floral and
scroll silver wire inlay to butt.

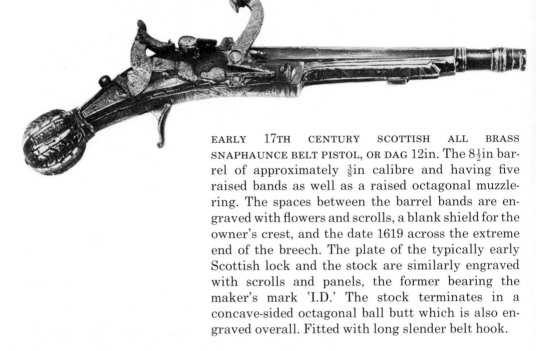

EARLY 17TH CENTURY SCOTTISH ALL BRASS SNAPHAUNCE BELT PISTOL, OR DAG 12in. The 8½in barrel of approximately ⅜in calibre and having five raised bands as well as a raised octagonal muzzle-ring. The spaces between the barrel bands are engraved with flowers and scrolls, a blank shield for the owner's crest, and the date 1619 across the extreme end of the breech. The plate of the typically early Scottish lock and the stock are similarly engraved with scrolls and panels, the former bearing the maker's mark 'I.D.' The stock terminates in a concave-sided octagonal ball butt which is also engraved overall. Fitted with long slender belt hook.

GEORGIAN COPY OF A SCOTTISH ALL METAL LEFT-HAND SNAPHAUNCE BELT PISTOL 18in. Barrel 12½in with bands of raised decoration, the typically early Scottish form of Snaphaunce lock bearing maker's mark 'R.G. Edr', dated 1615, and engraved overall with entwined Celtic strapwork. The lockplate, entire stock and octagonal globose butt are of brass deeply engraved overall with intricate entwined strapwork, and the extremity of the butt contains a screw-in pricker also with a globose brass head. Long slender engraved belt hook, steel ramrod with baluster turned end, and spirally fluted trigger.

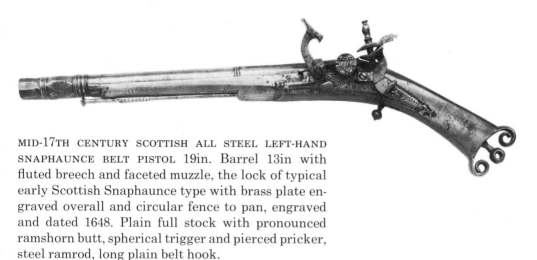

MID-17TH CENTURY SCOTTISH ALL STEEL LEFT-HAND
SNAPHAUNCE BELT PISTOL 19in. Barrel 13in with
fluted breech and faceted muzzle, the lock of typical
early Scottish Snaphaunce type with brass plate engraved overall and circular fence to pan, engraved
and dated 1648. Plain full stock with pronounced
ramshorn butt, spherical trigger and pierced pricker,
steel ramrod, long plain belt hook.

LATE 17TH CENTURY SCOTTISH ALL STEEL SNAPHAUNCE
BELT PISTOL 12½in. Rounded barrel 8in, with flared
octagonal muzzle and five engraved silver baluster
bands, the fence of the pan engraved 1674. Belt hook
on left of stock, lobe-shaped butt finial, ball trigger.

The Flintlock

The snaphaunce mechanism had certainly been an improvement but it was realised by many that it could be refined and simplified even further. The main drawback of the snaphaunce was that the pan-cover had to be pushed clear at the moment of firing and the inherent (concomitant) danger, that this might not function. The French gunmaker, Marin Le Bourgeoys, produced the flintlock mechanism, which combined the action of striking sparks while simultaneously uncovering the pan. This mechanism was to become standard, with various modifications, for the next two hundred years.

Le Bourgeoys also adopted the 'tumbler' mechanism. This was situated inside the lockplate and connected to the cock. The shaped section of the tumbler was designed to be engaged by the rear end of the mainspring. Pressing against the rear of the tumbler was a flat pointed sear which was again held under pressure by a small spring. As the tumbler rotated the point of the sear engaged with a notch. This held the firing mechanism until pressure was applied to the trigger.

The really new feature of this mechanism was that the sear swung vertically and had a point which engaged in two notches in the tumbler. This gave half-cock and full-cock and made the weapon much safer. It also made it an extremely practical military weapon.

The flintlock was much easier to load and fire than earlier weapons. The powder and ball were poured down the barrel, a pinch of priming powder placed in the pan. The pan cover closed and the cock pulled back until it locked. When the trigger was pressed it released the cock and the resulting sparks fired the charge.

Many gunmakers went straight from making wheellocks to flintlocks and hence the shape of many early flintlocks is extremely reminiscent of the wheellock with a large bulge at the end of the stock (which had been designed to hold the wheel). As this was no longer necessary this disappeared and the stocks became slimmer. The barrels were in general long and fired only a small diameter bullet but the great benefit of the flintlock was that it was fitted to every conceivable type of weapon, from great longarms to muff pistols. The second most popular type of flintlock (and earlier than the French lock) was the Miquelet lock, developed primarily in the Mediterranean. The cock was normally squat and angular and the jaws were secured by a set-screw which had a pivoted bar at the top. This ensured a firm grip. The most obvious distinguishing feature was that the mainspring was fitted on the outside of the lockplate. The safety position was secured by a small hook – the dog. This 'dog' engaged with a buffer as the pull needed on the French lock was extremely heavy.

The greatest advantage of the flintlock was that it was extremely reliable. It was much more a development than an invention, taking many features from the miquelet and snaphaunce but it was certainly an extremely successful development and as previously mentioned remained the most popular firearm action well into the 19th century.

POCKET PISTOLS – FLINTLOCK

Due to the introduction of the wheellock followed by the flintlock mechanisms weapons could be manufactured to any size. Gunmakers now sought to make a gun which would fit conveniently into the pocket.

Travel had increased enormously in the 16th and 17th centuries but it was extremely hazardous, whether in the country or in the town. It also became essential to have a small gun to protect oneself at home. Holster pistols were used when travelling on horseback but it was extremely cumbersome and inconvenient to have a large pistol when walking about. The 17th century pocket pistols were basically scaled-down replicas of the holster pistol of the period, with a few modifications, and also usually had a small ball trigger and no trigger guard.

The distinction between the pocket pistol (or sometimes overcoat pistol) and the muff pistol was mainly one of size. The smaller muff pistol was placed as the name suggests in the muff.

The main concern of the gunmakers was that these pistols should be streamlined enough not to catch in clothing, particularly as they would frequently be drawn in a hurry. The boxlock design was, therefore, adopted. This involved the lock being mounted centrally above the breech and the touch hole was drilled through the top of the barrel. Another identifying feature was that the frizzen spring was flush with the top of the barrel.

The boxlock pocket pistol could not be aimed but as it was primarily a weapon of personal defence and would be used for hand-to-hand combat, this was not deemed important.

Barrels were short and the ramrod was dispensed with. To load the pistol one merely unscrewed the barrel, inserted the powder and the ball directly into the breech and screwed on the barrel.

Since this pistol's main function was one of speed in a defence situation it had to be carried at half cock. One of its main initial dangers was that it would go off accidentally. Hence it was fitted with at least one safety catch and frequently two. The most common was the bar type which slipped forward to lock the frizzen. Another type was the sliding trigger guard which locked the action at half cock.*

These pistols were cheap and easy to manufacture and extremely popular and, hence, comparatively many have survived.

POCKET PISTOLS

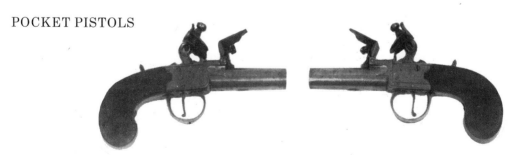

PAIR OF 40-BORE FLINTLOCK BOXLOCK POCKET PISTOLS
6¼in. Screw-off barrels 1¾in, by Forth, York. London proved, plain line-bordered frames, top thumb safeties, plain walnut slab butts.

* For pistols without trigger guards the trigger often operated on a spring which lowered the trigger when the pistol was cocked, returning to its recess when finger pressure was removed after firing.

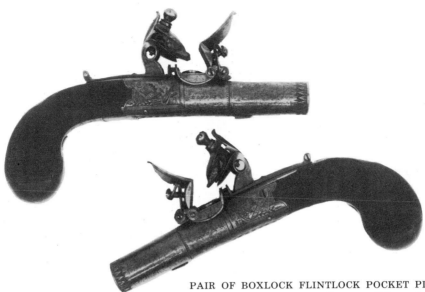

PAIR OF BOXLOCK FLINTLOCK POCKET PISTOLS by H.
Nock circa 1800 6½in. Screw-off barrels 1¾in, Birmingham proved, fern tip engraved muzzles. Rounded
frames, well engraved with Britannia shield trophies.
Top thumb safety bolts through to tension sprung
frizzens. Double friction rollers on frizzens concealed
triggers. Chequered butts with silver escutcheons
engraved with 'R'.

PAIR OF BRASS FRAMED AND BRASS BARRELLED FLINT-
LOCK BOXLOCK PISTOLS 7in. Screw-off barrels 2½in, by
Innes, Edinburgh, London proved. Frames engraved
with trophies of arms, hidden triggers, top thumb
safeties.

FLINTLOCK BOXLOCK POCKET PISTOL by Ino Richards 9in. Turn-off barrel 4in, London proved, frame engraved with military trophies and 'Ino Richards Strand London'. Sliding top thumb safety catch, tension sprung frizzen, concealed trigger, rounded walnut butt with silver grotesque buttmask and oval silver escutcheon.

FLINTLOCK BOXLOCK POCKET PISTOL 6¼in. Screw-off barrel 1½in with engraved bands at muzzle and breech, by Kimberley and Roberts, Birmingham, Birmingham proved. Frame engraved with trophies of arms, raised pan, folding trigger, top thumb safety catch through to frizzen, rollers on frizzen spring, plain rounded walnut butt with oval silver escutcheon.

BRASS FRAMED FLINTLOCK BOXLOCK POCKET PISTOL 6in. Barrel 1¾in, by R. Wilson, London, sideplates engraved with military trophies, sliding bar top thumb safety catch, slab sided diced wood butt inlaid with silver escutcheon, bearing owners initials, Birmingham proved, folding trigger.

FLINTLOCK BOXLOCK POCKET PISTOL by Jones and Co., with spring bayonet, 7¾in. Turn-off barrel 2½in, 3in sprung bayonet released by sliding trigger guard, London proved, trophy engraved frame with maker's name in oval, sliding top thumb safety catch through cock to tension sprung frizzen, slab walnut butt with silver escutcheon.

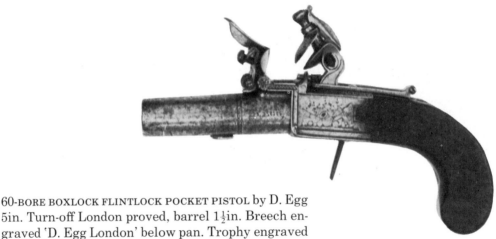

60-BORE BOXLOCK FLINTLOCK POCKET PISTOL by D. Egg 5in. Turn-off London proved, barrel 1½in. Breech engraved 'D. Egg London' below pan. Trophy engraved frame including a classical and a contemporary trophy of arms. Sliding top thumb safety catch through throat hole cock to double friction roller tension sprung teardrop frizzen. Raised pan, fine border engraving overall with laurel spray surrounding concealed trigger. Slab walnut butt.

FLINTLOCK BOXLOCK POCKET PISTOL 5½in. Barrel 1¼in, military trophies on sideplates, diced wood butt, sliding bar top thumb safety catch.

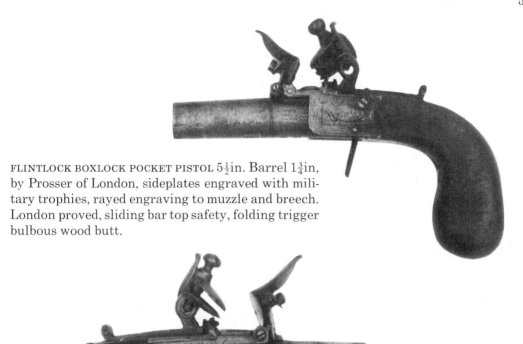

FLINTLOCK BOXLOCK POCKET PISTOL $5\frac{1}{2}$in. Barrel $1\frac{3}{4}$in, by Prosser of London, sideplates engraved with military trophies, rayed engraving to muzzle and breech. London proved, sliding bar top safety, folding trigger bulbous wood butt.

GOOD QUALITY 36-BORE FLINTLOCK BOXLOCK POCKET PISTOL $6\frac{1}{4}$in. Screw-off barrel $1\frac{1}{2}$in, by Dixon, Leicester, Birmingham proved. Frame engraved with trophies of arms, hidden trigger raised rectangular pan, top thumb safety catch through to frizzen, partly chequered walnut slab butt with white metal escutcheon.

BRASS BARRELLED AND BRASS FRAMED FLINTLOCK BOXLOCK BLUNDERBUSS POCKET PISTOL 7in. Slight swamped barrel $2\frac{1}{2}$in with octagonal breech bearing Birmingham proofs, by Hill, London, the frame engraved with trophies of flags, top thumb safety catch, plain slab butt.

BRASS BARRELLED AND BRASS FRAMED FLINTLOCK BOX-LOCK BLUNDERBUSS POCKET PISTOL 6½in. Bell-mouthed barrel, 2½in with octagonal breech bearing London proofs, by Oakes, London, the frame engraved with gadrooned laurel leaves, top thumb safety, steel trigger guard, brass tipped ramrod in two pipes beneath barrel, plain slab butt. Circa 1790.

CONTINENTAL MID-18TH CENTURY ALL STEEL FLINT-LOCK BOXLOCK POCKET PISTOL 5½in. Screw-off barrel 1½in, the frame simply engraved with Britannia shield, etc. and 'Segalas London', imitation London proofs at breech, scroll engraved steel butt, ring-neck cock. Originally fitted with sliding trigger guard, safety locking frizzen.

48-BORE FLINTLOCK CANNON BARRELLED BOXLOCK SIDECOCK POCKET PISTOL by Eubanck, circa 1685, 6¼in. Turn-off cannon barrel 2in, octagonal faceted breech, proved under ribbed trigger guard with London proofs and star over 'T.G.' Rounded cock and frizzen with L-shaped frizzen spring, signed 'Eubanck' beneath pan, scroll engraved top strap, walnut butt foliate carved at side and top, small star on bulbous butt.

52-BORE FLINTLOCK CANNON BARRELLED POCKET PIS-
TOL by I. Shorey, circa 1680, 7in. Turn-off cannon
barrel $2\frac{1}{4}$in, muzzle keyed for turning off, deep London proofs with maker's mark of a star over initials
'I.S.', foliate engraved ribbed breech. Linear engraved rounded banana-shaped lockplate with 'I.
Shorey'. Button trigger, foliate finialed sideplate and
trigger plate, walnut butt with foliate carving en-
veloping bulbous butt.

CANNON BARRELLED FLINTLOCK BOXLOCK POCKET PIS-
TOL, circa 1770, 8in overall. Screw-off barrel $2\frac{1}{4}$in,
London and 'foreigner's' proofs at breech, the frame
engraved with foliate scrolls and signed 'King, London'. Swan-necked cock, the top strap retained by pin
through butt, sliding walnut guard safety, frizzen
spring in top of breech, plain walnut slab butt.

PAIR OF BRASS FRAMED AND BARRELLED FLINTLOCK
BOXLOCK CANNON BARRELLED POCKET PISTOLS by
Freeman, circa 1780, 8in. Turn-off barrels $2\frac{1}{2}$in,
Tower proved, dog tooth border and scroll engraved
frames with 'Freeman, London', sliding trigger guard
safety catches, frizzen springs sunk in breech tops,
slab walnut butts inlaid with fine scroll and rocaille
silver wirework designs.

PAIR OF FRENCH CANNON BARRELLED BOXLOCK FLINT-
LOCK POCKET PISTOLS by Bizovard, circa 1780, 6in.
Turn-off barrels 1½in, finely engraved frames with
'Bizovard A Paris', foliate and border engraving,
necks and bellies of cocks engraved with serpents,
engraved frizzens, sliding trigger guard, safeties engraved with military trophies, rounded walnut butts
carved with a rose behind barrel tang.

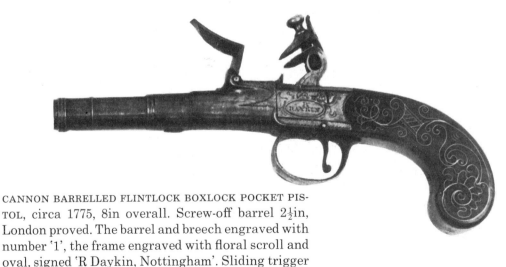

CANNON BARRELLED FLINTLOCK BOXLOCK POCKET PIS-
TOL, circa 1775, 8in overall. Screw-off barrel 2½in,
London proved. The barrel and breech engraved with
number '1', the frame engraved with floral scroll and
oval, signed 'R Daykin, Nottingham'. Sliding trigger
guard safety, frizzen spring in top of breech, the slab
butt inlaid overall with silver wire scrolls.

LATE 18TH CENTURY CANNON BARRELLED FLINTLOCK BOXLOCK POCKET PISTOL 7in. Screw-off barrel 2in by Allen, Poole, the frame engraved with rocailles and flowers and with Tower private proofs at breech. Flat frizzen spring on frizzen, slab butt inlaid overall with silver wire scrolls and with oval silver escutcheon.

48-BORE QUEEN ANNE STYLE CANNON BARRELLED FLINTLOCK BOXLOCK POCKET PISTOL by Ketland and Co., circa 1770, 8in. Turn-off barrel 2¼in, London proved, nicely scroll and linear engraved frame with maker's name. Frizzen spring sunk in top of barrel, scroll and rocaille silver wire inlaid with walnut butt.

18TH CENTURY CANNON BARRELLED FLINTLOCK BOXLOCK POCKET PISTOL 7¼in. Screw-off barrel 1¾in, by Grist and Son, Sarum, London proved, scroll engraved frame, sliding trigger guard safety, ring neck cock, plain walnut slab butt, with oval silver escutcheon.

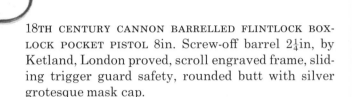

18TH CENTURY CANNON BARRELLED FLINTLOCK BOX-
LOCK POCKET PISTOL 8in. Screw-off barrel $2\frac{1}{4}$in, by
Ketland, London proved, scroll engraved frame, sliding trigger guard safety, rounded butt with silver
grotesque mask cap.

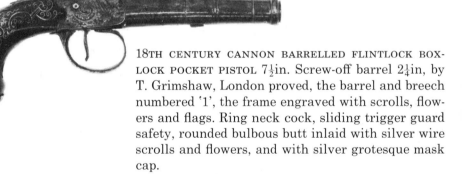

18TH CENTURY CANNON BARRELLED FLINTLOCK BOX-
LOCK POCKET PISTOL $7\frac{1}{2}$in. Screw-off barrel $2\frac{1}{4}$in, by
T. Grimshaw, London proved, the barrel and breech
numbered '1', the frame engraved with scrolls, flowers and flags. Ring neck cock, sliding trigger guard
safety, rounded bulbous butt inlaid with silver wire
scrolls and flowers, and with silver grotesque mask
cap.

BELGIAN ALL STEEL FLINTLOCK BOXLOCK POCKET PIS-
TOL 6in. Turn-off rifled cannon barrel $1\frac{1}{2}$in, sliding
trigger guard safety through to frizzen, frizzen spring
sunk in breech top. Rocaille and scroll engraved slab
butt and frame with maker's name 'I Corbusier' with
trace of address.

61

52-BORE CANNON BARRELLED FLINTLOCK BOXLOCK
POCKET PISTOL 8½in. Screw-off barrel 3in, by Pyke,
Bridgewater. London proved, frame engraved with
rocailles and maker's name within scrolls, frizzen
spring in top of barrel, plain mahogany slab butt.

PAIR OF ALL STEEL BELGIAN FLINTLOCK BOXLOCK POC-
KET PISTOLS engraved 'Segalis', circa 1750, retaining
all their original case colour hardened finish, 6in
overall. Turn-off cannon barrels 1½in. Engraved
overall with rocaille, scrolls and foliage, 'Segalis
London' within banners on frames. Sliding trigger
guard safety catches locking frizzens, frizzen springs
sunk in breeches.

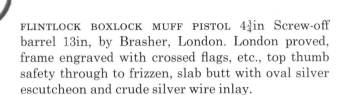

FLINTLOCK BOXLOCK MUFF PISTOL 4¾in Screw-off barrel 13in, by Brasher, London. London proved, frame engraved with crossed flags, etc., top thumb safety through to frizzen, slab butt with oval silver escutcheon and crude silver wire inlay.

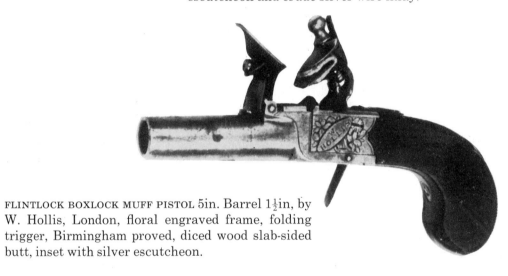

FLINTLOCK BOXLOCK MUFF PISTOL 5in. Barrel 1½in, by W. Hollis, London, floral engraved frame, folding trigger, Birmingham proved, diced wood slab-sided butt, inset with silver escutcheon.

FLINTLOCK BOXLOCK MUFF PISTOL, circa 1820, 4¼in. Screw-off barrel 18in with engraved bands at breech and muzzle, by C. Moore, London. London proved, scroll engraved frame, hidden trigger, top thumb safety catch through to frizzen, raised pan with rollers on frizzen spring, rounded chequered butt with rectangular silver escutcheon.

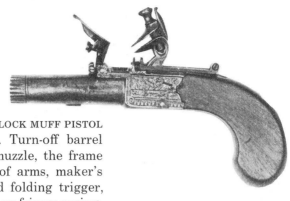

LATE 18TH CENTURY FLINTLOCK BOXLOCK MUFF PISTOL
by McLaughlan, Edinburgh, 5in. Turn-off barrel
1½in, fern tip engraved band at muzzle, the frame
engraved with military trophies of arms, maker's
name and 'Edinburgh'. Concealed folding trigger,
safety bar engaging frizzen, rollers on frizzen spring,
plain walnut slab-sided wood butt with blank silver
escutcheon.

LATE 18TH CENTURY FLINTLOCK BOXLOCK MUFF PISTOL
4½in. Screw-off barrel 1¼in, by D. Egg, London
proved. Frame engraved with trophies of arms and
strapwork borders, concealed cock screw, the cock
engraved with a fish or serpent, hidden trigger
surrounded by leaf engraving, top safety through
to frizzen, rollers on frizzen spring, plain walnut
slab butt.

OVERCOAT PISTOLS

SMALL 30-BORE IRISH FLINTLOCK OVERCOAT PISTOL by
Holland of Dublin 7in. Round barrel 3in, engraved
'Dublin' in sighting channel and stamped 'W.A. 348'
(census No). Full stocked, stepped lockplate foliate
engraved with 'Holland', French style cock, roller on
frizzen spring, engraved pineapple finialed trigger
guard, swivel ramrod, engraved silver buttcap and
escutcheon, deeply chequered rounded butt.

PAIR OF LATE 18TH CENTURY FLINTLOCK BOXLOCK OVER-
COAT POCKET PISTOLS 7¼in. Screw-off barrels 2in with
engraved borders at breeches, by Parker, London
proved. The frames engraved with flowers and
trophies of arms, raised pans, top safeties through to
frizzens. Slight swollen walnut slab butts with shield-
shaped silver escutcheons bearing owner's initials
'WW', and engraved silver buttcaps.

DOUBLE AND MULTI-BARREL FLINTLOCKS

The great majority of flintlock weapons produced were single shot but many
gunsmiths attempted to rectify this limitation by making double and multi-barrel
guns. Double barrel flintlocks are the most common and the small size variety were often scaled-down replicas of the double-barrel sporting longarms. One of the most
common arrangements was the tap action which was designed with two barrels which
were fitted one on top of the other. These barrels had a common breech block and were
connected by two separate tubes to a pan. A round metal block cut off the tube in the
lower barrel but this could be swung out to open the passage from breech to pan after
the upper barrel had been fired.

Multi-barrel guns were not a new invention as they had been made during the
wheellock and matchlock periods. Gunmakers had always felt that a single-shot
weapon had serious disadvantages. The design of the blunderbuss shows one method
of increasing the number of missiles that could be fired from one weapon. This relied
not on one shot following another but rather the spread of several bullets.

What is perhaps more interesting is the ingenuity shown by the gunmakers in their
design of three and four barrel guns. With four barrel guns the most popular design
was the alignment of two pairs of barrels on a pivoting block which alternatively
brought each pair of barrels into the firing position. As each pair fired the block could
be rotated to bring the other pair into the firing position. As a safety precaution most
of these pistols would have a catch which had to be released to disengage the empty
barrels and to re-engage the loaded barrels into the firing position.

An interesting variation on the multi-barrel theme was a pistol known as the
duck's foot pistol. This has an extremely amusing shape with four barrels all to be
fired simultaneously. This is basically the same concept as the blunderbuss design
and was particularly useful in a personal defence situation or for dispersing rioters.

Another attempt to make the flintlock pistol a more efficient weapon was to combine it with another weapon. The most common of such combinations was the sword-pistol. The pistol was usually mounted just below the cross guard of a short hunting sword. The most ingenious part of this design was the lock mechanism fitted in the hilt. This was followed at the end of the 18th century by the flintlock pistol being fitted with a sprung bayonet.

The multi-barrel guns did overcome many of the problems of the flintlock pistol but unfortunately probably they sacrificed accuracy and reliability.

One gun of this period certainly deserves some mention, for ingenuity and being far ahead of its time: the Puckle machine gun. It was designed by James Puckle who got a patent in 1718 for a 'portable gun or machine called a defence'. It was fired by a flintlock mechanism and had alternative cylindrical magazines, each holding up to eleven chambers, with a single barrel around three feet long. The most interesting feature of the Puckle gun was the racist or religiously biased choice of bullets – the conventional round bullets were to be used against Christian enemies but to fight the fiendish Turks a special square bullet was required!!

It was a very effective weapon and was recorded as having fired sixty-three shots in seven minutes. Unfortunately, this quite brilliant invention met with little success. And it was not until Gatling produced his famous machine gun at the time of the American Civil War that interest in machine guns was revitalised.

Although multi-barrel and combination flintlocks are not all that common they provide a fascinating study of the ingenuity and design of gunmakers of this period.

DOUBLE BARRELLED FLINTLOCK POCKET PISTOLS

MID-18TH CENTURY CONTINENTAL ALL STEEL DOUBLE BARRELLED SIDE BY SIDE FLINTLOCK BOXLOCK POCKET PISTOL $5\frac{3}{4}$in. Screw-off cannon barrels $1\frac{1}{4}$in, with London-type proofs at breech, flower engraved frames bearing the name 'Segalas London', bulbous slab-type butt engraved with scrolls.

CONTINENTAL STYLE ALL STEEL DOUBLE BARRELLED 60-
BORE SIDE BY SIDE FLINTLOCK BOXLOCK PISTOL 7$\frac{1}{2}$in.
Screw-off cannon barrels 2in with eight groove
rifling, frizzen springs in top of breeches, plain line
engraved frame and butt.

PAIR OF DOUBLE BARRELLED OVER AND UNDER TAP
ACTION FLINTLOCK BOXLOCK PISTOLS, circa 1800,
8in. Screw-off barrels 2$\frac{3}{4}$in with London proofs on
breeches of lower barrels, by Brasher, London. The
frames engraved with trophies of arms, top thumb
safeties, tap levers on left of frames, plain slab butts.

DOUBLE BARRELLED OVER AND UNDER TAP ACTION FLINTLOCK BOXLOCK PISTOL 8in. Screw-off barrels 3in with 3¼in spring bayonet beneath lower barrel, released by sliding trigger guard, by Gill, Richmond. The frame engraved with trophies of arms with entwined strapwork border, and sunbursts round selector tap, the ring neck cock engraved with serpent's head, top safety through to frizzen. Nicely figured walnut slab butt inlaid with silver wire wriggle and dot borders, scrolled designs, and shield-shaped escutcheon.

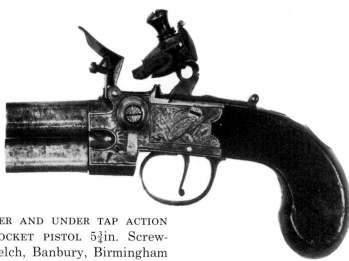

DOUBLE BARRELLED OVER AND UNDER TAP ACTION FLINTLOCK BOXLOCK POCKET PISTOL 5¾in. Screw-off barrels 1½in, by Welch, Banbury, Birmingham proved. The barrels and breeches numbered two and three, the frame engraved with trophies of arms and sunbursts, selector tap on left of frame, top thumb safety through to frizzen, slight swollen polished walnut slab butt with oval silver escutcheon.

DOUBLE BARRELLED OVER AND UNDER TAP ACTION
FLINTLOCK BOXLOCK PISTOL 8½in. Screw-off rifled barrels 3¼in, the frame engraved with stand of flags,
drums, etc. Selector tap on left of frame, ring neck
cock, chequered slab butt with remains of silver wire
inlay round top strap tang.

DOUBLE BARRELLED TAP ACTION FLINTLOCK BOXLOCK
POCKET PISTOL by J. Probin, circa 1780, 7in. Turn-off
barrels 2¼in, keyed at muzzles, London proved.
Frame engraved with military trophy and floral
trophy with 'J. Probin, London' within ovals. Throat
hole cock, sliding top thumb safety through to tension sprung, teardrop frizzen. Flattened walnut butt
with scroll and border silver wire inlay overall, oval
silver escutcheon.

DOUBLE BARRELLED OVER AND UNDER BRASS BAR-
RELLED FLINTLOCK BOXLOCK POCKET PISTOL 8in. Barrels 2¾in, by Simmons, brass frame engraved with
military trophies, turn-off lever to left of frame, sliding bar top safety, slab sided wood butt.

EARLY 19TH CENTURY FRENCH 38-BORE DOUBLE BAR-
RELLED OVER AND UNDER TAP ACTION FLINTLOCK BOX-
LOCK PISTOL 8in. Round barrels 3¼in with ramrod
pipes on right side, the frame engraved on both sides
with a bird on a branch. Selector tap on left of frame,
ring neck cock, top safety through to frizzen, semi-
slab type with chequered panels and raised oval
medallions.

BRASS FRAMED DOUBLE BARRELLED OVER AND UNDER
TAP ACTION FLINTLOCK BOXLOCK POCKET PISTOL 6in.
Screw-off barrels 1½in, by Williamson, Hull, Birmingham proved. The barrels and breeches numbered
three and four, the frame engraved with trophies of
arms, sunbursts, etc. Selector tap on left of frame, top
safety through to frizzen, plain walnut slab butt with
oval silver escutcheon.

BRASS FRAMED DOUBLE BARRELLED SIDE BY SIDE TAP
ACTION FLINTLOCK BOXLOCK POCKET PISTOL $6\frac{3}{4}$in.
Screw-off barrels 2in, by Jno Jones and Co, London,
Birmingham proved, the frame engraved with
trophies of arms, selector tap on left of frame, top
safety through to frizzen, slab butt inlaid with silver
wire scrolls.

MULTI BARRELLED FLINTLOCK POCKET PISTOLS

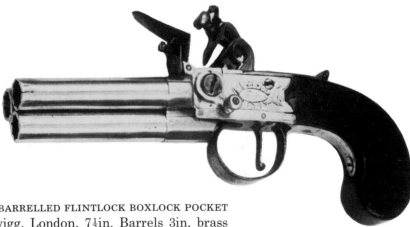

BRASS THREE BARRELLED FLINTLOCK BOXLOCK POCKET
PISTOL by Twigg, London, $7\frac{1}{2}$in. Barrels 3in, brass
frame engraved with trophies of arms, turn-off lever
to left of frame, sliding bar safety to top of frame, slab
sided wood butt.

THREE BARRELLED TAP ACTION FLINTLOCK BOXLOCK OVERCOAT PISTOL by Wallis of Hull, 8¾in. Turn-off barrels 3in muzzle slotted for key, London proved. Lower barrel fitted with spring bayonet operated by sliding trigger guard. Frame nicely engraved with military trophies and with Wallis. Sliding top safety bolt through to tension sprung frizzen. The tap fires each barrel individually. Slab wooden butt.

FOUR BARRELLED BOXLOCK FLINTLOCK TAP ACTION POCKET PISTOL by L. Samuel of Liverpool, circa 1800, 7in. Turn-off barrels 1¾in, muzzles cut for key and numbered consecutively with breech. London proved. Brass frame engraved with maker's name amid military trophies within ovals. Tension sprung frizzen, sliding top safety, steel tap slab walnut butt, oval silver escutcheon.

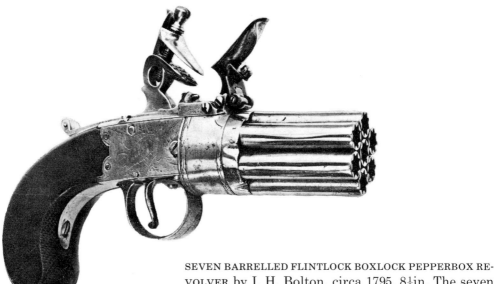

SEVEN BARRELLED FLINTLOCK BOXLOCK PEPPERBOX RE-
VOLVER by I. H. Bolton, circa 1795, 8½in. The seven
screw-off keyed barrels 2½in each numbered cor-
respondingly with the revolving breech block. Frame
floral engraved with maker's name in oval shield
within a trophy of arms and flags. Floral spray and
sunburst engraved on other side. Fern tip engraved
safety bolt through throat hole cock to frizzen. Tear
drop frizzen with double friction rollers and slightly
raised pan-rim. Sunburst engraved on trigger guard.
Butterfly nut on frame side to alter tension of revolving barrels, also a safety bolt locking the revolving
block to ensure perfect line up with vent and pan
and activating the central barrel. Slightly flattened
chequered grips.

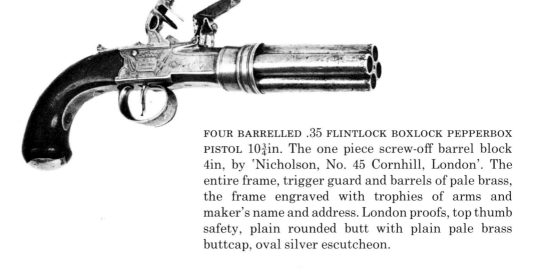

FOUR BARRELLED .35 FLINTLOCK BOXLOCK PEPPERBOX
PISTOL 10¾in. The one piece screw-off barrel block
4in, by 'Nicholson, No. 45 Cornhill, London'. The
entire frame, trigger guard and barrels of pale brass,
the frame engraved with trophies of arms and
maker's name and address. London proofs, top thumb
safety, plain rounded butt with plain pale brass
buttcap, oval silver escutcheon.

The Blunderbuss

The flintlock blunderbuss was developed in the 17th century and was used for a short time as a military weapon. The Austrian army and later the British employed this weapon but it was soon abandoned due to its lack of precision.

Its name reputably comes from 'donder busche' meaning 'thunder gun' – an apt description.

The blunderbuss could be taken to be the opposite of the rifle – which was designed to send a single bullet directly to a pre-determined target. The blunderbuss, by contrast, sent as much shot or other missiles as possible to cover as wide an area as possible. Not the weapon for a crack shot! – it was essentially a personal protection weapon used, for example, by butlers and caretakers of country houses, and guards on mail coaches. One can find a blunderbuss inscribed 'For His (or Her) Majesty's Coaches'.

The barrel of the blunderbuss was usually made of brass and the muzzle flared. In the early models, the bore gradually widened from the breech to the muzzle. The theory of this design was that the charge of powder (often 160 grains) would drive the shot (frequently a pound of buckshot) in a direction determined by the bore. The theory (later proved incorrect), that the spread would follow this path caused some late blunderbusses to take on quite grotesque shapes with monstrous muzzles! The average spread of the gun was about $\frac{1}{2}''$–$1''$ per foot.

Some blunderbusses had a spring bayonet attachment which worked on a spring-catch system. The weapon was designed to fire but once!

Many fine quality examples of the British gunsmiths craft are still to be found as the blunderbuss, although many were produced in other countries, remained a great favourite with the British.

Towards the end of its career a number of flintlock blunderbusses were converted to the percussion method but there was little need to adapt the weapon to this new method. By the mid-19th century the blunderbuss was made obsolete by a very much more effective method of self defence – the percussion revolver.

English

FLINTLOCK BOXLOCK BLUNDERBUSS PISTOL, circa 1780, 9¾in. Turn-off bell mouth barrel 4in, with provision for sprung bayonet to be released by sliding trigger guard. Frame linear and military trophy engraved. Sliding top thumb safety through to tension sprung frizzen. Slab wooden butt.

74

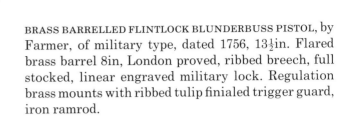

BRASS BARRELLED FLINTLOCK BLUNDERBUSS PISTOL, by
Farmer, of military type, dated 1756, 13½in. Flared
brass barrel 8in, London proved, ribbed breech, full
stocked, linear engraved military lock. Regulation
brass mounts with ribbed tulip finialed trigger guard,
iron ramrod.

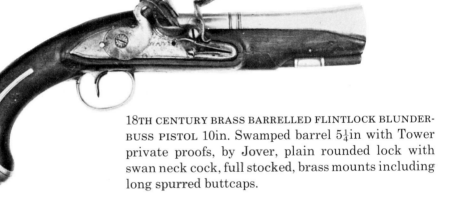

18TH CENTURY BRASS BARRELLED FLINTLOCK BLUNDER-
BUSS PISTOL 10in. Swamped barrel 5¼in with Tower
private proofs, by Jover, plain rounded lock with
swan neck cock, full stocked, brass mounts including
long spurred buttcaps.

LATE 17TH CENTURY BRASS BARRELLED FLINTLOCK
BLUNDERBUSS PISTOL 13½in. Swamped barrel 7¼in in
two stages, the muzzle rounded with leaf engraving,
the breech polygonal then octagonal, with strawberry leaf engraving. Early London proofs and
maker's proof ('BG' and anchor); the lock of later
date with swan neck cock and simple engraved decoration. Full stocked, brass mounts, long spurred
bulbous buttcap with strawberry leaf engraving,
slender brass trigger guard, and baluster ramrod
pipe.

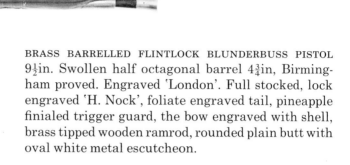

BRASS BARRELLED FLINTLOCK BLUNDERBUSS PISTOL
9½in. Swollen half octagonal barrel 4¾in, Birmingham proved. Engraved 'London'. Full stocked, lock
engraved 'H. Nock', foliate engraved tail, pineapple
finialed trigger guard, the bow engraved with shell,
brass tipped wooden ramrod, rounded plain butt with
oval white metal escutcheon.

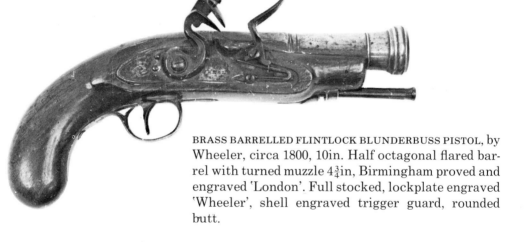

BRASS BARRELLED FLINTLOCK BLUNDERBUSS PISTOL, by
Wheeler, circa 1800, 10in. Half octagonal flared barrel with turned muzzle 4¾in, Birmingham proved and
engraved 'London'. Full stocked, lockplate engraved
'Wheeler', shell engraved trigger guard, rounded
butt.

BRASS FRAMED AND BARRELLED BOXLOCK FLINTLOCK
BLUNDERBUSS PISTOL, by Waters with patent spring
bayonet, 12½in. Flared barrel 7in, Tower proved,
sprung bayonet released by sliding catch within
trigger guard, sliding top thumb safety catch, horn
tipped whalebone ramrod with steel worm fitted to
side of barrel. Flattened, faceted walnut butt, frame
script engraved 'Waters and Co, Patent'.

PAIR OF BRASS BARRELLED BRASS FRAMED FLINTLOCK
BOXLOCK BLUNDERBUSS POCKET PISTOLS, by Jackson,
London, 6½in. Barrels 2¾in, with bell mouths and
octagonal breeches. London proved, sliding bar top
safeties, frames with simple decoration, plain slab
sided wood butts. Possibly used by the Navy or by a
coach driver.

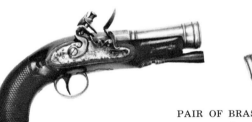

PAIR OF BRASS BARRELLED FLINTLOCK BLUNDERBUSS
PISTOLS, by Cox and Co, circa 1800, 9in. Probably
belonged to a naval officer. Half octagonal ribbed bell
mouthed barrels 4¾in, clearly struck Birmingham
proofs with factory stamp of '2' over lion, engraved
'Derby' on top flats. Full stocked in walnut, linear
engraved stepped lockplates with 'Cox and Co', sliding side safety bolts, rainproof pans, friction rollers
on frizzen springs. Brass furniture, roped sidenail
cups, pineapple finialed trigger guards engraved with
floral sprays. Wooden ramrods.

Continental

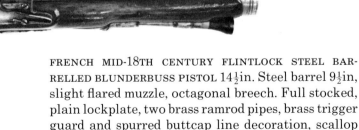

FRENCH MID-18TH CENTURY FLINTLOCK STEEL BAR-
RELLED BLUNDERBUSS PISTOL 14½in. Steel barrel 9½in,
slight flared muzzle, octagonal breech. Full stocked,
plain lockplate, two brass ramrod pipes, brass trigger
guard and spurred buttcap line decoration, scallop
decoration to buttcap terminal, brass engraved sideplate.

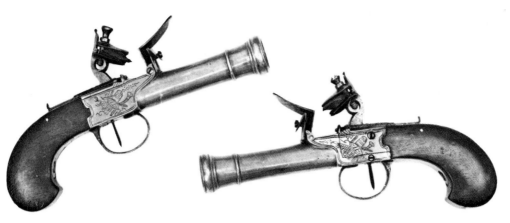

PAIR OF FRENCH BRONZE BARRELLED AND BRONZE
FRAMED FLINTLOCK BOXLOCK BLUNDERBUSS PISTOLS
7¾in. Bell mouth barrels 3in, the frames engraved
with stylised trophies of arms, top safeties through to
frizzens, ring neck cocks, star engraved trigger
guard, plain wood butts.

STEEL BARRELLED FLINTLOCK BLUNDERBUSS 32in. Bell
mouth barrel 16½in, with octagonal breech by Ketland and Co. Half stocked brass mounts, spring
bayonet beneath barrel released by catch in front
of trigger guard.

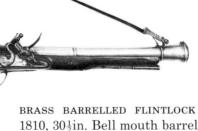

BRASS BARRELLED FLINTLOCK BLUNDERBUSS, circa
1810, 30½in. Bell mouth barrel 14½in with octagonal
breech bearing London proofs 13in spring bayonet on
top of barrel released by thumb catch on barrel tang,
plain flat lock with swan neck cock, plain butt and
full stock. Plain brass mounts including trigger
guard with acorn finial.

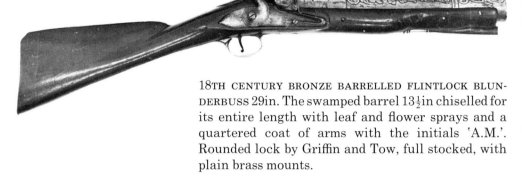

18TH CENTURY BRONZE BARRELLED FLINTLOCK BLUN-
DERBUSS 29in. The swamped barrel 13½in chiselled for
its entire length with leaf and flower sprays and a
quartered coat of arms with the initials 'A.M.'.
Rounded lock by Griffin and Tow, full stocked, with
plain brass mounts.

Continental

LATE 17TH CENTURY DUTCH FLINTLOCK DOGLOCK BLUN-
DERBUSS, from Rotterdam, circa 1675, 34½in. Brass
barrel of 'bottle' form, 19¾in, deeply struck at breech
with crossed anchors within circle (naval Ordnance
mark) and the crowned city arms of Rotterdam
within shield, ribbed muzzle. Full stocked, barrel
tang screw rising vertically from under bow of trigger guard, lock retained by three side screws. Iron
trigger guard with simple foliate finial, sheet brass
forecap and ramrod pipe, wooden ramrod.

Turkish

TURKISH FLINTLOCK BLUNDERBUSS 25in. Barrel 14in,
muzzle flared and decorated with inlaid brass patterns also at breech. Full stocked, brass mounts, trigger guard and buttplate engraved with various designs, the stock inlaid with silver wire decor, the butt
covered with inlaid silver foliate patterns within
circles.

TURKISH FLINTLOCK BLUNDERBUSS 21in. Barrel 11½in, muzzle flared and inlaid with brass designs of flowers, also at breech. Full stocked, brass trigger guard, buttplate chiselled with foliate patterns, brass side plate simply decorated and with saddle bar. Simple foliate pattern on hammer and lockplate.

Flintlock Travelling Pistols

Travel in the 17th and 18th centuries was long and arduous and extremely dangerous. As travel by horseback was practically the only mode of travel available to a gentleman or businessman of this period many carried large sums of money or valuables on their person. This made them the ideal victim of the many highwaymen and footpads who plagued the countryside.

For the town-dweller the most useful weapon was the pocket or muff pistol but the traveller on the roads usually preferred something more substantial. The flintlock mechanism was quickly adapted to satisfy this demand. The obvious advantages of the mechanism, including its reliability, economy of production and the fact that it was quite capable of withstanding hard wear, meant it suited this task perfectly.

Queen Anne pistols, made long after the monarch's death in 1714, were very popular as travelling pistols. They tended to be very graceful pistols, often quite tastefully decorated and with turn-off barrels. The great advantage of these pistols was that they could be loaded and prepared long before they were intended for use.

A travelling pistol could be concealed in the clothing of the traveller but more often, particularly as the 18th century progressed, and travelling by coach became the preferable alternative to horseback, most coach drivers, and many passengers, carried a large pair of quite weighty pistols in a box.

A boxed pair of flintlock travelling pistols with all accoutrements intact is a prize indeed and it is sometimes possible to find boxed sets consisting of a pair of travelling pistols with a pair of short pocket pistols, all of the same bore.

Such sets were extremely useful when the coach was ambushed when the pistols would prove excellent personal defence weapons.

BRITISH & IRISH

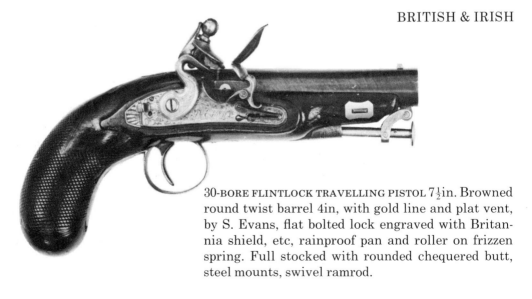

30-BORE FLINTLOCK TRAVELLING PISTOL 7½in. Browned round twist barrel 4in, with gold line and plat vent, by S. Evans, flat bolted lock engraved with Britannia shield, etc, rainproof pan and roller on frizzen spring. Full stocked with rounded chequered butt, steel mounts, swivel ramrod.

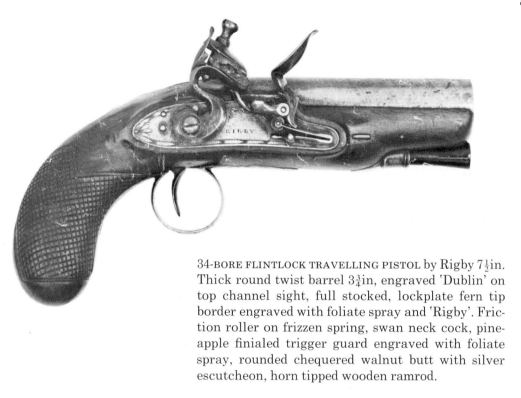

34-BORE FLINTLOCK TRAVELLING PISTOL by Rigby 7½in. Thick round twist barrel 3¾in, engraved 'Dublin' on top channel sight, full stocked, lockplate fern tip border engraved with foliate spray and 'Rigby'. Friction roller on frizzen spring, swan neck cock, pineapple finialed trigger guard engraved with foliate spray, rounded chequered walnut butt with silver escutcheon, horn tipped wooden ramrod.

30-BORE FLINTLOCK TRAVELLING PISTOL by Bunney and Sons, fitted with spring bayonet, 7¼in. Barrel 3½in, engraved 'Birmingham', 2¼in. hollow ground sprung bayonet, with roller bearing spring released by top thumb catch, stepped bolted lock engraved 'Bunney and Son', roller bearing frizzen spring. Full stocked, floral engraved brass trigger guard, pineapple finialed, horn tipped wooden ramrod with steel worm, horn foretip, rounded butt with flattened sides, oval silver escutcheon.

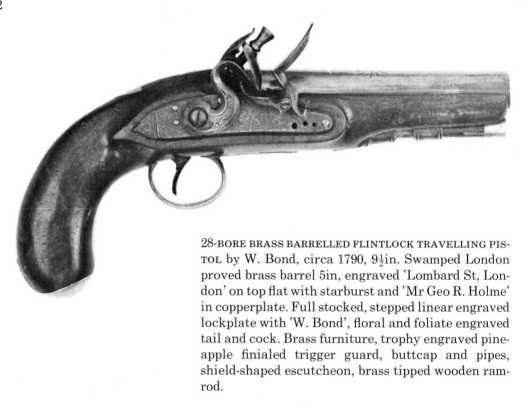

28-BORE BRASS BARRELLED FLINTLOCK TRAVELLING PIS-
TOL by W. Bond, circa 1790, 9½in. Swamped London
proved brass barrel 5in, engraved 'Lombard St, London' on top flat with starburst and 'Mr Geo R. Holme'
in copperplate. Full stocked, stepped linear engraved
lockplate with 'W. Bond', floral and foliate engraved
tail and cock. Brass furniture, trophy engraved pineapple finialed trigger guard, buttcap and pipes,
shield-shaped escutcheon, brass tipped wooden ramrod.

52-BORE FLINTLOCK BOXLOCK TRAVELLING PISTOL by
Gourlay of Glasgow, with spring bayonet, 7¾in. Turn-
off barrel 2½in, fern tip engraved muzzle slotted for
turn key, Birmingham proved with private maker's
mark, frame engraved 'Gourlay, Glasgow', within
ovals against military trophies. Bayonet released by
sliding trigger guard beneath barrel, friction roller
on bayonet spring, sliding top safety catch through
throat hole cock locking tension sprung frizzen,
slight rounded slab walnut butt with oval silver
escutcheon.

ENGLISH 24-BORE BRASS MOUNTED FLINTLOCK TRAVEL-LING PISTOL by Le Maire, circa 1700, 11½in. Barrel 7in, London proved, full stocked in well figured maple, rounded banana-shaped lockplate, linear engraved with 'Le Maire', early style cock, brass furniture, grimacing stylised lion's head mask buttcap with long pointed foliate finial. Foliate finialed trigger guard, foliate escutcheon and pierced sideplate with dragon's head. Baluster ramrod pipes, the stock swollen around throat pipe.

16-BORE IRISH FLINTLOCK TRAVELLING PISTOL 8½in. Octagonal twist barrel 4½in, engraved 'Maclean, Dublin' on top flat, gold line inlaid at breech. Full stocked, fern tip border engraved lock with 'Maclean', trophy engraved cock, friction roller on frizzen spring, trophy engraved pineapple finialed trigger guard, small flower head engraved buttcap plate, silver oval escutcheon.

PAIR OF BOXLOCK FLINTLOCK TRAVELLING PISTOLS by Knubley, circa 1820, 11¼in. Turn-off barrels 4½in, London proved, frames engraved with 'Knubley, London', within ovals surrounded by flag and drum trophies. Sliding top thumb safety catches through throat hole cocks locking tension sprung teardrop frizzens, trigger guards engraved with flower heads, slab walnut butts.

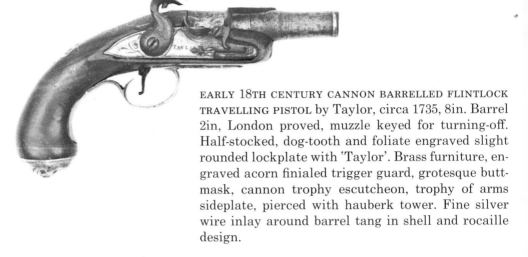

EARLY 18TH CENTURY CANNON BARRELLED FLINTLOCK TRAVELLING PISTOL by Taylor, circa 1735, 8in. Barrel 2in, London proved, muzzle keyed for turning-off. Half-stocked, dog-tooth and foliate engraved slight rounded lockplate with 'Taylor'. Brass furniture, engraved acorn finialed trigger guard, grotesque butt-mask, cannon trophy escutcheon, trophy of arms sideplate, pierced with hauberk tower. Fine silver wire inlay around barrel tang in shell and rocaille design.

PAIR OF FLINTLOCK BOXLOCK CANNON BARRELLED TRAVELLING PISTOLS by King, circa 1780, 8in. Turn-off barrels 2½in slotted at muzzle for key, Tower proved, barrels and frame of light coloured brass, scroll and rocaille engraved frames with 'King, London' within borders. Sliding brass trigger guard safety catches, frizzen springs sunk in breeches. Slab walnut butts inlaid with scroll and rocaille patterned silver wire, with some pique work on top scrolls.

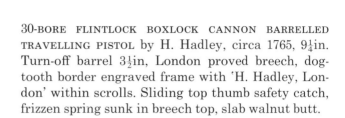

30-BORE FLINTLOCK BOXLOCK CANNON BARRELLED TRAVELLING PISTOL by H. Hadley, circa 1765, 9¼in. Turn-off barrel 3½in, London proved breech, dogtooth border engraved frame with 'H. Hadley, London' within scrolls. Sliding top thumb safety catch, frizzen spring sunk in breech top, slab walnut butt.

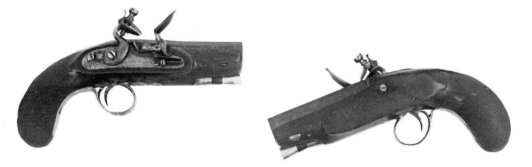

PAIR OF 34-BORE FLINTLOCK TRAVELLING PISTOLS, circa 1800, 7in. Browned octagonal twist barrels 3¼in with engraved bands at breeches, by Pepper, Dublin. Stepped bolted locks with some engraved decoration, raised pans, rollers on frizzen springs. Full stocked with rounded chequered butts, engraved steel trigger guards with pineapple finials, small rectangular silver escutcheons, brass tipped wooden ramrods.

PAIR OF 36-BORE FLINTLOCK TRAVELLING PISTOLS by Mortimer, 7¾in. Barrels 3¾in octagonal at breeches engraved 'H. W. Mortimer, London – Gun Makers to His Majesty'. Full stocked, stepped bolted locks engraved 'H. W. Mortimer and Son', rollers on frizzen springs, pineapple finialed trigger guards with Britannia shield trophies, brass tipped ebony ramrods.

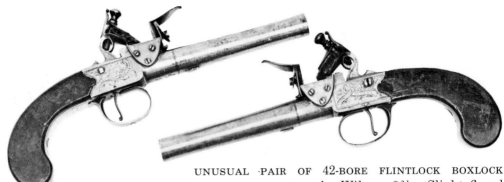

UNUSUAL ·PAIR OF 42-BORE FLINTLOCK BOXLOCK TRAVELLING PISTOLS by Wilson, 8¾in. Slight flared turn-off barrels 3¾in, Tower proved, frames engraved with birds upon rocailles, scrolls and flowers with 'Wilson' within scrolls. The sides of the pans have been fitted with shield-shaped plates; perhaps to enable the pistols to be better used for tinder, perhaps to eliminate the risk of burning grains of powder spilling onto the hand. Sliding trigger guard safety catches, locking tension sprung frizzens, slab walnut butts.

PAIR OF BRASS FRAMED AND BARRELLED FLINTLOCK BOXLOCK RIFLED TRAVELLING PISTOLS by John Richards, circa 1795, 7½in. Turn-off barrels 2¾in with eight groove, sharply twisting rifling, fern tip engraved muzzles, London proved breeches, frames boldly engraved 'John Richards, Strand, London' within banners amidst military trophies of arms, concealed triggers, fern tip engraved sliding top thumb safety catches through throat hole cocks, locking tension sprung frizzens, slight raised pans, slab wooden butts.

PAIR OF 28-BORE BOXLOCK FLINTLOCK TRAVELLING PIS-
TOLS by W. M. Mason, circa 1780, 11in. Turn-off barrels 4½in, London and Tower proved, scroll and rocaille engraved frames with dog-tooth borders, sliding
trigger guard safety, throat hole cock, frizzen springs
sunk in breeches, slab walnut butt.

CONTINENTAL

30-BORE CONTINENTAL BRASS BARRELLED FLINTLOCK
TRAVELLING PISTOL 10in. Octagonal barrel 4¾in with
turned swollen muzzle. Full stocked, steel furniture,
acorn finialed trigger guard, bow engraved with
trophy of arms, swollen longspur buttcap similarly
engraved, slab sideplate, floral carved apron behind
barrel tang, some simple scroll silver wire inlay, steel
ramrod.

SMALL FRENCH 70-BORE FLINTLOCK SIDELOCK TRAVEL-
LING PISTOL 7in. Barrel 3¼in in two stages, the round
muzzle separated from the fluted breech by a moulded
band, plain flat lock with swan neck cock. Full
stocked with bird's head butt, plain iron mounts.

PAIR OF 25-BORE FRENCH FLINTLOCK TRAVELLING
PISTOLS 10¼in. Slight flared octagonal barrels 5½in,
stamped with gilt St Etienne proofs. Full stocked,
plain locks, sheet steel furniture, two piece sideplates, swollen trigger guard finials, chequered butts.

50-BORE BELGIUM OR FRENCH FLINTLOCK BOXLOCK CAN-
NON BARRELLED TRAVELLING PISTOL 9½in. Turn-off
barrel 3½in, foliate, floral and rocaille engraved
frame with 'Farmer, London', sliding trigger guard
safety locking cock and frizzen, frizzen spring sunk in
breech, rounded walnut butt with scrolling silver
wire inlay.

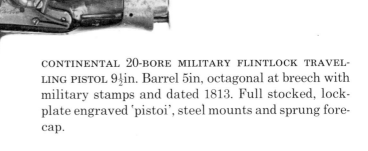

CONTINENTAL 20-BORE MILITARY FLINTLOCK TRAVEL-
LING PISTOL 9½in. Barrel 5in, octagonal at breech with
military stamps and dated 1813. Full stocked, lockplate engraved 'pistoi', steel mounts and sprung forecap.

56-BORE FRENCH OR ITALIAN FLINTLOCK TRAVELLING PISTOL 7in. Half octagonal barrel 3½in chiselled with rocaille and inlaid with punched brass. Full stocked, scroll engraved lock with foliate motif on tail, foliate and rocaille engraved steel furniture, stock carved around throat and barrel tang.

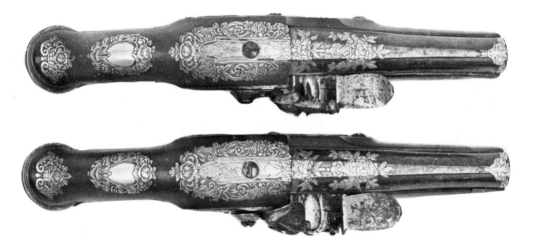

PAIR OF 27-BORE ITALIAN FLINTLOCK TRAVELLING PISTOLS 9in. Barrels 4½in, overlaid in gold at breeches and muzzles with floral and foliate trophies, flattened top ribs. Full stocks, lockplates engraved 'Frachetti a Minelli', one stamped 'M.B.F.', within heart, foliate engraving to tails and cocks. Floral and foliate engraved steel furniture, urn finialed trigger guards and throat pipes, longspur buttcaps with applied bosses, solid sideplates. Floral and foliate engraved silverplate inlaid around barrel tangs, escutcheons and above buttcaps. Horn forecaps and horn tipped wooden ramrods.

DOUBLE BARRELLED

DOUBLE BARRELLED OVER AND UNDER TAP ACTION BRASS FRAMED FLINTLOCK BOXLOCK TRAVELLING PISTOL by P. Bond, with sprung bayonet, 8¼in. Turn-off barrels 3in, Tower proved with sliding trigger guard releasing 3in bayonet with spring friction roller. Brass frame engraved 'P. Bond, No 45 Cornhill, London' within ovals, centred upon military trophies, lower shoulder of frame engraved 'C.S. Stubbing' (owner's name), sliding top thumb safety through throat hole cock locking double friction roller tension sprung, teardrop frizzen. Slab walnut butt with silver escutcheon.

DOUBLE BARRELLED SIDE BY SIDE 36-BORE FLINTLOCK TRAVELLING PISTOL by I. Probin 8in. Barrels 3½in, with silver escutcheon of I. Probin, London engraved on top strap with military trophies. Full stocked, steel mounts, foliate engraved cocks, bar safeties behind cocks, rainproof pans, roller on frizzen springs, pineapple finial to trigger guard, diced wood butt.

DOUBLE BARRELLED OVER AND UNDER FRENCH BOXLOCK FLINTLOCK TAP ACTION TRAVELLING PISTOL 8½in. Turn-off rifled barrels 3in, frame engraved with trophies of arms, sliding top thumb safety catch through throat hole locking tension sprung frizzen, arch-shaped tap lever, chequered butt.

Flintlock Belt Pistols

As previously discussed the flintlock mechanism was eminently suitable to adaptation to fit many different types of firearm. Although many laws were passed trying to outlaw the sale and possession of short pistols, these had little effect. Charles I attempted to stop this 'dangerous practice' in 1637 by decreeing that no pistol should be made with a barrel length of less than fourteen inches. This was presumably to halt the popularity of small concealed guns which were used as frequently for an attack as they were for defence. This law was completely ignored and did nothing to dampen the increasing demand for short pistols.

Flintlock belt pistols were extremely popular, both to the town-dweller and the traveller. Walking around the back streets of some of the main towns, at a time when there was no organised police force, was quite as hazardous as travelling on the country highways.

On horseback, a traveller would most likely rely on two methods of protection; firstly, a pair of long, quite bulky holster pistols in holsters affixed to the front of the saddle and, secondly, a smaller pair, attached to his belt by long hooks.

These weapons were more popular during the 17th century but remained in use throughout the age of the flintlock mechanism and tended to have national characteristics along with adaptations to their design which ran concurrently with developments and improvements to the mechanism.

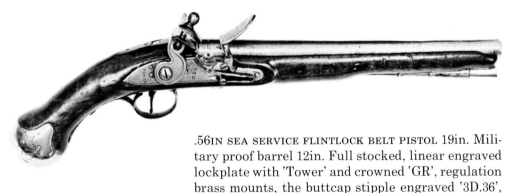

.56IN SEA SERVICE FLINTLOCK BELT PISTOL 19in. Military proof barrel 12in. Full stocked, linear engraved lockplate with 'Tower' and crowned 'GR', regulation brass mounts, the buttcap stipple engraved '3D.36', sprung steel belt hook, brass tipped wooden ramrod.

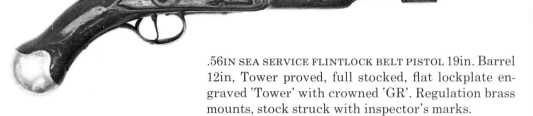

.56IN SEA SERVICE FLINTLOCK BELT PISTOL 19in. Barrel 12in, Tower proved, full stocked, flat lockplate engraved 'Tower' with crowned 'GR'. Regulation brass mounts, stock struck with inspector's marks.

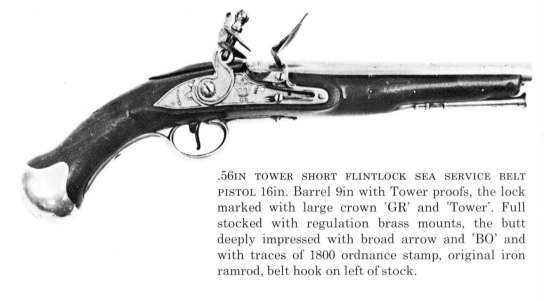

.56IN TOWER SHORT FLINTLOCK SEA SERVICE BELT PISTOL 16in. Barrel 9in with Tower proofs, the lock marked with large crown 'GR' and 'Tower'. Full stocked with regulation brass mounts, the butt deeply impressed with broad arrow and 'BO' and with traces of 1800 ordnance stamp, original iron ramrod, belt hook on left of stock.

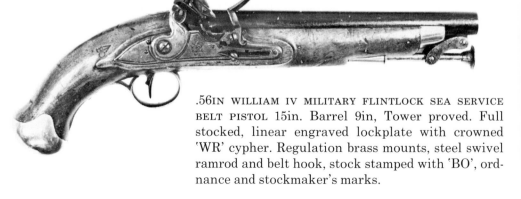

.56IN WILLIAM IV MILITARY FLINTLOCK SEA SERVICE BELT PISTOL 15in. Barrel 9in, Tower proved. Full stocked, linear engraved lockplate with crowned 'WR' cypher. Regulation brass mounts, steel swivel ramrod and belt hook, stock stamped with 'BO', ordnance and stockmaker's marks.

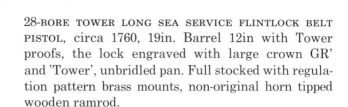

28-BORE TOWER LONG SEA SERVICE FLINTLOCK BELT PISTOL, circa 1760, 19in. Barrel 12in with Tower proofs, the lock engraved with large crown GR' and 'Tower', unbridled pan. Full stocked with regulation pattern brass mounts, non-original horn tipped wooden ramrod.

38-BORE FLINTLOCK BOXLOCK BELT PISTOL 8½in. Screw-off octagonal barrel 3in, the muzzle cut for barrel key bearing the maker's name 'Meredith and Moxham, London', in old-English on top flat of barrel, and with 4in spring bayonet on right of barrel released by thumb catch on frame. The left sideplate engraved with trophy of arms and with belt hook fitted, hidden trigger, top safety through to frizzen, rollers on frizzen spring, rounded chequered butt with plain oval escutcheon and simply engraved silver buttcap.

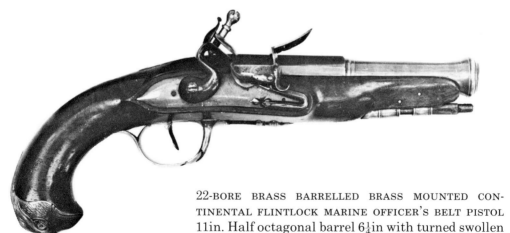

22-BORE BRASS BARRELLED BRASS MOUNTED CONTINENTAL FLINTLOCK MARINE OFFICER'S BELT PISTOL 11in. Half octagonal barrel 6¼in with turned swollen muzzle. Full stocked, brass lockplate, brass furniture, urn finialed trigger guard, rounded bar sideplate, chased bird's head buttcap, horn ramrod.

PAIR OF SPANISH 16-BORE MIQUELET FLINTLOCK BELT
PISTOLS 11in. Half round half octagonal barrels $6\frac{1}{2}$in,
the breeches engraved 'Fabricado en Eibar Ano d
1824' in silver and bearing the maker's gold poincon
'Urquiola', the locks signed 'VRGA'. Half stocks,
chequered butts, engraved steel mounts, the trigger
guards bearing the same poincons as on the breech,
belt hooks.

Flintlock Holster Pistols

Flintlocks were produced in a variety of designs and were fitted to many weapons throughout the mechanism's working life of over two hundred years.

Flintlock holster pistols changed much over this period and also evolved certain national characteristics. The earliest examples of flintlock holster pistols were made around the first quarter of the 17th century although these are extremely rare. These early examples had long barrels and moulded rings around the muzzle. One can also find examples of stepped barrels. The length of the barrel decreased as the century progressed.

One of the main functions of military pistols was for the use of the cavalry and obviously it was not easy for a man riding a horse to deal with a long cumbersome weapon. The introduction of the flintlock system, with its inherent benefits of reliability, economy of production and facility to be fitted to every conceivable form of firearm, meant that the cavalry could be provided with an accurate, dependable, short weapon. Two leather holsters were designed to carry the weapon and were fitted to the front of the saddle, hanging each side of the horse. This meant that the cavalryman would have his hands free but had his weapons in easy reach. Many holsters were strengthened with brass edging and later, in order to protect the pistols from damp and dust, a flap was fitted to cover the open top.

The main concern of the cavalryman was reliability and a weapon which could stand up to harsh use. The main concern of the military was economy and, as neither required a decorative weapon, most holster pistols were plain with little embellishment.

Holster pistols were also frequently used by civilian travellers. The only possible method of travelling was on horseback and most travellers would be armed as the highways were certainly not altogether safe, highwaymen and footpads all too ready to surprise the unprepared traveller. The traveller would probably have small pistols tucked into his belt and two long pistols, usually around twenty inches long, in holsters attached to the saddle-bow. At this time, holster pistols usually had long barrels of octagonal shape at the breech and fired a small diameter bullet.

As the 18th century progressed, holster pistols were frequently made in the Queen Anne style. The cannon barrels of such pistols were usually the turn-off kind and could be unscrewed. Another important development was the boxlock holster or coaching pistols, where the frizzen, cock and the pan were mounted centrally.

Towards the end of the 18th century, when more travel was done by coach, the civilian need for holster pistols declined and they were frequently replaced by coaching or travelling pistols.

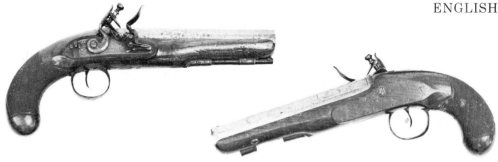

PAIR OF 11-BORE FLINTLOCK HOLSTER PISTOLS by H. Nock 12in. Octagonal barrels 7¼in engraved 'London'. Full stocked, stepped bolted locks with 'H. Nock' and roller bearing frizzen springs. Pineapple finialed trigger guards engraved with flowers and shield. Rounded chequered walnut butts with silver escutcheons.

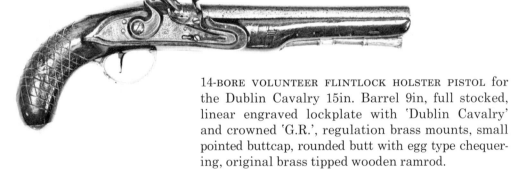

14-BORE VOLUNTEER FLINTLOCK HOLSTER PISTOL for the Dublin Cavalry 15in. Barrel 9in, full stocked, linear engraved lockplate with 'Dublin Cavalry' and crowned 'G.R.', regulation brass mounts, small pointed buttcap, rounded butt with egg type chequering, original brass tipped wooden ramrod.

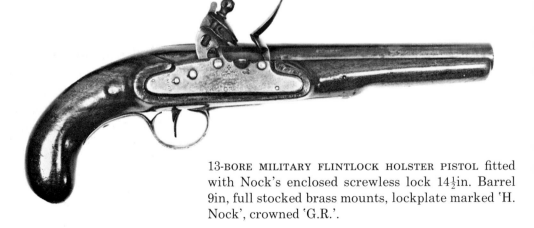

13-BORE MILITARY FLINTLOCK HOLSTER PISTOL fitted with Nock's enclosed screwless lock 14½in. Barrel 9in, full stocked brass mounts, lockplate marked 'H. Nock', crowned 'G.R.'.

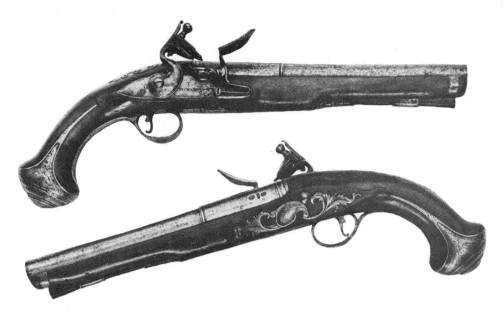

PAIR OF 14-BORE FLINTLOCK HOLSTER PISTOLS by T. Richards, circa 1750, 15½in. Stepped barrels 9¼in, London proved with maker's mark 'T.K.'. Full stocked, linear engraved lockplates with maker's name. Steel furniture, slightly engraved longspur buttcaps, tulip finialed trigger guards, pierced scrolled sideplates, shell finialed escutcheons. Steel ramrod pipes and wooden ramrods. Nicely shell carved behind barrel tangs. Fore-ends with steel band.

ROYAL HORSE GUARDS FLINTLOCK HOLSTER PISTOL .56in dated 1761 16½in. Barrel 10in, Tower proved, engraved 'Royal Horse Guards'. Full stocked, flat lockplate with bevelled edges engraved 'Tower 1761' with crowned 'G.R.'. Regulation brass mounts, longspur buttcap with grotesque mask boss, escutcheon engraved '1/3', slab sideplate, brass tipped wooden ramrod.

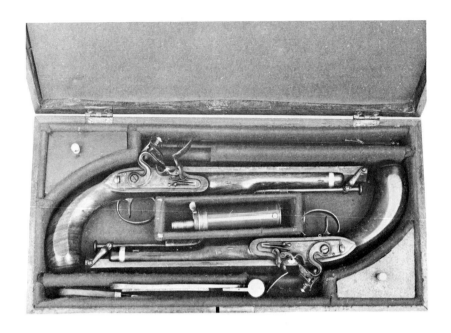

PAIR OF 16-BORE OFFICER'S FLINTLOCK HOLSTER PIS-
TOLS by Wogdon and Barton 14½in. Octagonal twist
barrels 9½in engraved 'Wogdon and Barton, London'
in script on top flats, unusual swivel ramrods bolting
to stopping lugs at muzzle sides, silver foresights.
Full stocked, stepped bolted detented locks engraved
'Wogdon and Barton' in script. Rainproof pans, roller
bearing frizzens, ramped frizzen springs, gold lined
vents. Engraved steel furniture, pineapple finialed
trigger guards with Britannia shields on floral
grounds, sunburst engraved buttcups. Rounded
walnut butts with flattened sides, fore ends inlaid
with silver bands.

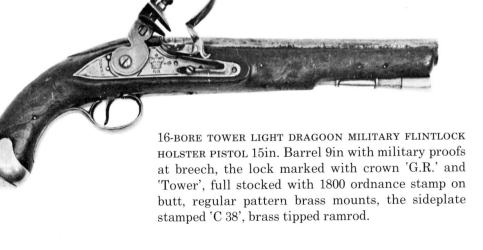

16-BORE TOWER LIGHT DRAGOON MILITARY FLINTLOCK
HOLSTER PISTOL 15in. Barrel 9in with military proofs
at breech, the lock marked with crown 'G.R.' and
'Tower', full stocked with 1800 ordnance stamp on
butt, regular pattern brass mounts, the sideplate
stamped 'C 38', brass tipped ramrod.

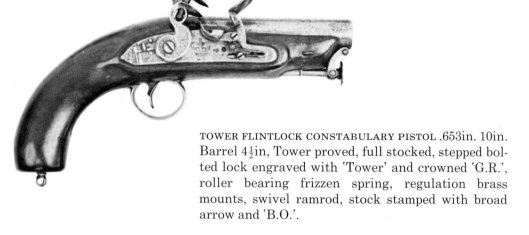

TOWER FLINTLOCK CONSTABULARY PISTOL .653in. 10in. Barrel 4½in, Tower proved, full stocked, stepped bolted lock engraved with 'Tower' and crowned 'G.R.', roller bearing frizzen spring, regulation brass mounts, swivel ramrod, stock stamped with broad arrow and 'B.O.'.

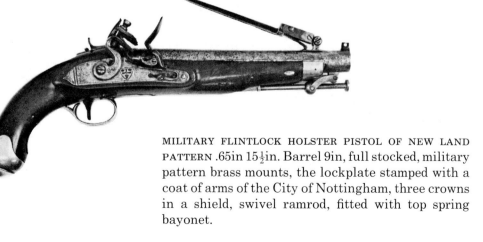

16-BORE TOWER NEW LAND PATTERN MILITARY FLINTLOCK HOLSTER PISTOL 15in. Barrel 9in with military proofs at breech, the lock stamped with crown 'G.R.' and 'Tower'. Full stocked, brass mounts, swivel ramrod.

MILITARY FLINTLOCK HOLSTER PISTOL OF NEW LAND PATTERN .65in 15½in. Barrel 9in, full stocked, military pattern brass mounts, the lockplate stamped with a coat of arms of the City of Nottingham, three crowns in a shield, swivel ramrod, fitted with top spring bayonet.

16-BORE MID-18TH CENTURY MILITARY CAVALRY HOL-
STER PISTOL 18½in. Barrel 12in, full stocked military
brass mounts, banana-shaped lockplate engraved
crown 'G.R.' and 'Smith, 1742', spurred buttcap, brass
escutcheon inset in butt. 'G.R.' stamp at breech.

PAIR OF 18-BORE FLINTLOCK HOLSTER PISTOLS, circa
1760, 12½in. London proved barrels 7in, with 'I.B.' and
engraved 'London Sucr to Mr Barbar' within teardrop. Full stocked, linear engraved lockplates with
'Clemmes Sling Lane'. Brass furniture, longspur buttcaps, florally engraved trigger guards, scrolled open
sideplates, shell finialed escutcheons. Brass pipes
and brass tipped wooden ramrods. Stocks carved
with tears behind barrel tangs.

SILVERGILT MOUNTED 21-BORE FLINTLOCK HOLSTER PIS-
TOL by Searles, circa 1800, 23in. Half octagonal barrel
17in, stepped and faceted with gold lines and engraving at breech and 'J.S. Searles, London' in copperplate script on top flat. Full stocked, linear engraved stepped lockplate with maker's name, gold
lined pan and vent roller on frizzen, rainproof pan.
Silvergilt Eastern style furniture chiselled with
classical trophies of arms, cornucopiae, flowers, foliate, etc, including throat pipe. Stock inlaid overall
with scrolling silver wire and engraved sheet silver
plaques.

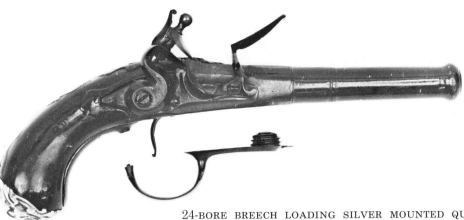

24-BORE BREECH LOADING SILVER MOUNTED QUEEN ANNE STYLE CANNON BARRELLED FLINTLOCK BOXLOCK SIDECOCK HOLSTER PISTOL by R. Rowland, Londini, circa 1720, 10¾in. Barrel 4½in to loading port with turned re-inforcing rings, breech stamped with London proof and maker's mark crowned 'R' within shield, part octagonal faceted breech engraved with frond tips. Trigger guard hinges and turns two and a half revolutions to reveal loading port. Squared flattened cock and frizzen, signed below L-shaped frizzen spring 'R – Rowland – Londini'. Rounded walnut butt silver furniture, grotesque mask buttcap, escutcheon with grotesque masks above and below engraved with family crest of the pelican upon a bar. Pierced scrolling foliate sideplate with mythical animals head. Butt carved with shallow foliate aprons around mounts and frame terminals. R. Rowland appears to have been one of the most successful manufacturers of breech loading weapons at the beginning of the 17th century and evidently took great pride in his speciality. A breech loading sporting gun by Rowland is in the Royal Sporting Gun Collection at Windsor.

36-BORE WHITE METAL FRAMED AND DOUBLE BARRELLED FLINTLOCK BOXLOCK HOLSTER PISTOL by King of London, circa 1770, 12¾in. Turn-off cannon barrels 5½in, muzzles slotted for key, Tower proved, dog-tooth border engraved frame with rocaille, scrolls and 'King, London', sliding single pan-cover to left, the sliding lever on left of frame. Frizzen spring sunk in breech top, sliding trigger guard safety, rounded butt with grotesque silver butt mask.

DOUBLE BARRELLED 16-BORE OVER AND UNDER FLINT-LOCK HOLSTER PISTOL CARBINE with detachable shoulder stock, by D. Egg 19in. Browned barrels 10in, gold lined vents, ramrod with chequered tip on right of barrels. London proved, stepped bolted lockplates signed 'D. Egg' in his classic script. Linear engraved lock with thunderbursts and Britannia shield, floral scrolls on cocks, steel mounts, engraved steel furniture, large bow on trigger guard, boldly chequered butt, slotted for shoulder stock, complete with its original detachable skeleton shoulder stock engraved on top strap 'D. Egg's patent butt'.

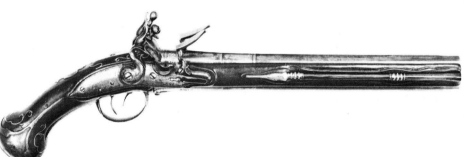

26-BORE DOUBLE BARRELLED OVER AND UNDER ENGLISH FLINTLOCK HOLSTER PISTOL by John Shaw, Londini, circa 1700, 20½in. Stepped barrels 13in, each stamped with maker's mark 'J.S.' and London proofs. Full stocked, down drooping rounded locks, twin line engraved borders engraved 'John Shaw, Londini', rounded cocks and unbridled frizzens, steel furniture, double trigger, ribbed trigger guard bow. Long-spur buttcap with grotesque mask boss, foliate finialed escutcheon, the butt inlaid with scroll silver wire.

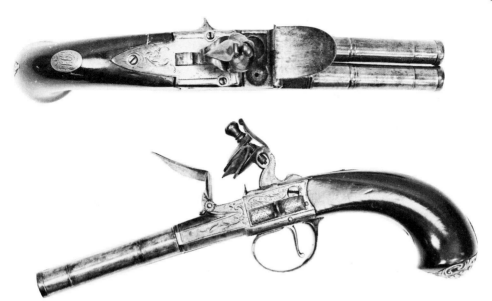

PAIR OF DOUBLE BARRELLED BOXLOCK FLINTLOCK CAN-
NON BARREL HOLSTER PISTOLS by Barbar, with sliding
pan-cutoffs, 11in. Turn-off cannon barrels 3½in,
Tower proved, dog-tooth border and scroll engraved
frames with 'Barbar, London' within banners, sliding
trigger guard safeties, side sliding pancovers to
left hand pans, frizzen springs sunk in breech tops,
rounded walnut butts with silver grotesque mask
buttcaps, oval escutcheons engraved 'J.I.'.

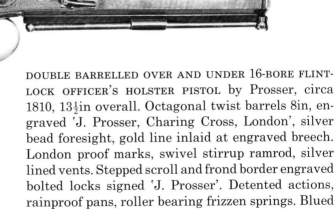

DOUBLE BARRELLED OVER AND UNDER 16-BORE FLINT-
LOCK OFFICER'S HOLSTER PISTOL by Prosser, circa
1810, 13½in overall. Octagonal twist barrels 8in, engraved 'J. Prosser, Charing Cross, London', silver
bead foresight, gold line inlaid at engraved breech.
London proof marks, swivel stirrup ramrod, silver
lined vents. Stepped scroll and frond border engraved
bolted locks signed 'J. Prosser'. Detented actions,
rainproof pans, roller bearing frizzen springs. Blued
trigger guard engraved with Britannia shield central
motif amidst scrolls. Finely figured walnut butt with
fine chequering. Vacant octagonal silver escutcheon.

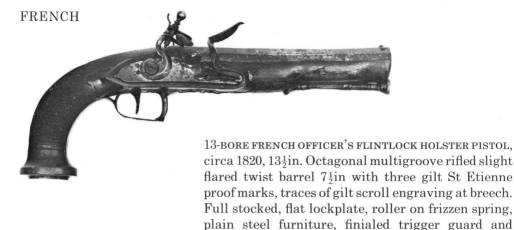

13-BORE FRENCH OFFICER'S FLINTLOCK HOLSTER PISTOL, circa 1820, 13½in. Octagonal multigroove rifled slight flared twist barrel 7½in with three gilt St Etienne proof marks, traces of gilt scroll engraving at breech. Full stocked, flat lockplate, roller on frizzen spring, plain steel furniture, finialed trigger guard and throat pipe, chequered butt, stock carved around trigger guard and ramrod pipes.

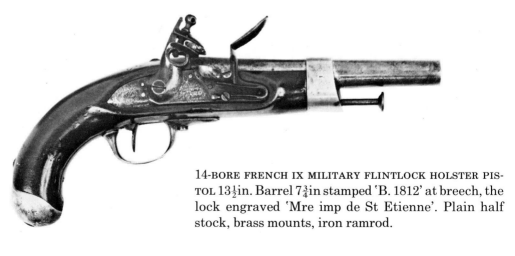

FRENCH 14-BORE MODEL 1777 CAVALRY FLINTLOCK HOLSTER PISTOL 13in. Barrel 7¼in marked '98' at breech, brass frame marked 'St Etienne' with crown and 'J' above the brass pan, trigger guard and butt-cap, butt bears traces of stamp 'Juillet 1786'.

14-BORE FRENCH IX MILITARY FLINTLOCK HOLSTER PISTOL 13½in. Barrel 7¾in stamped 'B. 1812' at breech, the lock engraved 'Mre imp de St Etienne'. Plain half stock, brass mounts, iron ramrod.

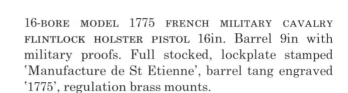

16-BORE MODEL 1775 FRENCH MILITARY CAVALRY
FLINTLOCK HOLSTER PISTOL 16in. Barrel 9in with
military proofs. Full stocked, lockplate stamped
'Manufacture de St Etienne', barrel tang engraved
'1775', regulation brass mounts.

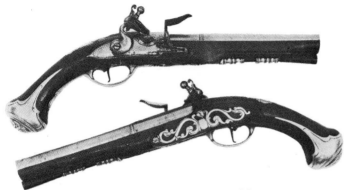

PAIR OF 16-BORE FRENCH SILVER MOUNTED FLINTLOCK
HOLSTER PISTOLS, circa 1720, 15½in. Half octagonal
swamped barrels 8¾in. Full stocked, slight rounded
lockplates with lipped borders en suite with cocks
and frizzens, silver furniture comprising longspur
buttcaps, with grotesque mask bosses, foliate finialed
trigger guards with ribbed bows, crowned foliate
escutcheons with portrait busts in low relief, baluster pipes, pierced scrolling sideplates each with
two rearing monsters. Horn forecaps, silver tipped
wooden ramrods.

LONG 21-BORE FRENCH FLINTLOCK HOLSTER PISTOL
21in. Barrel 14in stamped at chevron fluted breech
with proof mark, scroll and foliate engraved with
pellet borders. Full stocked, lock and cock engraved
and chiselled with scrolls in low relief. Brass furniture, longspur buttcap with interlaced scrollwork in
low relief. Pierced engraved foliate sideplate, trigger
guard engraved, stepped finials, engraved stepped
escutcheon, stock engraved around barrel tang.

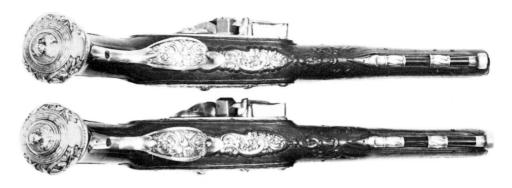

PAIR OF 24-BORE FRENCH SILVER MOUNTED FLINTLOCK
HOLSTER PISTOLS by Cassaignard à Nantes, circa
1770, 14in overall. Stepped slightly flared barrels in
two sections 8in, decorated with gold damascened
decoration of alternately rope twist flowers and foliage, rocaille scroll, and laurel wreaths upon blued
ground, silver foresights surrounded by gold damascened thunderbursts. Full stocked, flat bevelled lockplate with scrolled steps at tails engraved with military trophies, scrolls and 'Cassaignard à Nantes'.
Walnut full stocks, fine quality chased silver furniture, each struck with control mark of a standing
bird, comprising longspur buttcaps with military
trophies in relief, the bosses chased in relief with bust
portraits. Trigger guard terminals chased in relief
with flowers within rocaille, trophies on bows en
suite with sideplates. Ramrod pipes engraved as rope
twist, bone tipped whalebone ramrods. Stocks scroll
and rocaille carved around barrel tangs and throat
pipes.

ORMOLU MOUNTED 24-BORE FRENCH FLINTLOCK HOL-
STER PISTOL, circa 1715–20, 21in. Swamped faceted
barrel, 14½in, gold damascened overall with thunder
clap at saddle breech, extensive classical trophy of
arms incorporating a warrior surrounded by the in-
struments of war, foliate pattern on top flat, muzzle
with mounted knight with foliate surround, pellets
around muzzle face. Full stocked in mulberry wood,
engraved gilt furniture and backplate. Slight
banana-shaped flat lockplate engraved with scenes of
the chase, dogs and stag in a landscape, engraved
cock and frizzen, frizzen spring with much original
blued finish. Bulbous longspur buttcap with lobes,
also a lion's head boss, finely engraved with foliage
and stands of arms. Fine escutcheon chiselled as a
devil mask, pierced sideplate of two serpents opposed
on a grotesque mask. Foliate finialed and engraved
trigger guard, octagonal ramrod pipes. Stock with
some border and foliate carving. Wooden ramrod.

FRENCH MID-17TH CENTURY 28-BORE FLINTLOCK HOL-
STER PISTOL 22½in. Italian style barrel 16in with long
fluted octagonal section at breech. Flat lockplate
with fluted edges and traces of engraved decoration,
the tail chiselled in the form of a monster's head, the
cock chiselled in the form of a fish. Slender walnut
full stock with chiselled mounts, pierced ramrod pipes
and pierced and engraved trigger. Original iron
tipped ramrod.

LATE 18TH CENTURY FRENCH FLINTLOCK HOLSTER PISTOL 25in. Liege proved, barrel 17in with flat topped breech engraved with foliate sprays and 'France'. Rounded lock with raised pan and roller on frizzen spring, the plate engraved 'Georges Franzidis, Marseille'. Full stocked, with plain silver fore-end cap and ramrod pipe, all other mounts of heavy cast silver with raised trophies of arms, foliage, etc. Steel ramrod.

32-BORE FLINTLOCK HOLSTER PISTOL by Foullon of Nancy, circa 1670, 18½in. Part octagonal stepped swamped barrel 11¾in, proved with a tower at breech. Full stocked, rounded twin line engraved lockplate with foliage by cock and 'Foullon A Nancy', pellets engraved around rim of pan, swollen teat on back of frizzen. Polished steel furniture, longspur buttcap, ribbed trigger guard, swollen finial, baluster ramrod pipe, wooden ramrod carved and swollen stock at throat. Simple curved sideplate.

PAIR OF 36-BORE FRENCH OFFICER'S FLINTLOCK HOLSTER PISTOLS by Carl Starek, the locks by Griffin and Tow, 13½in. Octagonal multigrooved barrels 7½in sighted and engraved 'Carabine par peniet arq. Sier du Roy. Carl Starek in Wienn. Cour des F. traines au plais Royal à Paris'. Full stocked, stepped bolted lockplates. Engraved 'Griffin and Tow', with linear and floral decoration. Friction roller on frizzen high fence, gold lined pan and vent. Steel furniture, acorn finialed trigger guard, squared slab buttplate. Steel tipped ramrods. It would appear that these pistols were custom made with English locks.

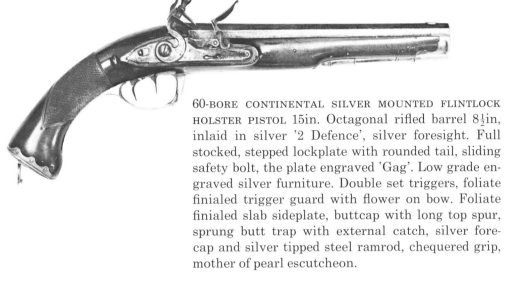

60-BORE CONTINENTAL SILVER MOUNTED FLINTLOCK
HOLSTER PISTOL 15in. Octagonal rifled barrel 8½in,
inlaid in silver '2 Defence', silver foresight. Full
stocked, stepped lockplate with rounded tail, sliding
safety bolt, the plate engraved 'Gag'. Low grade engraved silver furniture. Double set triggers, foliate
finialed trigger guard with flower on bow. Foliate
finialed slab sideplate, buttcap with long top spur,
sprung butt trap with external catch, silver forecap and silver tipped steel ramrod, chequered grip,
mother of pearl escutcheon.

Double Barrelled

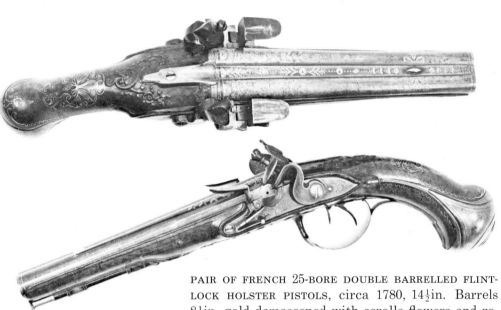

PAIR OF FRENCH 25-BORE DOUBLE BARRELLED FLINT-
LOCK HOLSTER PISTOLS, circa 1780, 14½in. Barrels
8¼in, gold damascened with scrolls flowers and rocaille, silver foresight. Full stocked, scroll engraved
locks and cocks, engraved steel furniture comprising foliate finialed trigger guards, bows engraved
with rocaille centred trophies of arms, longspur bulbous, foliate engraved buttcaps, the bosses engraved with suns-in-splendour. Steel tipped horn ramrods, walnut stocks foliate and floral carved around
furniture and barrel tangs, inlaid scrolling silver
wire escutcheons and buttcap borders.

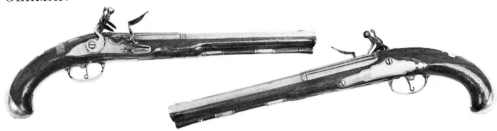

PAIR OF 27-BORE MID-18TH CENTURY GERMAN FLINT-
LOCK HOLSTER PISTOLS 18in. Barrels 12in with fluted
octagonal breeches, deeply impressed with mark of
'bear passing tree'. Flattened lockplate with bevelled
edges en suite with cocks and frizzens. Foliate engraved frizzen springs. Full stocked faceted brass
furniture. Trigger guards with long finials, octagonal
ramrod pipes, shaped escutcheons, ribbed pointed
buttcaps. Slab sideplates, foliate carved around barrel tangs and throat pipes, horn forecaps and horn
tipped ramrods.

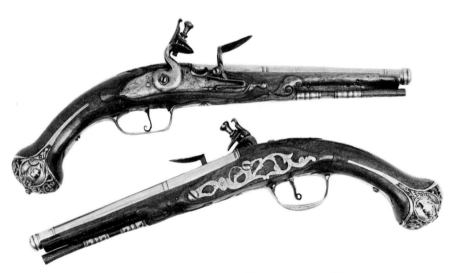

PAIR OF 48-BORE EARLY 18TH CENTURY GERMAN BRASS
BARRELLED FLINTLOCK HOLSTER PISTOLS 15in. Half
octagonal stepped brass barrels of slender form with
turned muzzles. Full stocked, foliate engraved slight
rounded lockplates. Brass furniture, pierced longspur buttcaps, deeply chiselled scroll in foliage, and
two portrait busts in relief, foliate engraved trigger
guard bows. Pierced scrolling sideplates. Baluster
ramrod pipes. Stocks foliate carved around barrel
tangs and throat pipes. Horn forecaps, wooden ramrods.

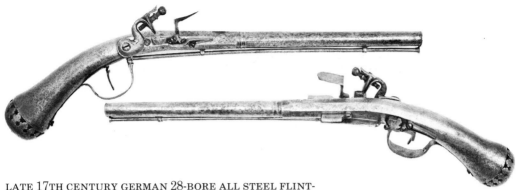

LATE 17TH CENTURY GERMAN 28-BORE ALL STEEL FLINT-
LOCK HORSEMAN'S PISTOL, circa 1680–90, 19in. Barrel
12in with narrow raised muzzle ring and octagonal
breech impressed with maker's initials and Saxon
guild mark, external mechanism with the pan and
frizzen spring assembly secured to right of breech by
two bolts. Round tapered butt with bolted on pierced
domed cap. Plain flat iron trigger guard, original
steel ramrod in two loops beneath barrel.

OTHER COUNTRIES OF ORIGIN   Austrian

14-BORE AUSTRIAN MILITARY FLINTLOCK HOLSTER PIS-
TOL 17in. Barrel 9¾in, Leige proved. Full stocked,
regulation lock struck with Imperial Eagle, regulation brass mounts, steel ramrod and lanyard
ring.

PAIR OF 14-BORE AUSTRIAN MILITARY FLINTLOCK HOL-
STER PISTOLS 18in. Barrels 11½in, octagonal at breech,
stamped with military proofs. Full stocked, stepped
lockplates, regulation brass mounts, slab sideplates,
rounded trigger guards, longspur buttcaps.

Dutch

Spanish

DUTCH 28-BORE DOUBLE BARRELLED OVER AND UNDER TURNOVER FLINTLOCK HOLSTER PISTOL, circa 1700, 18in. Barrels $10\frac{3}{4}$in in three stages, the octagonal breeches with traces of scroll engraving, separate pan and frizzen assemblies mounted on engraved plates. Full stocked with rammer on one side mounted in steel baluster ramrod pipes, foliate engraved back-action lock signed 'Herman', with matching steel sideplate. Plain figured walnut butt with engraved longspurred buttcap, plain trigger guard with flower engraved medallion, and shield-shaped escutcheon, sprung catch at front of trigger guard for releasing barrels.

EARLY 18TH CENTURY SPANISH 16-BORE RIPOLL MIQUELET FLINTLOCK HOLSTER PISTOL 12in. Barrel $7\frac{1}{2}$in with octagonal breech, moulded band, and raised muzzle ring, maker's marks including 'MAS' in rectangle at breech, the lock with shell design on frizzen spring cover and cock bridle, ribbed frizzen with impressed poincon of 'Vayaras'. Full stocked with spherical terminal to butt, plain iron sideplate and spurred trigger guard, brass mounts including scroll engraved fore-end cap, band round fore-end in front of lock, pierced and engraved brass overlay behind breech and on ball butt.

20-BORE EARLY 18TH CENTURY SPANISH MIQUELET FLINTLOCK HOLSTER PISTOL 15in. Three quarters octagonal barrel $8\frac{3}{4}$in. Full stocked, lock of classic form, striated frizzen stamped with maker's mark 'I. Bornio', steel buttcap and fluted trigger guard, sheet steel sideplate, brass tipped wooden ramrod.

Italian

14-BORE ITALIAN MILITARY FLINTLOCK CAVALRY HOL-STER PISTOL, similar to French AN IX, and possibly produced for use by the French Army of Occupation, 14in. Barrel 7½in, three quarter stocked, single brass barrel band, brass mounts, lockplate marked 'Mra Rle Di Napoli', butt stamped 'I.S. 81'. No provision for ramrod.

LATE 17TH CENTURY 16-BORE ITALIAN FLINTLOCK HOL-STER PISTOL, by Bergonze In Bresa, 19½in. Half octagonal barrel 12½in, engraved 'Vicenzo Cominazzo', silver foresight, the breech chiselled with grotesque mask in relief. Full stocked, slight rounded banana-shaped lockplate engraved 'Bergonze In Bresa', frizzen, pan, top jaw, cock and tail of lockplate chiselled with acanthus foliage. Longspur buttcap chiselled with scroll acanthus foliage and grotesque mask butt, trigger guard with pierced foliate terminals, chiselled with grotesque mask on bow, pierced scrolling serpent sideplate and grotesque mask. Baluster ramrod pipes and fore-end band, steel tipped wooden ramrod. Early 18th century rococo stock, carved with rocaille scrolls in relief.

Turkish

TURKISH 16-BORE FLINTLOCK HOLSTER PISTOL 25in. Barrel 17in, full stocked, four white metal foliate embossed large barrel bands. The butt decorated with white metal floral plaques with coloured stones, hammer engraved with frond decor, rainproof pan, roller on frizzen spring, Liege proved.

TURKISH 16-BORE SILVER MOUNTED FLINTLOCK HOL-
STER PISTOL 22½in. Barrel 14½in, full stocked. Three
large Eastern silver barrel bands embossed with foliate patterns, Eastern silver ramrod pipes, plain lock,
trigger guard, sideplate buttcap and breech mount of
embossed foliate Eastern sheet silver, silver wire
bound small of stock. Buttcap decorated with masks
within oval panels, military standards, etc.

TURKISH 20-BORE BALL BUTTED FLINTLOCK HOLSTER
PISTOL 21in. Barrel 14in, chiselled with foliate and
other patterns at breech. Full stocked, elaborately
chiselled lock, worked with foliate and other patterns. Large ball butt, the stock and butt intricately
inlaid with scrolled German silver wire patterns, and
pewter segment ditto in floral and other designs.

16-BORE TURKISH FLINTLOCK HOLSTER PISTOL 20in.
Barrel 13in, step chiselled at breech with poincon,
top rib slight silver inlaid. Full stocked. Intricately
geometric and scroll engraved stepped lock.

PAIR OF TURKISH OR BALKAN 21-BORE FLINTLOCK HOL-
STER PISTOLS in the Italian style, 20½in. Barrels 14in
with recessed scrolled panels at breeches and spuri-
ous signatures 'Lazari Cominas', rounded locks with
chiselled panels and stylised masks on tails. Full
stocked with floral carving round trigger guards, etc,
steel mounts including longspurred buttcaps, the
butts bound with silver wire in herringbone patterns,
chased sheet silver muzzle sheaths, barrel bands, and
covers to butts behind breeches, steel ramrods with
chased silver finials.

PAIR OF 20-BORE TURKISH FLINTLOCK HOLSTER PISTOLS
20in. Barrels 13in, inlaid in silver 'L. Lasarino', scroll
silver inlay at breech with imitation maker's poincon. Full stocked, carved overall with various foliate
patterns, brass trigger guards and elaborate spurred
buttcaps with silver tips, foliate engraved lockplates
and cocks with some gilt decoration. The butt inlaid
with silver wire and plaques mounted with three
stones.

Greek

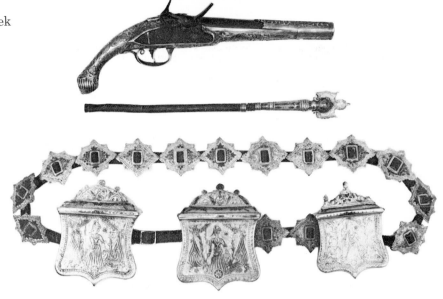

22-BORE GREEK NIELLOED WHITE METAL FLINTLOCK
HOLSTER PISTOL with its suite of accoutrements, 15in.
Barrel 9in, scroll chiselled stepped lockplate with
white metal inlaid band, striated frizzen. Full stocked
in floral and foliate nielloed bands, flowers, etc and
stylised human face. Large muzzle sheath. Nielloed
white metal ramrod suma, linear iron shaft (concealing a sprung dagger), handle incorporating faces,
suns and double headed eagles. Complete with its
belt containing a pair of chiselled and nielloed white
metal cartridge boxes depicting Britannia-style deity
amid trophies, a smaller sun box for priming powder
and fifteen white metal nielloed buckles depicting
faces and trophies, etc.

Albanian

ALBANIAN 18-BORE MIQUELET FLINTLOCK HOLSTER PIS-
TOL 22in. Barrel 14in with traces of chiselled decoration at breech, plain lock of traditional type,
carved wood fore-end. The large muzzle sheath and rat-
tail butt entirely of low grade silver, with deep relief
decoration overall, steel ramrod pipes and ramrod,
the latter with non-original ivory tip.

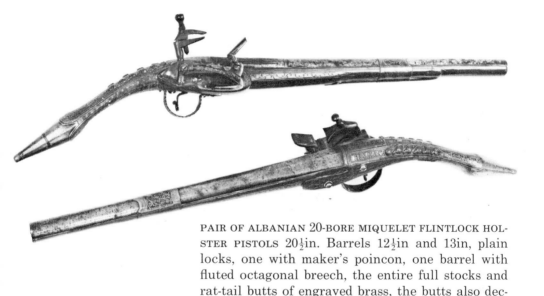

25-BORE ALBANIAN MIQUELET FLINTLOCK HOLSTER PIS-TOL stocked in engraved sheet brass, 21½in. Barrel 14in, full stocked, lockplate stamped with maker's mark. Decorative bridle, striated dovetailed frizzen, ribbed top jaw, turned screw, stock and rat-tail butt engraved with scrolls and geometric repeat patterns, pewter stud decoration, steel ramrod.

PAIR OF ALBANIAN 20-BORE MIQUELET FLINTLOCK HOL-STER PISTOLS 20½in. Barrels 12½in and 13in, plain locks, one with maker's poincon, one barrel with fluted octagonal breech, the entire full stocks and rat-tail butts of engraved brass, the butts also dec-orated with white metal pique studs, single brass barrel bands.

24-BORE ALBANIAN MIQUELET FLINTLOCK HOLSTER PIS-TOL 18½in. Barrel 10in, some inlaid foliate brass decoration, the stock sheathed in brass, two broad barrel bands of brass, decorated overall with scroll work, etc, lock with simple linear decoration and struck with mark, rat-tailed butt.

RUSSIAN COSSACK 18-BORE MIQUELET FLINTLOCK HOL-
STER PISTOL 19½in. Barrel 14in, plain lock with ribbed
frizzen, plain full stock and butt with ivory ball finial,
iron ball trigger.

20-BORE BALKAN FLINTLOCK HOLSTER PISTOL 18½in.
Barrel 11½in, damascened overall with scroll silver
and line of gold script. Full stocked, slight rounded
lock, scrolled chased with silver damascened decoration, nielloed silver buttcap with scrolls in relief,
the butt covered with silver filigree work and applied
shapes incorporating two pink corals, steel sideplates and trigger guard, large scroll embossed forecap.

34-BORE RUSSIAN COSSACK MIQUELET FLINTLOCK HOL-
STER PISTOL 16½in. Barrel 10¾in with ornamental brass
poincon and some foliate chiselling. Full leather-
covered stock with bone fore-end tip, lockplate of
classic type, bridle stamped with maker's poincon,
dovetailed striated frizzen, button trigger steel backstrap, ivory ball butt, two white metal barrel bands.

RUSSIAN 14-BORE MILITARY FLINTLOCK HOLSTER PISTOL
17in. Barrel 10in. Full stocked, brass mounts, arrow
arsenal mark appearing on some mounts, dated 1824
beneath lockplate, flatwood butt with spurred buttcap.

DOUBLE BARRELLED SIDE BY SIDE 36-BORE RUSSIAN
COSSACK MIQUELET FLINTLOCK HOLSTER PISTOL, circa
1800, 17in. Barrels 11in. Full stocked in black leather-
covered wood and overlaid with much arabesque
nielloed silver. Large bulbous buttcap, backstrap
with fretted edges, double button triggers, throat
pipe with beaded mouth.

BALKAN 22-BORE FLINTLOCK HOLSTER PISTOL 16in. Barrel 10¾in with imitation inscription and proof marks
at breech. Rounded lock of French form also engraved with curious inscription, leaf designs, etc.
Full stocked with carving round throat pipe, barrel
tang, and buttcap, dummy ramrod, steel mounts including engraved trigger guard and sideplate, and
chiselled buttcap.

BALKAN 20-BORE MIQUELET FLINTLOCK HOLSTER PISTOL
18in. Barrel 12½in, small plain lock with inset brass
poincon. The entire full stock and large ball butt
inlaid with white metal wire designs, mother of pearl
plaques and pieces of coral. No provision for ramrod,
small button trigger.

Caucasian

CAUCASIAN 20-BORE FLINTLOCK HOLSTER PISTOL 15½in. Spanish style barrel 9½in in two stages, the muzzle round with brass foresight, the breech octagonal with brass poincons and gold damascened, flowers, lines and 'Loadoa'. Engraved lock with swan neck cock, raised pan and roller on frizzen spring. Full stocked with dummy ramrod, scrolled carving, and silver wire inlay at muzzle, the butt profusely carved round barrel tang with stylised trophy of arms and inlaid with silver wire scrolls and leaves, silver damascened iron trigger guard, sideplate and ramrod pipe, the escutcheon and spurred buttcap of white metal embossed with trophies of arms.

CAUCASIAN MIQUELET FLINTLOCK HOLSTER PISTOL 19in. Barrel 14in, the breech with scrolled decoration and proof marks. Full stocked, three steel barrel bands, the stock covered in leather, the lockplate struck with armourer's mark. Ball finial to trigger, plain wooden ball butt.

Flintlock Duelling Pistols

Long after the introduction of firearms, the ritual test of honour – the duel – was fought with swords. There were recorded examples of pistol duels in the 17th century but it was not until the latter part of the 18th century the pistol replaced the sword.

In these early duels presumably any pistol was used but as literally life and death hung in the balance, every gentleman wanted pistols of the very best manufacture. The early pistols meant for these murderous purposes had little or no decoration. The duelling pistol as we know it was fully developed by the end of the 18th century. Basically, they had an octagonal barrel, the quadrant butts with exquisite chequering, mainly to afford a firm grip and the trigger guard often with a spur. All this to ensure a firm, steady hold as the butt was gripped with the thumb and two fingers, the index finger was through the trigger guard and the second finger around the spur. This pistol was made as a precision instrument, the barrel had to be precisely true, the ball a dead fit, the lock infallible and the balance perfect. Any defect would cost the owner his life.

French duelling pistols were usually rifled but this was not thought sporting in England where smooth-bores were required.

The etiquette of duelling required that the pistols came in matched pairs and the choice of pistols was given to the challenged party. Duelling pistols came in a wooden case, divided into compartments to hold, along with the pistols, such accessories as powder flask, screwdrivers, cleaning rods, bullet mould, etc. The fitting of the brass furniture in the boxes was of such quality and precision it was evidently done by the gunsmiths.

Frequent practice was, of course, essential to the dueller's art but it was unthinkable to wear out or abuse the precision-made duelling pistols. Very often a gentleman had a pair of target pistols made of the same balance and weight as his duelling pistols but with a very much smaller bore. These could be used in any room or in one of the pistol galleries in the large towns, where one's abilities were monitored and one's reputation heralded or disclaimed.

LATE 18TH CENTURY 20-BORE FLINTLOCK DUELLING PISTOL 14in. Blued octagonal barrel 9in with London proofs and silver star foresight, plain stepped lock signed 'Ketland and Co', roller bearing on frizzen spring and mainspring. Full stocked, with shell carving round barrel tang and flattened butt, flower engraved trigger guard with acorn finial, horn tipped wooden ramrod.

18-BORE FLINTLOCK DUELLING PISTOL 15½in. Octagonal barrel 9in, by William Wallis, full stocked, steel mounts, pineapple finial to trigger guard, rainproof pan, roller on frizzen spring, diced wood butt.

30-BORE FLINTLOCK DUELLING PISTOL by John Manton and Sons, London 15in. Octagonal barrel 10in, full stocked, steel mounts, lockplate well engraved with acanthus leaves, rainproof pan, roller on frizzen spring, gold lining to touch hole, bar safety to rear of cock.

18-BORE FLINTLOCK DUELLING PISTOL 15in. Heavy octagonal browned twist barrel 10in, with gold line and touch hole and gold inlaid 'Manton, London', plain stepped lock signed 'Manton', with rainproof pan and roller on frizzen. Full stocked with flat sided partly chequered butt, steel mounts including engraved trigger guard with pineapple finial.

PAIR OF 30-BORE FLINTLOCK DUELLING PISTOLS by P. Bond, circa 1780, 15in. Octagonal barrel 9¾in, engraved 'P. Bond, Cornhill and Lombard Street, London'. Full stocked, stepped bolted lockplates engraved with 'P. Bond'. Shell finialed blued trigger guards engraved with Britannia shield centred floral tributes, capstan screw set triggers. Boldly chequered rounded butts, silver barrel wedgeplates, wooden ramrods horn tipped with steel worm, and steel tipped with worm. Contained in their original green baize lined fitted mahogany case with P. Bond's illustrated trade label, containing leather-covered three-way flask, ball mould and cleaning rods.

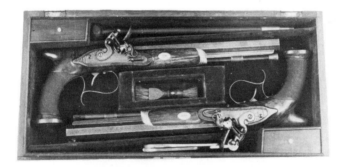

PAIR OF 30-BORE FLINTLOCK DUELLING PISTOLS, circa 1825, 15½in. Octagonal damascus barrels 10in, by T. Mortimer, London, the false breeches bearing oval silver plaques engraved with maker's name, the barrels engraved 'Gun Maker to His Majesty', flat bolted locks extremely well re-converted from percussion with rainproof pans and roller on frizzen springs, engraved fern leaf borders and trophy of arms on tail of lockplates. Half stocked with engraved silver fore end caps and flat engraved oval buttcaps, saw handle butts with rounded chequered grips, engraved steel trigger guards with pineapple finials, single set triggers.

PAIR OF 30-BORE SAW HANDLED FLINTLOCK DUELLING
PISTOLS by Tatham and Egg, circa 1825, 15½in.
Sighted slight browned twist octagonal barrels 9in,
gold lines to breech with gold poincon of Tatham and
Egg. Half stocked, stepped linear engraved lockplates
with safety bolts to rear of cocks, engraved 'Tatham
and Egg' with slight scroll engraving. Waterproof
gold lined pan, friction roller to frizzens, linear
engraved teardrop frizzens, sunburst engraved on top
jaw. Steel furniture with much original finish, fine
floral engraved buttplate with Tatham and Egg's 954
Improvement in gold with 'scale' engraved bands.
Sunburst to throat holes, linear engraved trigger
guards with trophies. Set triggers with capstan
screws, scroll, floral and sunburst engraving to
barrel tangs. Brass capped ramrods with worm and
powder measure. Silver barrel wedgeplates and silver
escutcheons engraved 'W.G.', chequered grips.

PAIR OF 28-BORE FLINTLOCK DUELLING PISTOLS, circa
1790, 14½in. Slender octagonal barrels 9½in, by
Wogdon, London, flat bolted locks, engraved with
maker's name, plain walnut full stocked, and slightly
flattened rounded butts. Steel mounts including engraved trigger guards with pineapple finials and
small engraved rounded buttcaps, one with plain
oval silver escutcheon between sidenails.

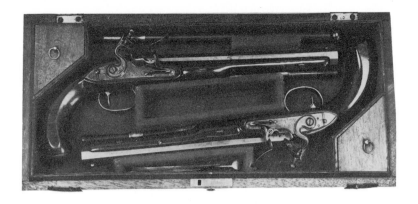

PAIR OF 26-BORE FLINTLOCK DUELLING PISTOLS, by Wogdon and Barton, 15in. Octagonal barrels 10in, engraved 'Wogdon and Barton' in script, silver foresights. Full stocked, stepped bolted locks, script engraved Wogdon and Barton, set triggers, engraved pineapple finialed trigger guards and flush rounded buttcaps, flattened grip sides.

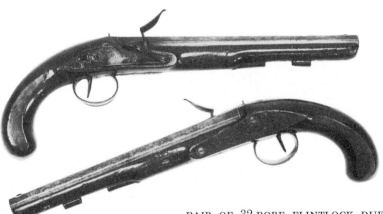

PAIR OF 32-BORE FLINTLOCK DUELLING PISTOLS, by Wogdon, 15in. Octagonal barrels 10in, silver foresights, top flats engraved 'Wogdon' in script, 'London' in capitals, pellet engraved breech, foliate, floral and scroll engraved barrel tangs. Full stocked, stepped lockplates engraved 'Wogdon' in script, simple flower heads on tails, sliding safety bolts, detented actions. Set triggers, acorn finialed trigger guards engraved with floral and foliate bouquets, buttcaps inlaid flush and engraved with shell, flowers and wreaths, wreath sidenail cups, rounded butts with flattened sides.

IRISH

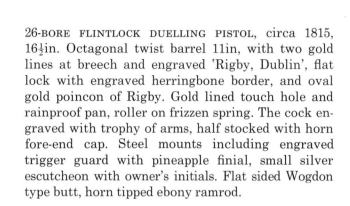

26-BORE FLINTLOCK DUELLING PISTOL, circa 1815, 16½in. Octagonal twist barrel 11in, with two gold lines at breech and engraved 'Rigby, Dublin', flat lock with engraved herringbone border, and oval gold poincon of Rigby. Gold lined touch hole and rainproof pan, roller on frizzen spring. The cock engraved with trophy of arms, half stocked with horn fore-end cap. Steel mounts including engraved trigger guard with pineapple finial, small silver escutcheon with owner's initials. Flat sided Wogdon type butt, horn tipped ebony ramrod.

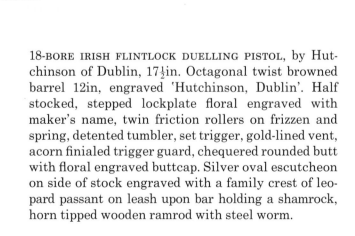

18-BORE IRISH FLINTLOCK DUELLING PISTOL, by Hutchinson of Dublin, 17½in. Octagonal twist browned barrel 12in, engraved 'Hutchinson, Dublin'. Half stocked, stepped lockplate floral engraved with maker's name, twin friction rollers on frizzen and spring, detented tumbler, set trigger, gold-lined vent, acorn finialed trigger guard, chequered rounded butt with floral engraved buttcap. Silver oval escutcheon on side of stock engraved with a family crest of leopard passant on leash upon bar holding a shamrock, horn tipped wooden ramrod with steel worm.

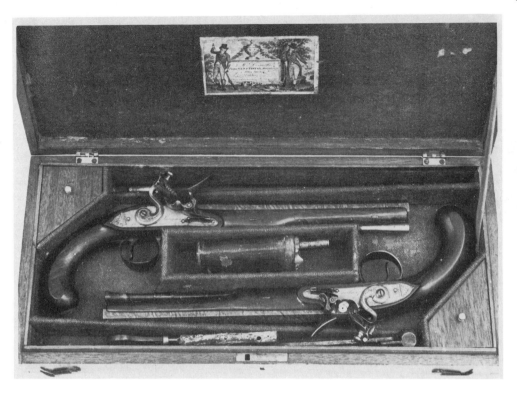

PAIR OF LATE 18TH CENTURY 20-BORE FLINTLOCK DUEL-LING PISTOLS 15in. Browned twist barrels 10in with gold touch holes and engraved gold lines at breeches, by Langson, Dublin. Flat locks with raised gold lined pans, rollers on frizzens, large sliding safeties on rear of lockplates and elegant swan neck cocks. Plain walnut full stocks and slight flattened butts with small plain oval silver caps. Steel mounts including flower engraved trigger guard with pineapple finials, one steel tipped ramrod with screw-off measure, the other with horn tip and worm. These pistols orig-inally belonged to Sir John Slade, first baronet who commanded the King's Dragoon Guards in 1800 and was a general in the Peninsular War.

Flintlock Sporting Guns

Hunting has always been one of man's main activities. Originally his motivation was necessity: he hunted to eat. The main criterion for the weapon he used was accuracy. In the 18th century the popularity of hunting grew as a sport for those with leisure and money. Some of the finest quality flintlock long arms were made for sporting purposes and large numbers of these weapons were made at this time due to the popularity of the sport.

Those who used a weapon for sporting purposes thought that the gun should be refined as much as possible and adorned with embellishments. Usually cost was not the most important factor and hence large sums of money were spent on deciding such things as the best length and type of barrel, the type and amount of powder, etc. Once a good accurate barrel was discovered, decoration was added. Early sporting guns were single-barrelled but in the latter part of the 18th century the double-barrel was produced.

The sporting gun became a status symbol and it became fashionable to buy a gun from a recognised gunmaker living in one of the best areas in London. Many famous families of gunmakers grew up, such as the Mantons and Eggs. Joseph Manton produced the raised aiming-rib between two side-by-side barrels. Many squires had remained faithful to their single barrel sporting guns claiming that the double barrel was less accurate. Manton's development, however, reversed this trend and set the shape of double-barrelled shotguns until the present day. One of the greatest makers of Flintlock Sporting Guns was the Frenchman Nicholas Boutet. He made his most excellent guns for Napoleon to give to favoured monarchs.

As money was of little import, precious metals, such as gold and platinum were used in the touch holes and pans as these resisted the corroding effect of the burning powder. As a great deal of thought and money went into the design of the barrel on English sporting guns, the colour and pattern was quite unrivalled. To ensure greater durability the barrel was formed by layers of steel and iron wrapped over one another. The resulting pattern makes an interesting variation. The barrels were also treated with chemicals to avoid rust, which coated them with a brownish protective skin. Many had pans designed to stay dry through rain.

One major development in shooting as a leisure pursuit was in the middle of the 18th century when shooting at flying birds gained in popularity as opposed to 'sitting' birds. Every gentleman prided himself in being able to shoot flying birds. This development meant that the guns had to be accurate and versatile and as light as possible.

The most beautiful adornment of sporting guns was carried out on the Continent. In Europe, gunmakers tended to specialise in exquisite carving, sometimes taken to extremes, as when the butt was fashioned into a grotesque head or gargoyle. The English stocks tended to be quite plain, more detail being paid to the accuracy and design of the barrel. The most common decoration was simple scrolls along the grip and some hatching on the butt which gave extra grip.

BRITISH

LATE 18TH CENTURY 15-BORE FLINTLOCK SPORTING GUN 44in. Round twist barrel 28in with gold poincon at breech, by Jas Dennis, London. Large roller on frizzen spring, half stocked with horn fore end cap, chequered fore-end and small of stock, engraved steel trigger guard, horn tipped wooden ramrod. Detachable butt which fits on to gun by means of a stout bayonet catch.

LATE 18TH CENTURY 15-BORE FLINTLOCK FOWLING PIECE OF SPANISH STYLE. Barrel 42in with octagonal breech bearing gold poincons of a crown above 'London' and a rampant griffin, by Griffin, London. Large flat lock bearing maker's name within a scroll, half stocked with take down fore end, steel mounts, with traces of engraved decoration, chequered small of stock, wooden ramrod in pipes beneath barrel.

16-BORE FLINTLOCK SPORTING GUN by Joseph Manton 48in. Barrel 33in, octagonal breech inlaid with silver, poincon of Joseph Manton, London. Half stocked, lockplate, hammer, trigger guard and buttplate well chiselled with foliage, etc, number '4731' (on trigger guard), rainproof pan, roller on frizzen spring, silver fore end tip.

19-BORE EARLY 19TH CENTURY DOUBLE BARRELLED FLINTLOCK SPORTING GUN 46in. Barrels 30in, gold lines at breech, by Sharp, Lancing, Sussex, the lockplates engraved with musical trophies, scroll engraved hammers, the trigger guard and buttplate engraved with trophies of arms, rainproof pans, rollers on frizzen springs, chequered small of stock, silver escutcheon in small of stock.

18TH CENTURY BREECH LOADING FLINTLOCK SPORTING RIFLE 50in. Rifled barrel 34in by Waters, full stocked, brass mounts engraved with foliage, etc, brass foliate escutcheon, the breech plug above which unscrews for loading, the ears of the plug form the rearsight when in position. Maker's proofs, the barrel and butt stamped with Irish registration mark.

DOUBLE BARRELLED EARLY 19TH CENTURY 22-BORE FLINTLOCK SPORTING GUN 52in. Barrels 36in, octagonal at breech, by Wogdon and Barton, steel mounts, rollers on frizzen springs, rainproof pans, chequered small of stock, wooden cheek piece on butt, gold touch holes and lines at breech, silver oval escutcheon in small of stock.

EARLY 19TH CENTURY DOUBLE BARRELLED 28-BORE FLINTLOCK SPORTING GUN 47½in. Round twist barrels 31½in, by Stubman, flat locks with rainproof pans and rollers on frizzen springs. Half stocked with chequered wrist, steel mounts including large trigger guard with pineapple finial, old iron ramrod.

30-BORE FLINTLOCK TRADE GUN 62in. Slender barrel 45½in with Birmingham proofs, military type lock stamped with elephant and castle and 'Warranted'. Plain three quarter stock and slender butt, the latter with impressed mark of 'Johnston and Co Ltd, Glasgow', brass mounts, non-original iron ramrod.

64-BORE SINGLE BARRELLED CONTINENTAL FLINTLOCK
SPORTING RIFLE, circa 1740, 43in. Octagonal barrel
27in, inlaid at breech in silver with hunter and dogs
above scrolls. Full stocked, stepped lock faintly engraved, dog tooth border and '. . . . . . Ler Paris', good
quality bronze furniture finely engraved with dog
and deer in arborial landscape. Buttcap and trigger
guard with urn and acorn finials repeated as carving
on stock, cheek piece carved with vulture and prey,
sliding butt trap, silver shield-shaped escutcheon,
brass tipped steel ramrod, set double triggers.

20-BORE EARLY 18TH CENTURY GERMAN FLINTLOCK
SPORTING GUN 50¾in. Half octagonal stepped barrel
36½in, half stocked, slight rounded banana-shaped
lockplate, scroll and foliate engraved, foliate chiselled tail, iron furniture, pierced scrolling sideplate
with roaring dragon's head. Ribbed trigger guard
bow with bulbous terminals, baluster ramrod pipes,
throat pipe finial en suite with trigger guard terminals. Walnut stock carved around furniture and
cheek piece with rococo scrolls and rocaille in low
relief, horn forecap and horn tipped wooden ramrod.

16-BORE GERMAN FLINTLOCK SPORTING GUN, circa
1750, 49in. Octagonal barrel 33½in, engraved 'Damian
Malder in Coblentz'. Half stocked, stepped lockplate
engraved 'Devillers' on bevelled edge. Good quality
brass furniture, foliate finialed spurred trigger guard
with grotesque mask in low relief, buttcap spur with
foliage in low relief, pierced foliate sideplate with
two monsters heads. Stock carved with cheek piece,
and foliage around furniture, horn forecap, wooden
ramrod.

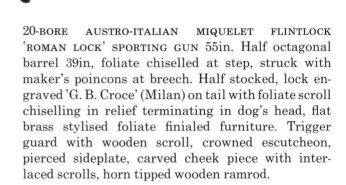

20-BORE AUSTRO-ITALIAN MIQUELET FLINTLOCK 'ROMAN LOCK' SPORTING GUN 55in. Half octagonal barrel 39in, foliate chiselled at step, struck with maker's poincons at breech. Half stocked, lock engraved 'G. B. Croce' (Milan) on tail with foliate scroll chiselling in relief terminating in dog's head, flat brass stylised foliate finialed furniture. Trigger guard with wooden scroll, crowned escutcheon, pierced sideplate, carved cheek piece with interlaced scrolls, horn tipped wooden ramrod.

20-BORE EARLY 18TH CENTURY DUTCH DOUBLE BARRELLED TURNOVER FLINTLOCK SPORTING GUN of Wender type 62½in. Barrels 46in octagonal at breeches with traces of proof marks, detachable pan and frizzen units, scroll engraved back-action lock, full length two piece 'fore ends', one side with four baluster pipes and wooden ramrod. Border engraved breech, pierced foliate sideplate, barrels released for turnover by sprung catch in front of trigger guard bow. Steel buttcap.

Flintlock Muskets and Carbines

The Flintlock musket was well established in England by the time of the Civil Wars but the infantry still preferred the matchlock and this was still their chief weapon. The musket became the sole weapon for infantry after the invention of the bayonet around the 1650's. The first bayonets produced were plug bayonets but by the 1700's socket bayonets were introduced and this made the flintlock musket the standard weapon. Prior to this the flintlock had primarily been reserved for cavalry carbines.

The First 'Brown Bess' musket appeared in the 1720's and this remained the main arm of the British Infantry for well over a century. The military did not place accuracy of aim as their main criterion and the infantry relied more on rapid fire of platoons of troops. While elaborate decoration was usually the order of the day for the civilian, the military man was much more concerned with accuracy and reliability. Military flintlocks were plain, serviceable and totally lacking in frills or excess decoration. Prior to 1764 the musket usually bore the makers name and date on the lockplate but after this they had a Crowned G.R., perhaps a regimental number and the word 'Tower'.

The Brown Bess of this early period was a large conventional flintlock, secured by three screws and having a wooden ramrod beneath a 46″ barrel. By the middle of the 18th century the standard Brown Bess, the Long Land pattern, had evolved. The fittings were usually brass, with a large butt plate, pipes, side plate and trigger guard. Later the barrel length was reduced to 42″ to make the musket easier to carry. This was known as the Short Land Pattern.

It is a frequent misconception that a carbine was a short musket but the earliest examples were as long as the Land Muskets, only the bore was smaller. It was well into the 18th century before short barrels were adopted. Cavalry carbines had two main distinguishing features, the sling ran freely through a ring on a rod joined to the side of the stock, making it easier for the horseman to fire without having to unsling. Secondly, during the Napoleonic Wars the ramrod housing was improved and had a swivel fitted to the muzzle, this enabled the rod to be swung round and pushed down the barrel. This eliminated the danger of the rod being dropped.

The Government standard for military flintlocks was quite high and hence gunmakers tended to shy away from Government orders. It was also said that the Government were the worst payers! In the early years of the 19th century this proved a great problem as an invasion by France seemed imminent the Government was forced to turn to the largest private organisation with a suitable stock of firearms – The East India Company. The 'India Pattern' muskets with their 39″ barrel were cheaper and easier to produce and were found to be as reliable as the previous designs especially due to the improvements in gunpowder. They were sound, plain guns and suited for mass production at the time of the Napoleonic Wars and later. By 1830 nearly a million of this pattern were in the Tower. By this time too, all muskets were fitted with a socket bayonet with a short blade, about 15–17″ long.

Continental flintlock muskets were very similar to the British manufactured weapon with one major difference. The British remained faithful to the lug and pin method of fixing the musket barrel to the stock. This was much less efficient than the method evolved on the Continent, where barrel bands slipped over the stock and barrel.

ENGLISH

16-BORE ELLIOT'S PATTERN VOLUNTEER CAVALRY FLINT-LOCK CARBINE, circa 1800, 44in. Barrel 28in with Tower private proofs, plain flat lock with swan neck cock with double line engraved borders, and impressed 'Mather, Newcastle'. Nicely figured walnut full stock with standard pattern military brass mounts, steel saddle bar and ring on left of stock, steel ramrod. With its original triangular socket bayonet by Woolley and Deakin, in brass mounted leather scabbard.

LATE 18TH CENTURY 32-BORE CAVALRY OFFICER'S FLINTLOCK CARBINE 44in. Octagonal barrel 29in by Wogdon, London. Full stocked, three brass ramrod pipes, foliate engraved trigger guard and buttplate, the trigger guard engraved with officer's name 'Captain William Wrightson', saddle bar and ring.

10-BORE 42in BROWN BESS VOLUNTEER FLINTLOCK MUS-KET 58in. Barrel 42in, Tower proved, maker's mark 'S.P.', engraved 'London'. Full stocked, rounded lock engraved 'Clark', regulation brass mounts, buttcap spur engraved 'NY 24', steel sling swivels.

VOLUNTEER FLINTLOCK BAKER RIFLE ·70in, 46in. Barrel 30½in, full stocked, plain brass mounts by Dunderdale and Mabson, scrolled brass trigger, two ramrod pipes, blade rearsight. Rainproof pan roller on frizzen spring, blank oval brass escutcheon in small of stock, wooden cheek piece to butt, buttplate engraved 'E/2 A.R.'.

14-BORE EAST INDIA COMPANY MILITARY FLINTLOCK FUSIL 52in. Barrel 37in, full stocked, brass mounts, three ramrod pipes, lockplate dated '1809', butt stamped 'An 623', East India Company lion on lockplate.

EAST INDIA COMPANY 4-BORE FLINTLOCK RAMPART GUN 73in. Barrel 54in with London and maker's proofs by Moore, London, bearing maker's name, East India Company mark and date '1793' on lock and barrel, large flat lock with ring neck cock. Full stocked, brass military pattern mounts, heavy steel ramrod, East India Company mark impressed on the butt.

OTHER COUNTRIES OF ORIGIN

20-BORE KURDO BALKAN MIQUELET FLINTLOCK CARBINE 38½in. Half octagonal barrel 25in. Full stocked in engraved steel and brass sheets. Striated frizzen sighted barrel retained by four brass capucines. Steel ramrod. Slender butt with disc engraved mother of pearl inlay.

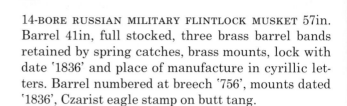

14-BORE RUSSIAN MILITARY FLINTLOCK MUSKET 57in. Barrel 41in, full stocked, three brass barrel bands retained by spring catches, brass mounts, lock with date '1836' and place of manufacture in cyrillic letters. Barrel numbered at breech '756', mounts dated '1836', Czarist eagle stamp on butt tang.

GERMAN 14-BORE MILITARY FLINTLOCK MUSKET 57½in. Barrel 42in with London proofs on octagonal breech, the lockplate stamped 'P.S. US Suhl'. Full stocked with three steel barrel bands, steel mounts, sling loop on trigger guard, brass tipped steel ramrod.

LATE 18TH CENTURY BELGIAN 14-BORE MILITARY FLINT-LOCK MUSKET 60in. Barrel 45in stamped 'HY 13' and 'Number 142 4 TE Co. I TS A'. Lockplate with brass pan engraved 'Liege Manufte Imple' and stamped with crowned 'G 13'. Full stocked with steel mounts and steel ramrod. All steel parts stamped with Liege Armoury mark.

24-BORE CONTINENTAL MILITARY FLINTLOCK MUSKET (probably Austrian) 49in. Barrel 33in, full stocked, two plain steel barrel bands retained by spring catches, steel mounts, lockplate dated '1856'.

CAUCASIAN 26-BORE MIQUELET FLINTLOCK RIFLE 51½in.
Watered Persian barrel 40in, with gold damascened
decoration at breech and muzzle, small lock with gold
poincon on bridle, and gold mark on lockplate. Plain
ebonised full stock, and straight butt with walrus
ivory heelplate, plain button trigger.

NORTH ARMENIAN 16-BORE MIQUELET FLINTLOCK GUN
72½in. Octagonal barrel 57in, with raised brass band
and rearsight at breech, the full breech tray covered
with scroll engraved brass, the breech also impressed
with triangles of punch marks and unintelligible
signature, the large curved lock partly over-laid with
engraved sheet brass. The three quarter stock inlaid
with twelve engraved silver rosettes and two large
pierced and engraved silver plaques, plain butt with
engraved brass cap and trigger plate, and brass ball
trigger, no provision for trigger guard.

LATE 17TH CENTURY 12-BORE DUTCH FLINTLOCK RIFLE
44½in. Octagonal barrel 29½in with twelve groove
rifling, foliate finialed rear-sight with steel cover.
Full stocked, slight rounded lock engraved with
floral and rocaille decoration with 'Van Vtrecht',
semi-circular sheet steel buttcap, foliate finialed
faceted spurred trigger guard, pierced scrolling
sideplate engraved with figures supporting mask.
Butt carved with cheek pieces on each side, inlaid
with finely engraved sheet steel plaques in silhou-
ette. Stock carved with grotesque mask beind barrel
tang, inlaid mother of pearl eyes.

Scottish pistols

Scottish pistols were quite distinctive from their English counterparts. The earliest type of pistol had wooden stocks with a tulip-shaped pommel. These pistols were made in Dundee and are extremely rare. These are not, however, the most well known Scottish pistols. That distinction is held by a pistol made in a small town near Stirling, called Doune. It was quite usual in Scotland at this time for one small town to have a complete monopoly in a certain craft. The monopoly in Doune lasted well over a century; a craftsman passing on his art to his son.

It became a social expectation for a Scottish nobleman and soldier to carry a Doune pistol at his belt. The Doune pistol as it was developed was all-steel with a curved butt ending in two rams-horns. Most pistols had a tongue opposite the hammer to place over the belt. One of the most distinctive features of this pistol, which sets it apart from English firearms of the time, is its lack of a trigger guard. Obviously the prime consideration in its design was speed rather than safety. There was no other safety device on the pistol except for the half-cock, but despite this it was accepted as the deadliest weapon of its time – well suited to the Highlander's purposes.

The real popularity of the Doune pistol came when the Black Watch, under General Wade, were issued with it as standard. Volunteers for all other Scottish Regiments raised had to be promised a pair of Doune Pistols. The Board of Ordnance allowed each Colonel £1 15s 7d per pair for each soldier. A classically bad tactic! The system was so prone to abuse that many colonels took the opportunity of buying in cheap replicas, mainly from Birmingham. There are hence many fakes around, many with pseudo Scottish names. These can be distinguished from the 'real thing' purely by the lack of the fine finish and quality.

By the end of the 18th century a soldier carried a pistol more for decoration as the musket and bayonet had superseded it as the main weapon of offence, and by the mid 1790's most Highland Regiments had discarded this fine weapon. A pair of Doune pistols would be almost too good to hope for for most collectors but some of the replicas are fine pieces in their own right.

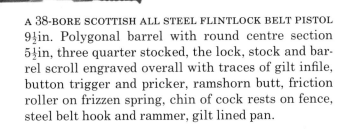

A 38-BORE SCOTTISH ALL STEEL FLINTLOCK BELT PISTOL 9½in. Polygonal barrel with round centre section 5½in, three quarter stocked, the lock, stock and barrel scroll engraved overall with traces of gilt infile, button trigger and pricker, ramshorn butt, friction roller on frizzen spring, chin of cock rests on fence, steel belt hook and rammer, gilt lined pan.

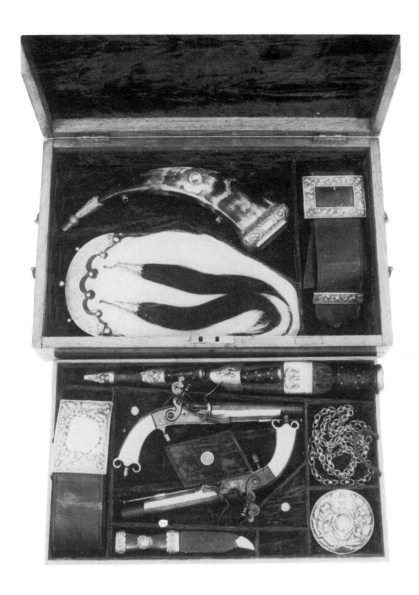

SET OF LATE GEORGIAN SCOTTISH DRESS ACCOUTRE-
MENTS, complete pair of 32-bore Highland type flintlock belt pistols by Donald Currie 10½in. Barrels 6¾in
with flared muzzles and twelve sided breeches, the
scroll engraved locks with horizontal scears and rollers on frizzen springs, pierced circular combs to
cocks, the full stocks and ramshorn butts silver
plated overall and decorated with engraved thistles,
acorn triggers and prickers, plain steel ramrods
and belt hooks. Dirk by MacLeod, College Street,
Edinburgh. Blade 12½in, dark wood hilt carved with
thistles and strapwork in its leather sheath with
companion knife and fork, engraved silver plated
mounts overlaid with thistles, paste pommels.

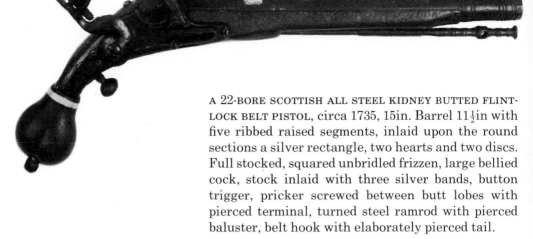

A 22-BORE SCOTTISH ALL STEEL KIDNEY BUTTED FLINT-
LOCK BELT PISTOL, circa 1735, 15in. Barrel 11½in with
five ribbed raised segments, inlaid upon the round
sections a silver rectangle, two hearts and two discs.
Full stocked, squared unbridled frizzen, large bellied
cock, stock inlaid with three silver bands, button
trigger, pricker screwed between butt lobes with
pierced terminal, turned steel ramrod with pierced
baluster, belt hook with elaborately pierced tail.

Percussion weapons

Flintlocks worked well generally but had still quite a few disadvantages. The flint used was frequently of poor quality and wore out more quickly than the average 30 strikes. There was also considerable wear at the frizzen. The two main disadvantages were misfires and also hangfire. This was particularly dangerous for hunters and competitive shooters. 'Hangfire' was the term used for the delay between pressure being applied to the trigger and the actual explosion.

Another development was needed to provide a quicker and more consistent means of ignition. An Aberdeenshire minister, The Reverend Alexander Forsyth, was possessed of more than an evangelical religion; he had a passion for shooting, was an excellent chemist and a first-rate mechanic. He was particularly concerned with the problem of hangfire as he was a fanatical duck-shooter. He was aware that a group of unstable chemical compounds known as fulminates had interesting explosive qualities. Fulminates had been tried as an equivalent to gunpowder but they had wrecked the gun rather than fired the bullet. These fulminates exploded on impact and Forsyth thought that it might be possible to cause a minor explosion which would set off the larger explosion. He produced his famous 'scent bottle' which deposited a few grains of fulminate in the touch hole, and he patented this system in 1807.

Although this system pointed the way to a more efficient idea his scent bottle was too sensitive and complex and the mechanism would not sustain rough usage.

Many methods of getting the fulminate into the touch hole were tried, from fulminate-filled discs, pills, tubes and quills. At the beginning wax was used to bind the pills of fulminate but this was problematic due to its low melting point.

An American, Dr. Guthrie, produced a binding material using a gum arabic base. These pills were placed in a groove over the touch hole and a sharply pointed hammer was designed to break the casing. Joseph Manton in England used the same idea but fitted the pills to the head of the hammer.

These pills were quite effective but had one major problem – their size. They were extremely difficult to handle and were impossible in bad weather. Many solutions were tried – the capsules were fitted into the centre of discs of paper, card or thin metal and then thinly coated. Others developed the idea of placing the fulminates in small tubes of metal or quills. Some even fixed a series of tiny spots of fulminate in a tape exactly the same idea as a roll of caps for a child's gun. This last system was quite successful as it enabled a rapid rate of fire.

However, all these systems had drawbacks and in the 1820's the copper percussion caps were designed. There is a dispute about who actually discovered them but it is quite possible that many gunmakers were working along the same lines. These caps were generally a short closed copper tube with the fulminate inside. The weapon designed to use these caps had a small metal tube fitted into the breech. The tube was drilled through and so positioned that it was struck by the sharp-nosed hammer. Over this tube called the nipple was placed the copper cap. It was a reasonably simple action, the hammer fell, struck the cap, produced a small explosion and a flash which passed through the nipple into the breech and fired the charge. The hammer was recessed so that as it fell it was totally enclosed by the hammer head. This ensured that if the cap splintered it would not fly off and possibly injure the user. Another safety precaution was in the construction of the cap, it was made of thin-ribbed copper to ensure it split easily.

A large number of these pocket pistols were produced at Liège and Birmingham. They were extremely cheap, single shot and using the newly developed percussion caps. These had a very low incidence of misfires and were not affected by bad weather.

The system was very quickly adopted by most gunmakers but it took the British Army until 1838 to officially adopt the system.

The introduction of the percussion cap began the rapid development of modern firearms.

Breech-loading was not a startling new concept of the mid-19th century, the idea had been around a long time. Early cannons were breech-loading, with the powder and shot inserted at the rear of the barrel and other examples include Henry VIII's famous wheellock breech-loading pistols and Ferguson's breech-loading rifle. This was, however, a difficult principle to apply to short firearms, as the gunmakers came across the limiting factors of expense and complexity along with the practical problems of escaping gas, causing an erractic fire. This also was dangerous to the firer and could render the weapon itself useless.

There was, however, continued efforts to produce an effective breech-loading gun as all previous systems had two major disadvantages; they were, in the main, muzzle-loading and single-shot.

The solution to the problem revolved round the introduction of a cartridge inserted into the breech, which would also seal it. Lefaucheux had developed a system where the fulminate was inserted in a separate cap which was placed in a metal cartridge. This was activated by the hammer striking a metal pin which penetrated through the side of the metal case, striking the fulminate and detonating it. This was called pinfire but did not overcome all the problems.

The final step was taken by Rollin White who took out a patent for a breech-loading revolver in 1855. His system had a cylinder drilled right through with a small metallic cartridge at the rear end. The fulminate was placed on the inside edge of the cartridge and was detonated by a blunt-nosed hammer.

After Rollin White's patent expired many other gunmakers produced their own breech-loading weapons and there was a flood of these in the early 1870's.

One major problem remained – that of ejecting the cartridge. In the early breech-loaders this was done manually but a more efficient system was sought. Finally, this problem was overcome with the introduction of the centrefire cartridge. The only difference in this type of cartridge was that the detonating cap was located in the middle of the base of the cartridge. This, with the introduction of the hammerless ejector, made possible within a few years such weapons as repeating rifles and machine guns. It also made possible the most famous Colt: the Colt Army Single Action. It is important to note, however, that Colt did not have a monopoly over the hand-gun market and Smith & Wesson and Remington were also producing a large number of successful weapons.

Breech-loading longarms were accepted by the British Board of Ordnance in 1865 but they decided that, since no system available gave the final answer, they would convert Enfields to the breech system. The conversion was designed by an American, Snider, and the Enfield-Snider appeared. This was made a viable weapon by the self-sealing cartridge designed by a Colonel Boxer. The Americans had the Henry Rifle which was later developed into the 'gun that won the West' – the famous Winchester. In Britain, many improvements were made and in 1871 Ordnance issued the Martini-Henry hammerless rifle. Following this, two individuals' work was combined in one rifle when the British Government decided to take James Lee's magazine and William Metford's barrel and make the Lee-Metford rifle. By the end of the 19th century, the rifling of the Lee-Metford was improved at the Royal Small Arms Factory at Enfield and Metford's name was forgotten, to be replaced by the Lee-Enfield Rifle.

Percussion Holster and Belt Pistols

When one thinks of holster pistols of this period one immediately thinks of the legendary Wild West and shoot-outs at dusk! Certainly one of the important developments that accompanied the introduction of the percussion system was that horse holster pistols ceased to be in such demand and were replaced particularly if not solely in America, by belt holster pistols.

In the early part of the 19th century the design and production of, firstly, the pepperbox, then the transitional revolver and, finally, the Colt revolver removed the need for two pistols. Obviously, when one relies on a single-shot system, the advantages of having two weapons need little expansion. In fact, the introduction of the revolver completely changed the concept of personal defence and one revolver was generally recognised as, certainly potentially, more dangerous than two flintlock horse holster pistols.

This meant that a man on foot or on horseback could carry one multi-shot weapon and belt holsters replaced the saddle holsters for short guns. A man on horseback would frequently have a rifle in a type of holster attached to his saddle.

Not only Colts were carried in belt holsters and it is possible to get a wide variety of revolvers used in this way as it was very much a matter of personal preference which was used.

These belt holsters were normally worn quite high at the waist despite the popular misconception which depicts the Western gunman with his holster low on his thigh.

PERCUSSION HOLSTER PISTOLS

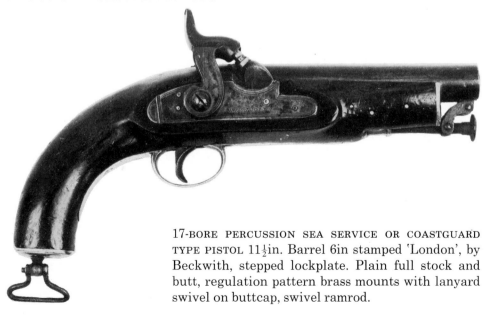

17-BORE PERCUSSION SEA SERVICE OR COASTGUARD TYPE PISTOL 11½in. Barrel 6in stamped 'London', by Beckwith, stepped lockplate. Plain full stock and butt, regulation pattern brass mounts with lanyard swivel on buttcap, swivel ramrod.

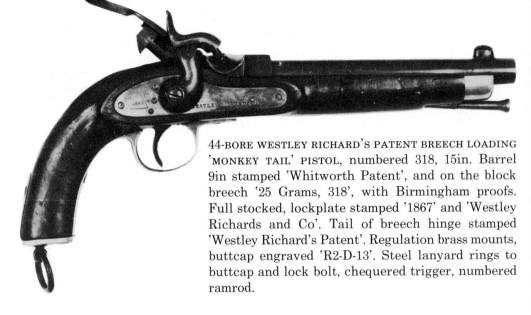

44-BORE WESTLEY RICHARD'S PATENT BREECH LOADING 'MONKEY TAIL' PISTOL, numbered 318, 15in. Barrel 9in stamped 'Whitworth Patent', and on the block breech '25 Grams, 318', with Birmingham proofs. Full stocked, lockplate stamped '1867' and 'Westley Richards and Co'. Tail of breech hinge stamped 'Westley Richard's Patent'. Regulation brass mounts, buttcap engraved 'R2-D-13'. Steel lanyard rings to buttcap and lock bolt, chequered trigger, numbered ramrod.

ALL METAL 40-BORE PERCUSSION PISTOL 14in. Part octagonal barrel 8¾in with turned muzzle inlaid 'London' in silver amidst bluebell drops and scrolls. Three quarter stocked in white metal scroll engraved dolphin hammer, lockplate and segment of stock (as in Scottish all metal pistols) nicely scroll and linear engraved overall with sprays of thistles, roses and shamrocks. Large Anglo-American trophy and American crest (Large eagle perched on a shield of stars and stripes) below a sunburst. Steel ramrod and button trigger, hinged butt trap.

14-BORE MILITARY PERCUSSION HOLSTER PISTOL 9¾in. Birmingham proved barrel 5½in, full stocked, twin line border engraved lockplate stamped with crown and Tower. Full stocked, regulation brass mounts, steel ramrod.

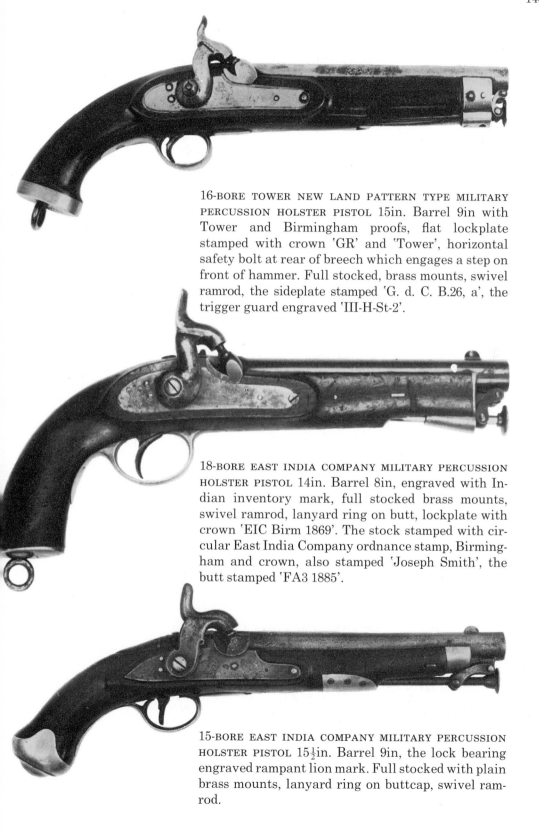

16-BORE TOWER NEW LAND PATTERN TYPE MILITARY PERCUSSION HOLSTER PISTOL 15in. Barrel 9in with Tower and Birmingham proofs, flat lockplate stamped with crown 'GR' and 'Tower', horizontal safety bolt at rear of breech which engages a step on front of hammer. Full stocked, brass mounts, swivel ramrod, the sideplate stamped 'G. d. C. B.26, a', the trigger guard engraved 'III-H-St-2'.

18-BORE EAST INDIA COMPANY MILITARY PERCUSSION HOLSTER PISTOL 14in. Barrel 8in, engraved with Indian inventory mark, full stocked brass mounts, swivel ramrod, lanyard ring on butt, lockplate with crown 'EIC Birm 1869'. The stock stamped with circular East India Company ordnance stamp, Birmingham and crown, also stamped 'Joseph Smith', the butt stamped 'FA3 1885'.

15-BORE EAST INDIA COMPANY MILITARY PERCUSSION HOLSTER PISTOL 15½in. Barrel 9in, the lock bearing engraved rampant lion mark. Full stocked with plain brass mounts, lanyard ring on buttcap, swivel ramrod.

34-BORE DOUBLE BARRELLED OVER AND UNDER PER-
CUSSION HOLSTER PISTOL, by Blake, 10¾in. Barrels
5¼in, London proved engraved 'I.A. Blake and Co,
London'. Scroll engraved back-action locks and dolphin hammers. Scroll engraved long backstrap and
trigger guard. Swivel ramrod, rounded chequered
walnut butt.

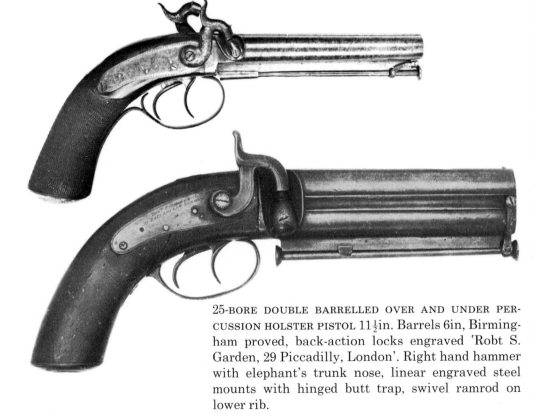

DOUBLE BARRELLED SIDE BY SIDE 32-BORE PERCUSSION
SIDELOCK HOLSTER PISTOL 11in. Twist barrels 5in, by
E. and W. Bond, Cornhill, London. London proved.
Swivel rammer beneath barrel, scroll engraved back-
action locks and hammers, round chequered walnut
butt, with engraved steel cap. Continental hinged
trigger. Scroll engraved steel trigger guard.

25-BORE DOUBLE BARRELLED OVER AND UNDER PER-
CUSSION HOLSTER PISTOL 11½in. Barrels 6in, Birmingham proved, back-action locks engraved 'Robt S.
Garden, 29 Piccadilly, London'. Right hand hammer
with elephant's trunk nose, linear engraved steel
mounts with hinged butt trap, swivel ramrod on
lower rib.

PAIR OF PERCUSSION HOLSTER PISTOLS, by Hayson and Co of Doncaster, with interchangeable 52-bore smooth bore barrels and 52-bore rifled barrels, 14¾in. Deeply etched damascus twist barrels 9in with silver foresights, each signed 'Doncaster' on breech, integral lower ribs. Half stocked, scroll engraved bolted detented locks. Scroll engraved stylised pineapple finialed trigger guards, capstan screw set triggers. Brass tipped ebony ramrods with brass capped worms, rounded chequered butts, silver escutcheons and barrel wedgeplates and escutcheons.

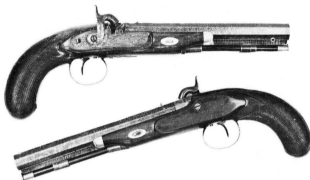

PAIR OF 30-BORE BACK-ACTION PERCUSSION HOLSTER PISTOLS, by Jones, 12in. Octagonal browned barrels 7in, scroll engraved locks, hammers and pineapple finialed trigger guards. Full stocked, white metal barrel wedgeplates and diamond-shaped escutcheons, chequered rounded butts.

PAIR OF 16-BORE BACK-ACTION PERCUSSION HOLSTER PISTOLS by W. Richards and Co, 13½in. Browned octagonal twist barrels 7½in, engraved 'W. Richards and Co, London', scroll engraved colour hardened breeches inlaid with two German silver lines. Full stocked, scroll engraved colour hardened locks and dolphin hammers with maker's name. Blued scroll engraved trigger guards, swivel ramrods, white metal barrel wedges, plates and escutcheons. Rounded chequered butts.

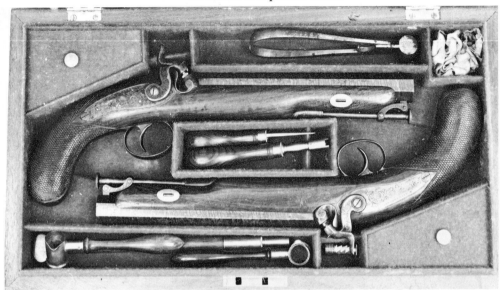

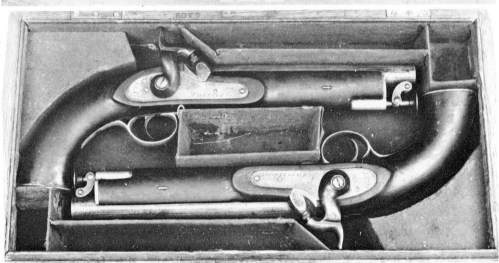

PAIR OF 16-BORE MILITARY PERCUSSION HOLSTER PISTOLS 15in. Barrels 9in, with Birmingham proofs, the locks engraved in large lettering 'Maybury and Sons 1857'. Full stocked with plain military pattern brass mounts, swivel ramrods.

PAIR OF 32-BORE DOUBLE BARRELLED BACK-ACTION PER-CUSSION HOLSTER PISTOLS by H. Tatham Jnr., circa 1845, 11½in overall. Octagonal case colour hardened barrels 6in, London proved, engraved 'H. Tatham Jnr., Charing Cross, London' on top flats, fern tip engraved muzzles. Silver inlaid safety plugs, breech integral with lower frame spur. Scroll and foliate engraved bolted locks signed 'H. Tatham Jnr.', dolphin hammers, case colour hardened overall en suite with barrels. Scroll and foliate engraved blued trigger guards, and hinged butt traps. Blued swivel ramrods on lower ribs. Finely chequered walnut butts with oval silver escutcheons.

Irish

30-BORE DOUBLE BARRELLED PERCUSSION HOLSTER PISTOL by Rigby, number 5738, 12in. Damascus twist barrels 7in, engraved 'Rigby, Dublin' on top rib with 'DU 8354', four gold lines at patent breech, silver safety plug. Half stocked in figured walnut, finely engraved detented locks and dolphin hammers, with repeated dolphin scroll motif, finely engraved trigger guard and buttcap, horn tipped wooden ramrod, gold escutcheon engraved with stag on bar with initials 'G.R.', chequered butt.

Continental

13-BORE CONTINENTAL MILITARY PERCUSSION HOLSTER PISTOL 14½in. Barrel 8in. Half stocked, flattened lockplate, regulation brass mounts.

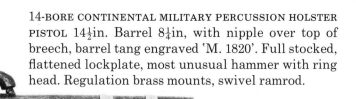

14-BORE CONTINENTAL MILITARY PERCUSSION HOLSTER PISTOL 14½in. Barrel 8¼in, with nipple over top of breech, barrel tang engraved 'M. 1820'. Full stocked, flattened lockplate, most unusual hammer with ring head. Regulation brass mounts, swivel ramrod.

LONG PAIR OF CONTINENTAL 17-BORE PERCUSSION HOLSTER PISTOLS 18in. Round barrels 12in, with imitation twist, engraving at breech and traces of gold lines. Vine and tendril engraved hammers and back-action locks. Full stocked with rounded butts terminating in carved grotesque masks with glass eyes, the butts and fore ends inlaid with German silver wire scrolls, German silver mounts including embossed trigger guards with trophies of arms, brass tipped wooden ramrods.

FRENCH 14-BORE BREECH LOADING PERCUSSION HOLSTER PISTOL 12½in. Octagonal twist barrel 7½in, with traces of name 'Le Page, Paris', the barrel released to swing sideways by spring loaded button beneath fore end, boxlock type action enclosed in plain rounded walnut butt, plain steel mounts, trap in buttcap with hinged cover and lanyard ring. Presumably designed to take a combustible cartridge.

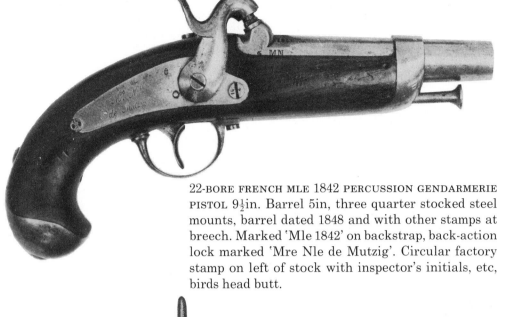

22-BORE FRENCH MLE 1842 PERCUSSION GENDARMERIE
PISTOL 9½in. Barrel 5in, three quarter stocked steel
mounts, barrel dated 1848 and with other stamps at
breech. Marked 'Mle 1842' on backstrap, back-action
lock marked 'Mre Nle de Mutzig'. Circular factory
stamp on left of stock with inspector's initials, etc,
birds head butt.

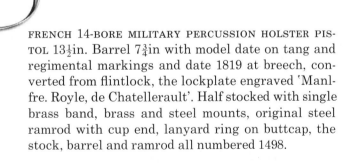

FRENCH 14-BORE MILITARY PERCUSSION HOLSTER PIS-
TOL 13½in. Barrel 7¾in with model date on tang and
regimental markings and date 1819 at breech, converted from flintlock, the lockplate engraved 'Manl-
fre. Royle, de Chatellerault'. Half stocked with single
brass band, brass and steel mounts, original steel
ramrod with cup end, lanyard ring on buttcap, the
stock, barrel and ramrod all numbered 1498.

FRENCH 21-BORE DOUBLE BARRELLED LONG PER-
CUSSION HOLSTER PISTOL 18in. Barrels 12½, half
stocked, finely foliate engraved steel mounts, plain
hammers, back-action locks engraved with mythical
serpents, trigger guard finely chiselled with scallop
design and a bird, urn finial. Fine chequering to butt,
buttplate with facets, steel ramrod.

152

PAIR OF FRENCH 26-BORE RIFLED PERCUSSION HOLSTER
PISTOLS, circa 1830, 11in. Slight swamped octagonal
barrels 6in, with St Etienne proofs, plain flat locks
and steel mounts. Walnut half stocks and rounded
chequered butts, original horn ramrods, one with
iron worm.

German

GERMAN 12-BORE MILITARY PERCUSSION HOLSTER PIS-
TOL 15in. Barrel 9in with crown at breech, large,
plain lock with traces of 'Hamburg'. Three quarter
stock with plain steel mounts and no provision for
ramrod.

GERMAN 32-BORE RIFLED PERCUSSION HOLSTER PISTOL
14in. Browned octagonal barrel 8½in, gold inlaid at
breech 'Suhl' within wreath, converted from flintlock
by breech drum method. Flatlock engraved with
roped border and eagle holding a wreath, hinged
nipple protector operated by original frizzen spring
with roller. Full stocked with horn fore end cap,
slight flattened rounded chequered butt carved with
foliage around barrel tang, and with raised borders
around mounts some silver wire inlay around buttcap, steel mounts with engraved decoration, single
set trigger, horn tipped wooden ramrod.

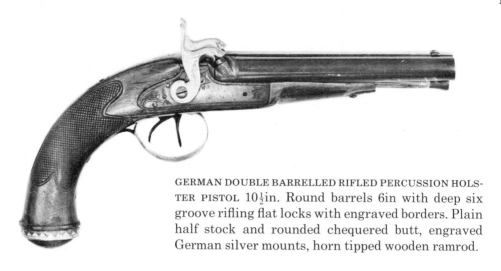

GERMAN DOUBLE BARRELLED RIFLED PERCUSSION HOLS-
TER PISTOL 10½in. Round barrels 6in with deep six
groove rifling flat locks with engraved borders. Plain
half stock and rounded chequered butt, engraved
German silver mounts, horn tipped wooden ramrod.

PAIR OF MID-19TH CENTURY GERMAN OFFICER'S 14-BORE
PERCUSSION HOLSTER PISTOLS 13in. Browned twist
barrels 8½in, with raised concave top ribs, plain flat
locks engraved around hammers 'Forstner in Carls-
ruhe'. Plain half stocks and steeply angled fluted
butts, plain blued steel mounts, oval German silver
barrel wedgeplates, brass tipped steel ramrods.

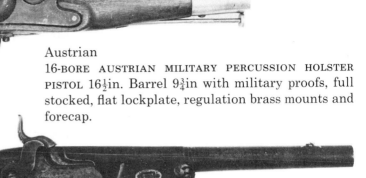

Austrian

16-BORE AUSTRIAN MILITARY PERCUSSION HOLSTER PISTOL 16½in. Barrel 9¾in with military proofs, full stocked, flat lockplate, regulation brass mounts and forecap.

AUSTRIAN 20-BORE PERCUSSION HOLSTER PISTOL 16in. Barrel 10in, in two stages, round with fluted octagonal breech and moulded band between, the tang engraved 'Number 2', white metal foresight, large flat lock engraved 'Timner' in script. Half stocked with carved fore end finial, rounded chequered butt with flared end, plain steel mounts including spurred trigger guard.

30-BORE AUSTRIAN MODEL 1863 MILITARY PERCUSSION LOREZ PISTOL 16in. Rifled barrel 10½in, stamped with military proof marks and 'Zeilinger'. Half stocked, lockplate struck with Imperial Eagle (en suite with barrel) and (1) '864'. Regulation iron mounts, swivel safety on lock, lanyard ring on butt.

30-BORE AUSTRIAN MILITARY PERCUSSION HOLSTER PISTOL 16in. Rifled barrel 10in, three quarter stocked, single steel barrel band and plain steel mounts. Plain lockplate stamped with Austrian eagle and numeral 863 and fitted with swivel safety.

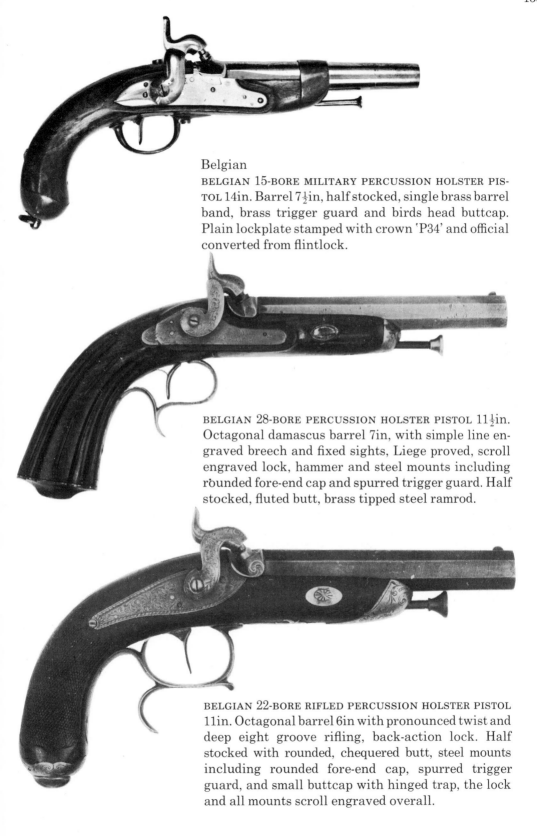

Belgian

BELGIAN 15-BORE MILITARY PERCUSSION HOLSTER PIS-
TOL 14in. Barrel 7½in, half stocked, single brass barrel
band, brass trigger guard and birds head buttcap.
Plain lockplate stamped with crown 'P34' and official
converted from flintlock.

BELGIAN 28-BORE PERCUSSION HOLSTER PISTOL 11½in.
Octagonal damascus barrel 7in, with simple line engraved breech and fixed sights, Liege proved, scroll
engraved lock, hammer and steel mounts including
rounded fore-end cap and spurred trigger guard. Half
stocked, fluted butt, brass tipped steel ramrod.

BELGIAN 22-BORE RIFLED PERCUSSION HOLSTER PISTOL
11in. Octagonal barrel 6in with pronounced twist and
deep eight groove rifling, back-action lock. Half
stocked with rounded, chequered butt, steel mounts
including rounded fore-end cap, spurred trigger
guard, and small buttcap with hinged trap, the lock
and all mounts scroll engraved overall.

27-BORE BELGIAN RIFLED PERCUSSION OFFICER'S HOL-STER PISTOL 11½in. Octagonal barrel 6¾in with multi groove rifling and slight flared muzzle. Full stocked, by Rennes, steel mounts part engraved with foliage, engraved classical urn terminal to trigger guard, diced wood butt, horn tipped ramrod.

PAIR OF BELGIAN 20-BORE RIFLED PERCUSSION HOLSTER PISTOLS 14in. Octagonal twist barrels 8¾in, with Liege proofs and deep multi groove rifling, small en-graved side locks. Plain half stocks and rounded chequered butts with carved flared terminals, en-graved steel mounts, traps in butts with large shell caps, original steel ramrods.

PAIR OF BELGIAN 13-BORE RIFLED PERCUSSION HOLSTER PISTOLS 13½in. Octagonal barrels 8in, half stocked foliate engraved steel mounts. Back-action locks, foliate engraved hammers. Liege proved. Diced wood butts.

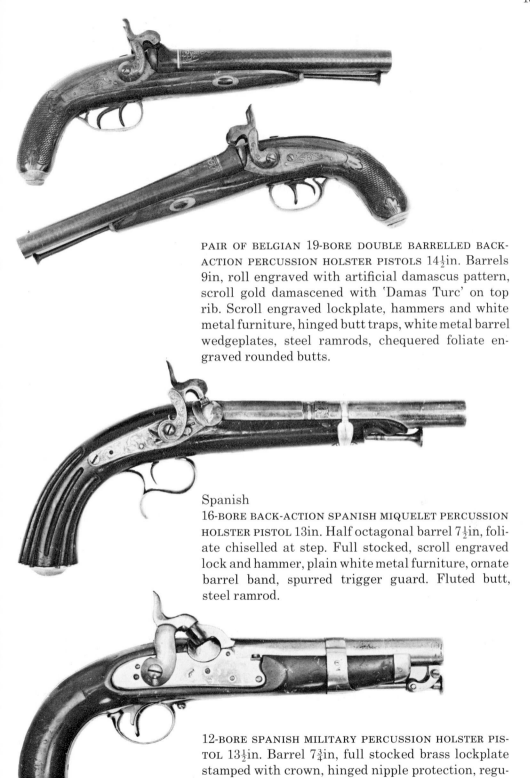

PAIR OF BELGIAN 19-BORE DOUBLE BARRELLED BACK-ACTION PERCUSSION HOLSTER PISTOLS 14½in. Barrels 9in, roll engraved with artificial damascus pattern, scroll gold damascened with 'Damas Turc' on top rib. Scroll engraved lockplate, hammers and white metal furniture, hinged butt traps, white metal barrel wedgeplates, steel ramrods, chequered foliate engraved rounded butts.

Spanish
16-BORE BACK-ACTION SPANISH MIQUELET PERCUSSION HOLSTER PISTOL 13in. Half octagonal barrel 7½in, foliate chiselled at step. Full stocked, scroll engraved lock and hammer, plain white metal furniture, ornate barrel band, spurred trigger guard. Fluted butt, steel ramrod.

12-BORE SPANISH MILITARY PERCUSSION HOLSTER PISTOL 13½in. Barrel 7¾in, full stocked brass lockplate stamped with crown, hinged nipple protection, regulation brass mounts and backstrap, steel swivel ramrod.

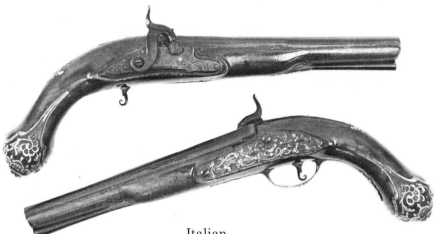

Italian

PAIR OF MID-18TH CENTURY ITALIAN 17-BORE HOLSTER PISTOLS, converted to percussion by breech drum method, 15in. Barrels $9\frac{1}{4}$in, with fluted top ribs and octagonal breeches with Spanish type poincons of C. Banchi, rounded locks with chiselled tails and scroll engraved flats (the latter executed at the time of their conversion), raised silver bands at breeches, the engraved breech tangs with fold-flat 'V' rearsights. Full stocks with fine quality chiselled silver mounts incorporating leaf and tendril designs, compact spurred buttcaps, solid wavy sideplates, trigger guards, escutcheons, and ramrod throat pipes, plain black wood ramrods.

Prussian

PRUSSIAN 20-BORE 'POTSDAM' MILITARY PERCUSSION HOLSTER PISTOL $15\frac{1}{2}$in. Barrel $9\frac{1}{4}$in, with octagonal breech bearing crowned 'FW' stamp, large lock with spring loaded hinged nipple protector/safety, the plate engraved with crown and 'Potsdam GS'. Half stocked with heavy brass mounts, the buttcap bearing regimental markings and with lanyard ring, the sideplate dated 1831.

PRUSSIAN 'POTSDAM TYPE' MILITARY PERCUSSION HOLSTER PISTOL $14\frac{1}{2}$in. Barrel $8\frac{3}{4}$in with muzzle ring and octagonal breech, the latter stamped 'FW' and dated '1851', the lock stamped with crown and 'Saarn', sprung hinged nipple protector safety. Half stocked with single brass barrel band, brass mounts including spurred trigger guard and buttcap with lanyard ring.

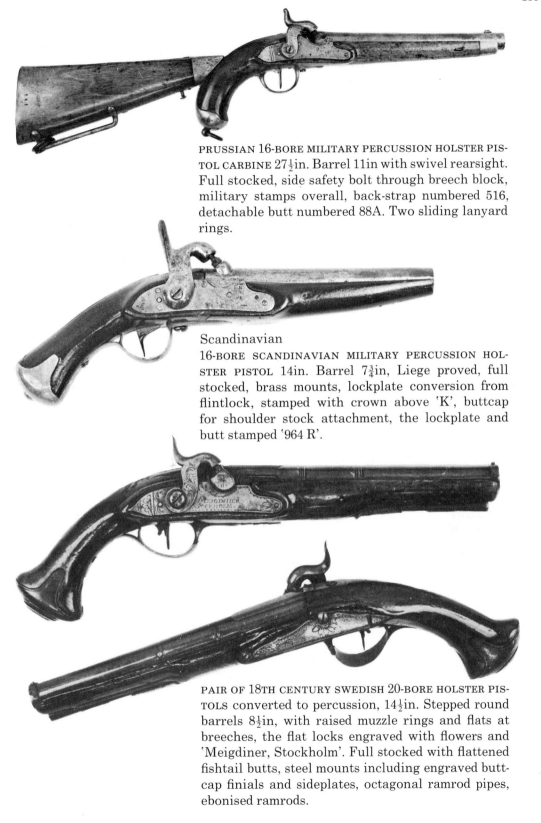

PRUSSIAN 16-BORE MILITARY PERCUSSION HOLSTER PIS-
TOL CARBINE 27½in. Barrel 11in with swivel rearsight.
Full stocked, side safety bolt through breech block,
military stamps overall, back-strap numbered 516,
detachable butt numbered 88A. Two sliding lanyard
rings.

Scandinavian

16-BORE SCANDINAVIAN MILITARY PERCUSSION HOL-
STER PISTOL 14in. Barrel 7¾in, Liege proved, full
stocked, brass mounts, lockplate conversion from
flintlock, stamped with crown above 'K', buttcap
for shoulder stock attachment, the lockplate and
butt stamped '964 R'.

PAIR OF 18TH CENTURY SWEDISH 20-BORE HOLSTER PIS-
TOLS converted to percussion, 14½in. Stepped round
barrels 8½in, with raised muzzle rings and flats at
breeches, the flat locks engraved with flowers and
'Meigdiner, Stockholm'. Full stocked with flattened
fishtail butts, steel mounts including engraved buttcap finials and sideplates, octagonal ramrod pipes,
ebonised ramrods.

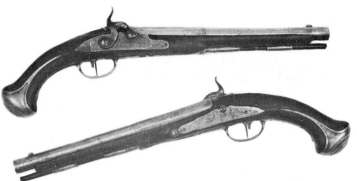

PAIR OF SWEDISH 28-BORE PERCUSSION HOLSTER PIS-
TOLS 17½in. Half round barrels 11in, with flat sided
breeches and half length flattened sighting ribs, converted from flintlock by breech drum method, the flat
lockplates engraved 'F. Meidinger, Stockholm'. Dark
wood full stocks with simple carved panels round
ramrod pipes, breech tangs, etc, steel mounts including leaf finialed trigger guards, and longspurred
buttcaps.

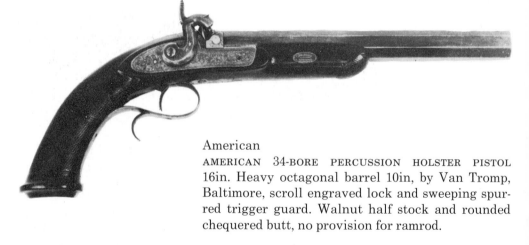

American
AMERICAN 34-BORE PERCUSSION HOLSTER PISTOL
16in. Heavy octagonal barrel 10in, by Van Tromp,
Baltimore, scroll engraved lock and sweeping spurred trigger guard. Walnut half stock and rounded
chequered butt, no provision for ramrod.

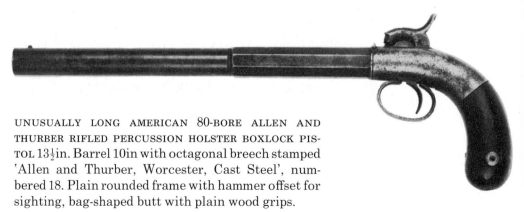

UNUSUALLY LONG AMERICAN 80-BORE ALLEN AND
THURBER RIFLED PERCUSSION HOLSTER BOXLOCK PIS-
TOL 13½in. Barrel 10in with octagonal breech stamped
'Allen and Thurber, Worcester, Cast Steel', num-
bered 18. Plain rounded frame with hammer offset for
sighting, bag-shaped butt with plain wood grips.

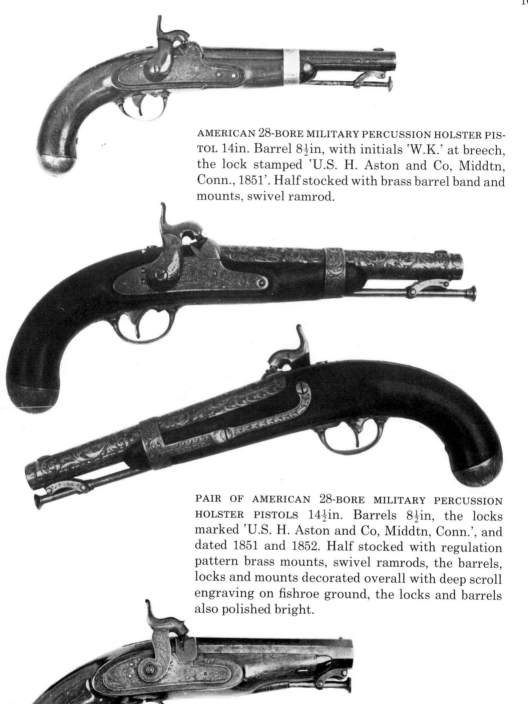

AMERICAN 28-BORE MILITARY PERCUSSION HOLSTER PISTOL 14in. Barrel 8½in, with initials 'W.K.' at breech, the lock stamped 'U.S. H. Aston and Co, Middtn, Conn., 1851'. Half stocked with brass barrel band and mounts, swivel ramrod.

PAIR OF AMERICAN 28-BORE MILITARY PERCUSSION HOLSTER PISTOLS 14½in. Barrels 8½in, the locks marked 'U.S. H. Aston and Co, Middtn, Conn.', and dated 1851 and 1852. Half stocked with regulation pattern brass mounts, swivel ramrods, the barrels, locks and mounts decorated overall with deep scroll engraving on fishroe ground, the locks and barrels also polished bright.

Canadian

CANADIAN 22-BORE PERCUSSION HOLSTER PISTOL 10½in. Octagonal barrel 5½in, by Walker, Montreal, foliate engraved lock, hammer, and steel trigger guard. Full stocked with plain rounded butt and horn fore-end cap, swivel ramrod.

Continental
21-BORE FRENCH MODEL 1837 PERCUSSION NAVAL BELT
PISTOL 12in. Barrel 6in with military proofs, barrel
tang engraved 'M 1837'. Back-action lock, steel belt
hook and swivel ramrod, regulation brass mounts,
steel lanyard ring, buttcap stamped with anchor,
rounded stock.

FRENCH 22-BORE MODEL 1849 PERCUSSION NAVAL BELT
PISTOL 12in. Barrel 7in. Three quarter stocked, single
brass barrel band, trigger guard and buttcap, barrel
dated '1851' at breech, backstrap marked 'Mle 1849',
single blade rearsight. Back-action lock marked 'Mre
Nle de Chatellerault', swivel ramrod with chain
swivel, belt hook, butt bears circular 'M.N.' stamp,
buttcap with anchor stamp.

15-BORE ITALIAN MILITARY PERCUSSION BELT PISTOL
13½in. Barrel 8in, stamped with three proof marks —
crown, eagle and crowned shield. Full stocked, lockplate stamped 'Fabb A.R.A. In Torino', breech
stamped 'P.A. 1845'. Regulation brass mounts, sideplate stamped 'FoC', steel belt hook, brass tipped
swivel ramrod, brass links. Stock stamped 'D.F.'.

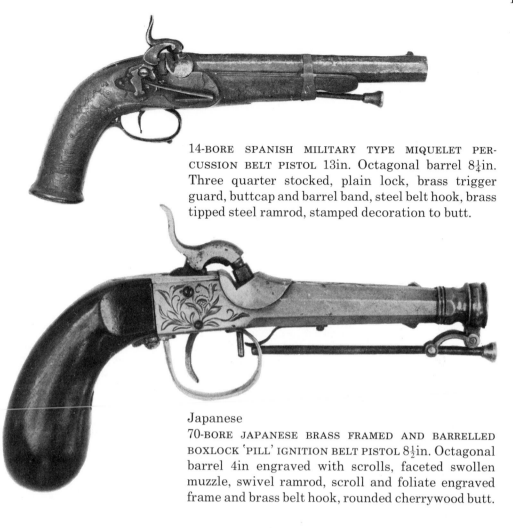

14-BORE SPANISH MILITARY TYPE MIQUELET PER-
CUSSION BELT PISTOL 13in. Octagonal barrel 8¼in.
Three quarter stocked, plain lock, brass trigger
guard, buttcap and barrel band, steel belt hook, brass
tipped steel ramrod, stamped decoration to butt.

Japanese
70-BORE JAPANESE BRASS FRAMED AND BARRELLED
BOXLOCK 'PILL' IGNITION BELT PISTOL 8½in. Octagonal
barrel 4in engraved with scrolls, faceted swollen
muzzle, swivel ramrod, scroll and foliate engraved
frame and brass belt hook, rounded cherrywood butt.

English
14-BORE BACK-ACTION PERCUSSION BELT PISTOL by
Monalet of London, 13in. Thick octagonal barrel
7½in engraved 'London', white metal line inlaid at
scroll engraved breech. Full stocked, scroll engraved
lock and steel furniture, engraved 'Monalet le Gem'.
Spurred pineapple finialed trigger guard, sprung belt
hook, swivel ramrod, rounded chequered butt, white
metal barrel wedgeplates and escutcheon.

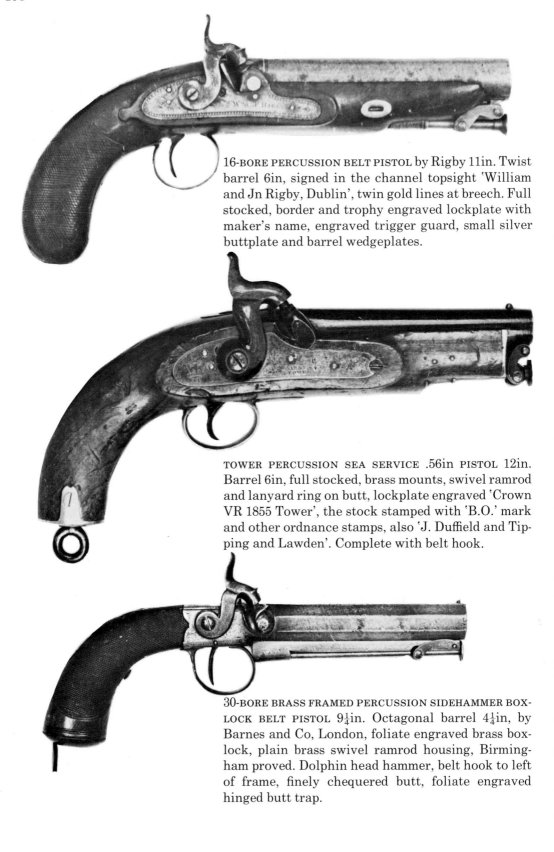

16-BORE PERCUSSION BELT PISTOL by Rigby 11in. Twist barrel 6in, signed in the channel topsight 'William and Jn Rigby, Dublin', twin gold lines at breech. Full stocked, border and trophy engraved lockplate with maker's name, engraved trigger guard, small silver buttplate and barrel wedgeplates.

TOWER PERCUSSION SEA SERVICE .56in PISTOL 12in. Barrel 6in, full stocked, brass mounts, swivel ramrod and lanyard ring on butt, lockplate engraved 'Crown VR 1855 Tower', the stock stamped with 'B.O.' mark and other ordnance stamps, also 'J. Duffield and Tipping and Lawden'. Complete with belt hook.

30-BORE BRASS FRAMED PERCUSSION SIDEHAMMER BOX-LOCK BELT PISTOL 9¼in. Octagonal barrel 4¼in, by Barnes and Co, London, foliate engraved brass box-lock, plain brass swivel ramrod housing, Birmingham proved. Dolphin head hammer, belt hook to left of frame, finely chequered butt, foliate engraved hinged butt trap.

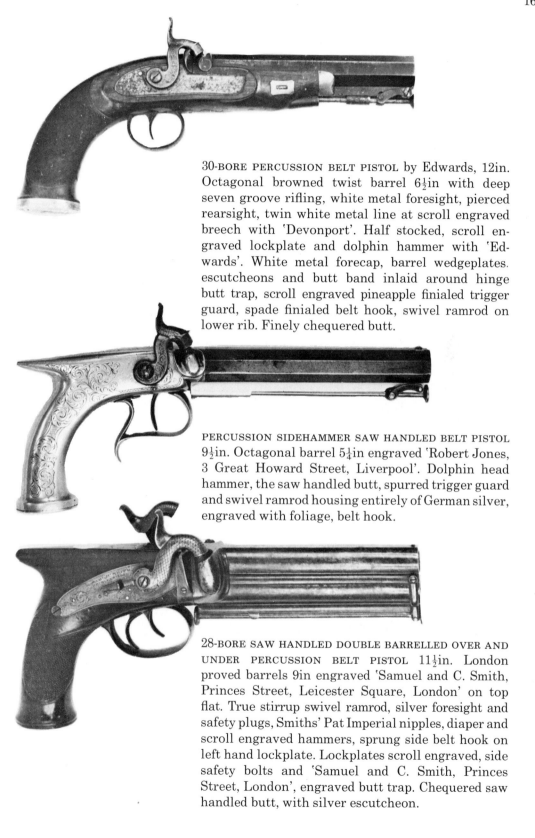

30-BORE PERCUSSION BELT PISTOL by Edwards, 12in. Octagonal browned twist barrel 6½in with deep seven groove rifling, white metal foresight, pierced rearsight, twin white metal line at scroll engraved breech with 'Devonport'. Half stocked, scroll engraved lockplate and dolphin hammer with 'Edwards'. White metal forecap, barrel wedgeplates. escutcheons and butt band inlaid around hinge butt trap, scroll engraved pineapple finialed trigger guard, spade finialed belt hook, swivel ramrod on lower rib. Finely chequered butt.

PERCUSSION SIDEHAMMER SAW HANDLED BELT PISTOL 9½in. Octagonal barrel 5¼in engraved 'Robert Jones, 3 Great Howard Street, Liverpool'. Dolphin head hammer, the saw handled butt, spurred trigger guard and swivel ramrod housing entirely of German silver, engraved with foliage, belt hook.

28-BORE SAW HANDLED DOUBLE BARRELLED OVER AND UNDER PERCUSSION BELT PISTOL 11½in. London proved barrels 9in engraved 'Samuel and C. Smith, Princes Street, Leicester Square, London' on top flat. True stirrup swivel ramrod, silver foresight and safety plugs, Smiths' Pat Imperial nipples, diaper and scroll engraved hammers, sprung side belt hook on left hand lockplate. Lockplates scroll engraved, side safety bolts and 'Samuel and C. Smith, Princes Street, London', engraved butt trap. Chequered saw handled butt, with silver escutcheon.

166

PAIR OF 10-BORE MILITARY STYLE PERCUSSION BELT
PISTOLS by Tatham, 11in. Barrels 6in, Birmingham
proved. Full stocked, lockplates stamped with maker's
name, regulation brass trigger guards and forecaps,
steel belt hooks and swivel ramrods.

PAIR OF 14-BORE BACK-ACTION PERCUSSION BELT PIS-
TOLS by George and John Deane, circa 1850, 10¾in
overall. Browned twist London proved barrels 5½in,
engraved 'George and John Deane (Makers to H.R.H.
Prince Albert), 30 King William Street, London
Bridge'. Dovetailed leaf foresights. Blued swivel ramrods, lower ribs, and sprung belt hooks. Back-action
bolted locks signed George and John Deane, finely
scrolled engraved with roped borders, case colour
hardened en suite with scroll engraved trigger
guards and hinged buttcaps. Chequered triggers.
Finely chequered figured walnut butts with silver
vacant escutcheons. These pistols exhibit certain
slightly unusual features, such as forward leaning
hammer spurs, chequered triggers, large trigger
guard bow mountings, tail of locks secured by bolt
and cup through butts.

PERCUSSION TRAVELLING PISTOLS

English
48-BORE BOXLOCK PERCUSSION SIDEHAMMER TRAVEL-
LING PISTOL by Smith of London, 7¾in. Birmingham
proved, turn-off deeply rifled barrel 3in, engraved at
muzzle and breech, scroll engraved frame, top plate
and hammer. Concealed trigger, partly chequered
butt with white metal escutcheon.

26-BORE BACK-ACTION PERCUSSION TRAVELLING PISTOL
8in. Rounded browned twist rifled barrel 4in. Full
stocked, scroll engraved bolted lock and dolphin
hammer with 'Southall'. Scroll engraved pineapple
finialed trigger guard. Swivel ramrod, horn forecap,
German silver barrel wedgeplates and escutcheon.
Chequered rounded butt.

WHITE METAL STOCKED SAW HANDLED PERCUSSION
TRAVELLING PISTOL 8½in. Turn-off octagonal rifled
barrel 3½in. Birmingham proved, well scroll engraved white metal stock, sidehammer, hinged butt
trap fore caps.

36-BORE BOXLOCK SIDEHAMMER PERCUSSION TRAVEL-
LING PISTOL 8in. Octagonal barrel 3½in, Birmingham
proved. Scroll engraved frame and dolphin hammer,
swivel ramrod on lower rib. Chequered rounded walnut butt with white metal escutcheon.

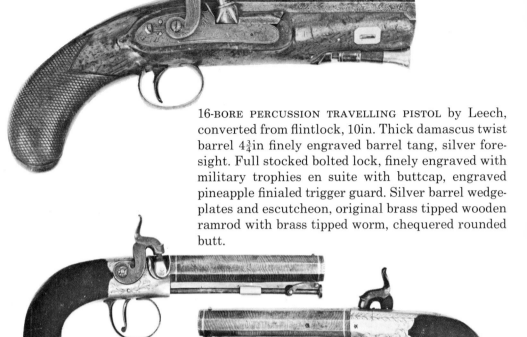

16-BORE PERCUSSION TRAVELLING PISTOL by Leech, converted from flintlock, 10in. Thick damascus twist barrel 4¾in finely engraved barrel tang, silver foresight. Full stocked bolted lock, finely engraved with military trophies en suite with buttcap, engraved pineapple finialed trigger guard. Silver barrel wedge-plates and escutcheon, original brass tipped wooden ramrod with brass tipped worm, chequered rounded butt.

PAIR OF 52-BORE BOXLOCK SIDEHAMMER PERCUSSION TRAVELLING PISTOLS made for export, circa 1840, 9in. Octagonal twist barrels 4½in, with inlaid white metal lines. Scroll engraved white metal frames, swivel ramrods on white metal lower ribs. Scroll engraved dolphin hammers, blued trigger guards, chequered walnut butts with engraved white metal bands and twin vacant escutcheons.

Continental

CONTINENTAL 60-BORE RIFLED PERCUSSION TRAVELLING PISTOL 9in. Tapered octagonal barrel 4½in with scroll engraved breech and 'M. Wachter in Memmingen' on top flat, fixed front and adjustable rearsights, scroll engraved lock and hammers. Plain half stock and rounded butt, steel mounts including nailplate engraved with two ducks, single set trigger.

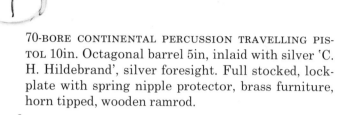

70-BORE CONTINENTAL PERCUSSION TRAVELLING PIS-
TOL 10in. Octagonal barrel 5in, inlaid with silver 'C.
H. Hildebrand', silver foresight. Full stocked, lockplate with spring nipple protector, brass furniture,
horn tipped, wooden ramrod.

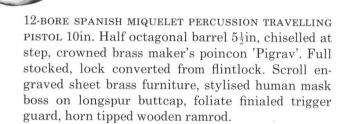

12-BORE SPANISH MIQUELET PERCUSSION TRAVELLING
PISTOL 10in. Half octagonal barrel $5\frac{1}{2}$in, chiselled at
step, crowned brass maker's poincon 'Pigrav'. Full
stocked, lock converted from flintlock. Scroll engraved sheet brass furniture, stylised human mask
boss on longspur buttcap, foliate finialed trigger
guard, horn tipped wooden ramrod.

FRENCH 30-BORE PERCUSSION TRAVELLING PISTOL $7\frac{1}{2}$in.
Octagonal barrel $3\frac{3}{4}$in with gold damascus line at
muzzle and scrolls at breech (worn), St Etienne
proved, plain flatlock, hammer and steel mounts, including domed buttcap. Plain walnut full stock with
no provision for ramrod, rounded partly chequered
butt.

GERMAN PERCUSSION SIDEHAMMER TRAVELLING PISTOL
7½in. Octagonal barrel 4in, multi groove rifling and
slight flared muzzle, engraved 'Ulrich Zu Oberndorf',
numbered '2' at barrel tang and key slot for adjusting
leaf rearsight. Full stocked, plain steel trigger guard
and mounts, lockplate engraved round edges with
roped pattern. Finely chequered butt, left of stock
inset with silver shield engraved with 'H', set trigger.

American
AMERICAN .88in BORE PERCUSSION TRAVELLING PISTOL
with German silver lock, furniture and barrel, 8½in.
Multi groove rifled octagonal barrel 4½in, integral
with lower rib. Half stocked, scroll engraved German
silver furniture and lockplate, sprung shell hinged
butt trap, chequered butt, shield-shaped escutcheon.

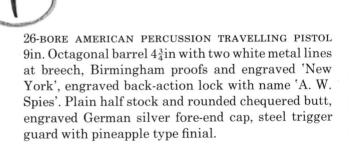

26-BORE AMERICAN PERCUSSION TRAVELLING PISTOL
9in. Octagonal barrel 4¾in with two white metal lines
at breech, Birmingham proofs and engraved 'New
York', engraved back-action lock with name 'A. W.
Spies'. Plain half stock and rounded chequered butt,
engraved German silver fore-end cap, steel trigger
guard with pineapple type finial.

PAIR OF 34-BORE PERCUSSION TRAVELLING PISTOLS by
Mabson, Labron and Mabson, 11in. Browned octagonal twist barrels 6in, colour hardened breeches.
Full stocked, scroll engraved locks and hammers.
Foliate and border engraved blued pineapple finialed
trigger guard. Blued throat pipes, brass tipped ebony
ramrods with brass capped steel worms. Rounded
chequered butts, white metal barrel wedgeplates and
escutcheon. Contained in their blue velvet lined fitted mahogany case with brass carrying handle, containing copper powder flask embossed with foliage
and diamond-shaped studs.

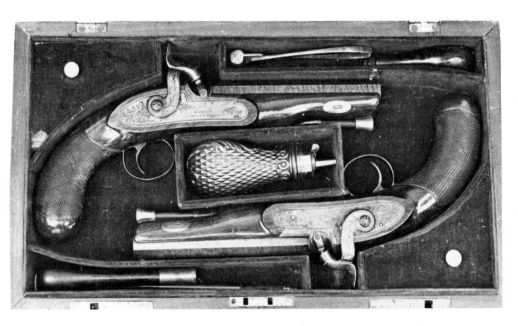

Japanese

UNUSUAL PERCUSSION BOXLOCK TRAVELLING PISTOL
11¼in. Quarter octagonal barrel 6½in, turned swollen
muzzle, frame stamped with Japanese characters,
swivel ramrod secured in baluster pipe integral with
trigger guard, swivel foresight of disc form, sharply
down drooping chequered butt.

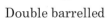

Double barrelled

DOUBLE BARRELLED OVER AND UNDER 80-BORE PER-
CUSSION SIDELOCK TRAVELLING PISTOL 7½in. One piece
elongated octagonal barrel block, 3in, gold inlaid
with scroll engraved 'William Smith, London' and
sprays of foliage. The muzzles engraved with fern
leaf border, small silver foresight. The lower barrels
bearing two sets of London proofs, engraved spray of
foliage and lightly impressed with Irish registration
number. The side by side locks expertly converted
from flintlock,. external mainsprings and hammers,
safety bolts, fern leaf engraved borders and scrolled
decoration, hall marked silver (Birmingham 1820),
trigger guard engraved with Britannia shield
amidst foliage and toothed border. Finely chequered
rounded butt with small finely engraved silver cap,
containing screw-in brass tipped steel ramrod.

DOUBLE BARRELLED OVER AND UNDER 56-BORE PER-
CUSSION TRAVELLING PISTOL by D. Egg, 8½in. Colour
hardened octagonal barrels 3½in, fern tip engraved
muzzle, silver foresight, swivel ramrod on lower rib.
London proved. Finely scroll engraved frame and
dolphin hammers, sliding side safety bolts, topstrap scroll engraved with 'D. Egg, Pall Mall, London', within lozenge. Spurred trigger guard, finely
chequered butt in Continental style with fluted terminal and oval silver escutcheon.

DOUBLE BARRELLED OVER AND UNDER 38-BORE PER-
CUSSION TRAVELLING PISTOL 8½in. Octagonal barrels
4in, by Kavanagh, 11 Dame Street, Dublin, scroll
engraved back-action locks, hammers and trigger
guard, the locks also with fern tip borders. Long
hinged trap on back of butt concealing cavities for
two balls and two caps, flattened partly chequered
butt with plain oval silver cap, swivel ramrod, three
bents to tumbler.

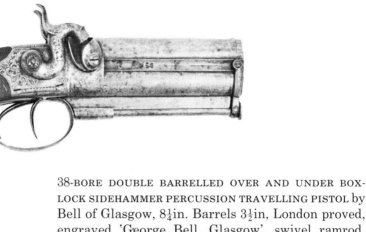

38-BORE DOUBLE BARRELLED OVER AND UNDER BOX-
LOCK SIDEHAMMER PERCUSSION TRAVELLING PISTOL by
Bell of Glasgow, 8¼in. Barrels 3½in, London proved,
engraved 'George Bell, Glasgow', swivel ramrod.
Finely scroll engraved frame, dolphin hammers, trigger guard and hinged butt trap. Finely chequered
walnut butt with chamfered oblong silver escutcheon.

30-BORE DOUBLE BARRELLED BACK-ACTION PERCUSSION
TRAVELLING PISTOL 10in. Twist barrels 5in. Full
stocked, scroll engraved locks and dolphin hammers. Scroll engraved pineapple finialed trigger guard,
swivel ramrod. White metal escutcheon and barrel
wedgeplates, chequered rounded butt.

25-BORE DOUBLE BARRELLED BACK-ACTION PERCUSSION
TRAVELLING PISTOL fitted with spring bayonet, 11in.
Twist barrels 5½in, engraved 'T. Tipping' on top rib.
Sliding top thumb safety catch releases 3½in roller
bearing sprung bayonet. Scroll engraved back-action
locks with dolphin hammers engraved 'T. Tipping'.
Full stocked, scroll engraved trigger guard, swivel
ramrod, silver barrel wedgeplates and escutcheon,
rounded chequered butt.

PERCUSSION TARGET AND DUELLING PISTOLS

The percussion system was quickly adopted for duelling pistols. With such a deadly business a fraction of a second was crucial and, hence, with any new system which proved faster it was imperative that any participant had the newest and most improved weapon. The percussion system was fractionally quicker in fire than even the best flintlock. As speed and accuracy were of prime importance adaptations were made to the weapon. Upon being struck by the hammer a flash was sent directly to the powder and cut out any delay caused by the touch hole.

Perhaps one of the most important adaptations to the weapon was made at this time – the spur trigger. This was primarily to save the trigger finger from having to do any steadying of the weapon. The spur trigger was basically a curved tail to the trigger guard which was fixed rigid. This certainly added to the efficiency of the weapon which now also assumed its final shape with a long, curved butt.

One of the most telling developments at this time was that the duel itself was going out of fashion. Public opinion certainly swung against duels particularly after such notable duels between eminent statesmen. People felt that such responsible statesmen who were of great importance should not attempt to kill each other because of some possibly quite imaginary affront to their honour. There was also the feeling that the duel no longer had the same 'gentleman' status, as duels had been fought in France by men who did not uphold the honour tradition. Such magazines as *Punch* continually poked fun at duelling in such conditions. It was quite generally felt that a verbal affront was little reason for such a deadly combat.

There was also the influence of Prince Albert who was outspoken in his condemnation of the practice of duelling which he considered quite barbaric. At this time, the views of Royalty had a strong effect on the English gentleman. This was added to by *The Times* which gradually guided public opinion.

In 1844, two army officers fought a duel and a Colonel Fawcett was killed. An Army Council Order came out completely prohibiting duelling, both the issuing and accepting of a challenge.

The percussion duelling pistols that were produced during this period were of the same standards of perfection as the flintlock particularly those made by the great gunsmiths such as Joseph Manton. The percussion duelling pistols had an even more elaborate set of tools than the flintlock, including equipment for pressing and shaping the caps as well as all the normal tools for loading and cleaning. A boxed pair with all their accoutrements is one of the greatest prizes for a collector.

English PAIR OF 40-BORE PERCUSSION DUELLING PISTOLS 14½in. Heavy octagonal twist barrels 10in, with multi groove rifling and engraved 'J. Purdey, 314½ Oxford Street, London', flat bolted locks with good quality scroll engraving and bearing maker's name. Half stocked with horn fore-end caps and acutely angled rounded chequered butts with flared ends terminating in flat oval caps, engraved with rope work borders and flower centres. Steel mounts including engraved trigger guards with shell decorated finials, brass tipped ebony ramrods, with concealed worms, single set triggers.

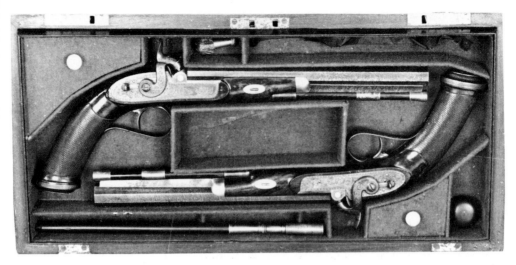

PAIR OF 34-BORE PERCUSSION TARGET PISTOLS by Gough and Bowen, 16in. Octagonal damascus twist barrels 10in, with eighteen groove rifling, with traces of original brown finish engraved 'Gough and Bowen', breeches scroll engraved with silver line inlay. Half stocked, scroll and border engraved bolted locks, detented actions, set triggers. Scroll engraved ovoid buttcaps, finely scroll engraved trigger guard bows with stylised pineapple finials. Silver forecaps, barrel wedgeplates and escutcheons. Brass tipped ebony ramrods with brass capped steel worms highly polished chequered walnut butts.

PAIR OF 36-BORE PERCUSSION DUELLING PISTOLS by Williams, circa 1840, 15½in. Heavy octagonal twist barrels 9¾in, browned and engraved 'Williams, 67 Threadneedle Street, London', silver plugs, lines at breeches and foresights. Half stocked, scroll engraved lockplates with bolt safeties to dolphin hammers. Large flash shields. Capstan screw set triggers, engraved and spurred trigger guards. Silver forecaps, sidenail plates and escutcheons engraved with crest. Brass tipped wooden ramrods with brass capped worms. Chequered butts.

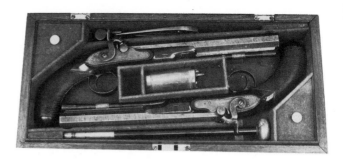

PAIR OF 25-BORE PERCUSSION DUELLING PISTOLS 15$\frac{1}{2}$in. Octagonal twist barrels 10in, with gold line at breeches and gold inlaid 'Manton, London', converted from flintlock by breech drum method, flat locks with fern tip engraved borders, maker's name, and small spray of foliage on tails of plates. Half stocked with horn fore-end caps, rounded chequered butts, engraved trigger guards with pineapple finials and with serial number 4454, horn tipped wooden ramrods.

PAIR OF 30-BORE PERCUSSION DUELLING PISTOLS 15in. Browned octagonal barrels 9$\frac{3}{4}$in, with gold lined and scroll engraved breeches, by Wogdon, London. Converted from flintlock with new breeches, flat scroll engraved hammers and bolted locks. Plain full stocks and slight flattened rounded butts, single set triggers, blued steel mounts including flower engraved buttcaps and trigger guards, with acorn finials, small silver escutcheons.

PAIR OF 36-BORE PERCUSSION DUELLING PISTOLS by J. Manton, converted from flintlock by the maker, number 4220, 15in. Octagonal twist barrels 10in, silver foresights, breech lines, safety plugs and maker's stamp 'Crowned Joseph Manton Patent'. Half stocked, lockplates engraved 'Joseph Manton, London' with fern tip borders, thunderflash and simple floral spray around sliding safety bolts. Detented tumblers, steel furniture, pineapple finialed trigger guards, border and trophy engraved bows, border and floral engraved buttcaps. Silver escutcheons and barrel wedgeplates. Brass tipped, wooden ramrods with brass tipped worms. Chequered butts, horn forecaps.

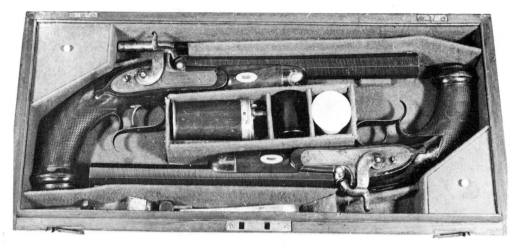

PAIR OF 38-BORE PERCUSSION DUELLING PISTOLS by Joseph Egg, 16in. Octagonal browned twist barrels 10in, engraved 'Joh Egg, London', silver foresights. Half stocked in figured walnut, scroll and border engraved bolted locks and rounded dolphin hammers (detented) signed 'Joseph Egg' and 'London' in script. Scroll engraved breeches with silver safety plugs. Scroll engraved, blued steel furniture including spurred trigger guards, set triggers, unusual rounded fore end caps, hinged butt traps with flower head engraved lids, rope engraved sidenail cups. Silver oval escutcheons engraved with a crest within garter motto 'Francas non Flectes' above initials 'C.S.'. Silver barrel wedgeplates and inlet plates at breech to protect woodwork. Chequered butts.

PAIR OF 32-BORE PERCUSSION DUELLING PISTOLS 15in. Heavy browned octagonal twist barrels 10in, engraved 'J. Purdey, 314½ Oxford Street, London', flat bolted locks, with good quality scroll engraving, bearing maker's name. Half stocked, with horn fore end caps, plain rounded chequered butts, steel mounts including engraved trigger guards with pineapple finials, wooden ramrods with brass covered worms and long hollow brass tips, for use as powder measure.

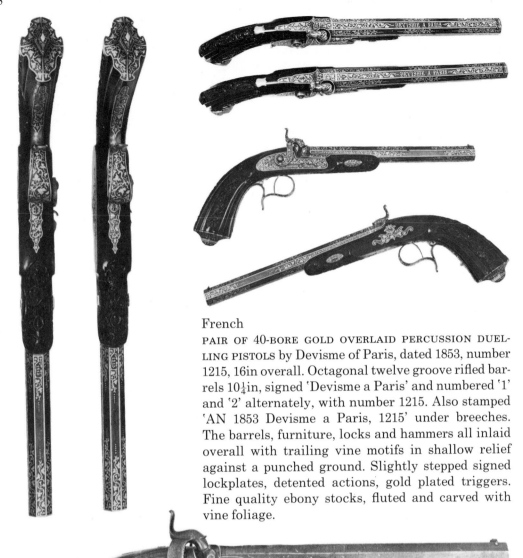

French

PAIR OF 40-BORE GOLD OVERLAID PERCUSSION DUEL-LING PISTOLS by Devisme of Paris, dated 1853, number 1215, 16in overall. Octagonal twelve groove rifled barrels 10¼in, signed 'Devisme a Paris' and numbered '1' and '2' alternately, with number 1215. Also stamped 'AN 1853 Devisme a Paris, 1215' under breeches. The barrels, furniture, locks and hammers all inlaid overall with trailing vine motifs in shallow relief against a punched ground. Slightly stepped signed lockplates, detented actions, gold plated triggers. Fine quality ebony stocks, fluted and carved with vine foliage.

30-BORE PERCUSSION DUELLING PISTOL in the English manner, by Lesoinne and Pirlot of Liege, 15¼in. Octagonal twist multi groove rifled barrel 9½in, engraved 'N.M. Lesoinne and Pirlot, Fils a Liege' in italic script with flourishing capitals. Half stocked, scroll and border engraved, detented lock and dolphin hammer with maker's name. Scroll engraved pineapple finialed spurred trigger guard and buttcap, set trigger, white metal forecap, barrel wedgeplates and escutcheon, chequered butt, brass tipped wooden rammer.

PAIR OF FRENCH 38-BORE PERCUSSION DUELLING PIS-
TOLS 15½in. Octagonal twist barrels 10in, with fine
multi groove rifling engraved back-action locks, marked 'Fni par Henry A Paris'. Half stocked with shell
carved fore-end caps, rounded chequered butts terminating in small oval steel caps, scroll engraved steel
trigger guards, with extra spur grips, single set triggers. In their close fitted baize lined mahogany case
with a good quality embossed copper flask by B. A.
Paris, pincer mould, combination nipple key and
turnscrew with trap for spare nipples, loading rod,
cleaning rod with brush, mallet, oil bottle and turned
wood box for caps.

PAIR OF 85-BORE FRENCH PERCUSSION DUELLING OR
TARGET PISTOLS by Ferdinand Claudin of Paris, 17½in.
Octagonal sighted deeply blued barrels 11in. Seven
groove rifling, engraved 'Fnt P. Fa. Claudin, Brevete
boulevard des Italiens 38, Paris'. Half stocked in
finely figured walnut, lockplates with small contour
step on tails, closely scroll engraved. Detented locks.
Deeply colour hardened en suite with furniture.
Scroll engraved scrolled trigger guards, faceted
baluster finialed buttcaps. Fluted butts, scroll carved
at fore-ends.

PAIR OF MID-19TH CENTURY FRENCH 44-BORE RIFLED
PERCUSSION DUELLING PISTOLS 16½in. Octagonal barrels 10½in, engraved 'Fni par Gastinne Renette a
Paris', and with multi groove rifling, numbered '1'
and '2' at breeches, plain side locks with elegant
hammers, plain steel mounts, including spurred trigger guards. Half stocked with leaf carved fore ends
and fluted butts. In their original close fitted green
baize lined oak case, with 'Gastinne Renette, Paris'
in gold lettering in the lid, complete with bullet
mould, turnscrew, nipple key, mallet, loading and
cleaning rods, and two wood boxes.

36-BORE FRENCH PERCUSSION TARGET PISTOL by Postel of Dieppe, 13¼in. Octagonal twist hair groove rifled barrel 7in, engraved 'Postel Arquer a Dieppe' within ovals. Half stocked in curly grained walnut, floral and foliate engraved lock, capstan screw set trigger, floral and foliate engraved steel furniture. Foliate finialed spurred trigger guard, ovoid buttcap, chequered grip, shell carved fore-end, oval silver escutcheon.

27-BORE FRENCH PERCUSSION TARGET PISTOL, circa 1850, 15in. Part octagonal, part polygonal barrel 9½in with some flutes and seven groove rifling, gold damascened at breech with number '1' and 'Acier Fondu'. Adjustable rearsight, half stocked in scroll, rocaille and flute carved walnut, rocaille engraved lock and steel furniture with spurred trigger guard incorporating some gold damascened game and a dog.

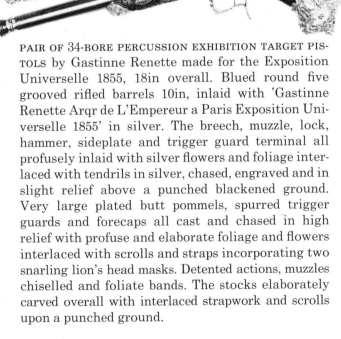

PAIR OF 34-BORE PERCUSSION EXHIBITION TARGET PISTOLS by Gastinne Renette made for the Exposition Universelle 1855, 18in overall. Blued round five grooved rifled barrels 10in, inlaid with 'Gastinne Renette Arqr de L'Empereur a Paris Exposition Universelle 1855' in silver. The breech, muzzle, lock, hammer, sideplate and trigger guard terminal all profusely inlaid with silver flowers and foliage interlaced with tendrils in silver, chased, engraved and in slight relief above a punched blackened ground. Very large plated butt pommels, spurred trigger guards and forecaps all cast and chased in high relief with profuse and elaborate foliage and flowers interlaced with scrolls and straps incorporating two snarling lion's head masks. Detented actions, muzzles chiselled and foliate bands. The stocks elaborately carved overall with interlaced strapwork and scrolls upon a punched ground.

PAIR OF 40-BORE PERCUSSION TARGET PISTOLS by Lefaucheux of Paris, 16½in. Polygonal sectioned fluted blued barrels 9¾in with ten groove rifling, gold inlaid 'Lefaucheux rue Vivienne a Paris' at breeches with numbers '1' and '2' respectively twice repeated. Half stocked in ebony carved with interlaced scrolls with fluted butts. Detented actions, locks, hammers and steel furniture all profusely and finely engraved with best rocaille, scrolls and floral decoration. Octagonal faceted spurred trigger guards with scrolled supports, lobed buttcaps with four facets terminating in turned button finials.

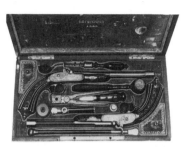

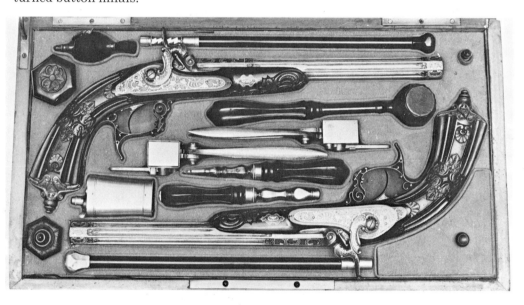

PAIR OF 36-BORE GOLD INLAID FRENCH PERCUSSION TARGET PISTOLS 15¾in overall. Fluted octagonal barrels 10in with twelve groove rifling, gold inlaid at muzzles and breeches with rocaille and scroll decoration upon engraved grounds. Half stocked in rocaille and scroll carved ebony with fluted butts. Detented actions, the locks, hammers and furniture profusely inlaid with gold rocaille scrolls and flowers en suite with barrels. Spurred trigger guards with intricately pierced scroll supports, scroll chiselled inlaid buttcaps with turned button finials.

Belgian

PAIR OF BELGIAN 36-BORE PERCUSSION DUELLING PIS-
TOLS 16½in. The deeply rifled 10½in barrels of fine
damascus steel gold inlaid at breeches with numbers
'1' and '2' and 'Damas Superfin'. The locks scroll
engraved overall and gold inlaid 'Gilson a Anvers',
the steel spurred trigger guards, buttcaps and sidenail plates also scroll engraved overall. Ebony half
stocks with foliate carved fore-ends and sweeping
fluted 'Gothic' butts. In their close fitted and red
velvet lined dark walnut veneered case with brass
escutcheon in the lid and inlaid with brass strips,
containing pine cone embossed copper flask, pincer
mould, ebony mallet, nipple key with compartment in
handle, loading rod, cleaning rod.

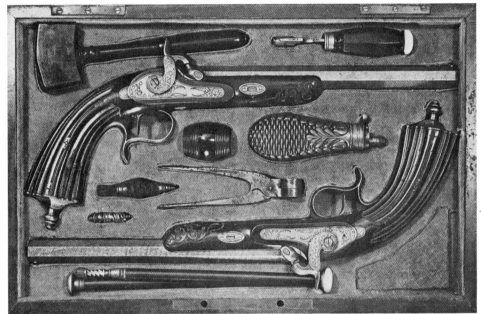

30-BORE BACK-ACTION BELGIAN PERCUSSION TARGET
PISTOL 15½in. Octagonal damascus twist multi groove
rifled barrel 9½in, Liege proved. Half stocked in finely
figured maple, scroll engraved lock and hammer inlaid with gold and silver tendrils, white metal furniture. Scroll engraved spurred trigger guard, hinged
shell butt trap, foliate sidenail cup, shield-shaped
escutcheon, oval barrel wedgeplate. Shell carved
ebony forecap and foliate carved ebony butt terminal.

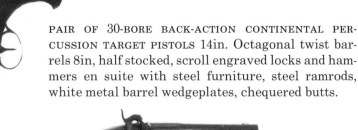

PAIR OF 30-BORE BACK-ACTION CONTINENTAL PER-CUSSION TARGET PISTOLS 14in. Octagonal twist barrels 8in, half stocked, scroll engraved locks and hammers en suite with steel furniture, steel ramrods, white metal barrel wedgeplates, chequered butts.

German, Austrian, Bavarian

PAIR OF 32-BORE GERMAN BACK-ACTION PERCUSSION TARGET PISTOLS 13in. Half octagonal browned barrels 7½in, white metal foresights, scroll engraved barrel tang, scroll engraved detented locks, dolphin hammers and steel furniture, locks with swivel safeties. Full stocked, horn forecaps, white metal barrel wedgeplates, foliate carved chequered wood grips, horn tipped wooden ramrods.

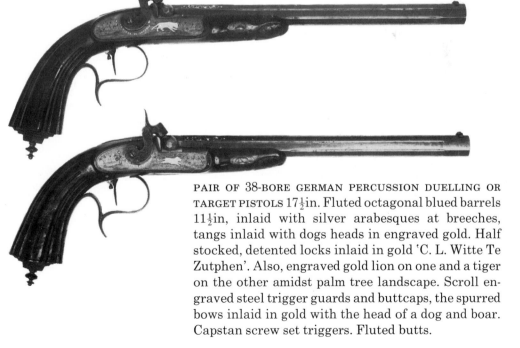

PAIR OF 38-BORE GERMAN PERCUSSION DUELLING OR TARGET PISTOLS 17½in. Fluted octagonal blued barrels 11½in, inlaid with silver arabesques at breeches, tangs inlaid with dogs heads in engraved gold. Half stocked, detented locks inlaid in gold 'C. L. Witte Te Zutphen'. Also, engraved gold lion on one and a tiger on the other amidst palm tree landscape. Scroll engraved steel trigger guards and buttcaps, the spurred bows inlaid in gold with the head of a dog and boar. Capstan screw set triggers. Fluted butts.

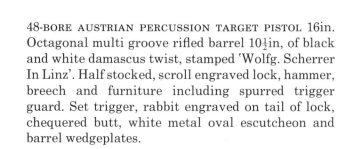

48-BORE AUSTRIAN PERCUSSION TARGET PISTOL 16in. Octagonal multi groove rifled barrel 10½in, of black and white damascus twist, stamped 'Wolfg. Scherrer In Linz'. Half stocked, scroll engraved lock, hammer, breech and furniture including spurred trigger guard. Set trigger, rabbit engraved on tail of lock, chequered butt, white metal oval escutcheon and barrel wedgeplates.

GERMAN OR AUSTRIAN RIFLED PERCUSSION TARGET PISTOL in the French style, 14in. Octagonal barrel 8¾in with engraved breech and silver inlaid with simple scroll work and 'Guss Stahl', scroll engraved lock and flat hammer with pierced decoration, the lock originally fitted with horizontal safety bolt acting on cut-out in front of hammer. The bolt is now removed and the hole filled. Fixed front and adjustable rearsights, half stocked with carved terminal and no provision for ramrod, fluted butt, steel mounts including scroll engraved spurred trigger guard and shaped buttcap with pierced finial.

American
'KENTUCKY' 90-BORE UNDERSTRIKER PERCUSSION TARGET PISTOL 14in. Heavy barrel 10in, with octagonal breech and multi groove rifling. Single blade rearsight, traces of maker's name at breech 'ington', probably for 'Remington'.

PERCUSSION POCKET PISTOLS

Flintlock pocket pistols were extremely efficient weapons and were very popular as methods of defence. One of their main drawbacks, however, was that they were at the mercy of the weather. As one could not possibly know where or when one was going to be attacked this was a major disadvantage.

As soon as Forsyth had produced his famous scent bottle there was a demand for pocket pistols to be made using this new method. The mechanics of the percussion system were much simpler than the flintlock as there was no need for a cock, the adjustable top jaw, the frizzen or the frizzen spring.

In the beginning the pocket pistols produced tended to be rather complex requiring dexterity to deal with the small pills of fulminate. This was obviously not the ideal method for a weapon which was to be used in a confrontation situation. After the introduction of the copper percussion cap, however, it became much simpler to produce effective and cheap pocket pistols in large numbers. Birmingham and Liege became centres of production of these cheap but very useful percussion pocket pistols. Usually they had slab butts and used a mechanism reminiscent of the boxlock, with the hammer and nipple situated centrally over the breech. This did away with the need for a touch-hole and made firing fractionally quicker. This method of production tended to do away with the high quality gun in place of these inexpensive but extremely efficient small firearms and demand grew.

The percussion cap had many advantages as it was a good size and was safe and reliable. Even in the case of a misfire the cap could be removed and replaced very quickly.

English pocket pistols tended to be rather plain and in general these guns tended to have very little decoration but some continental examples are extremely ornate.

Of course these types of pocket pistols were to be replaced by imported Derringers which were even more useful as secret concealed weapons of protection and then by the rapid development of the revolver. But the shift in emphasis from British produced pocket pistols to American produced revolvers was indicative of a changing pattern. The introduction of a national police force and the banning of duelling tended to decrease the demand for pocket pistols in Britain whereas in America there was an ever-increasing demand.

English and Irish
54-BORE BOXLOCK SIDEHAMMER PERCUSSION POCKET PISTOL by Rigby, the butt fitted to take spare balls, 6in. Damascus twist octagonal barrel 2in engraved 'Dublin', sprung swivel ramrod on lower rib. Finely border and scroll engraved frame and hammer with 'Wm and Jn Rigby', inlaid silver safety plug, three bents to tumbler. Foliate engraved hinged backstrap revealing three compartments for cartridges. Flattened slight round walnut butt.

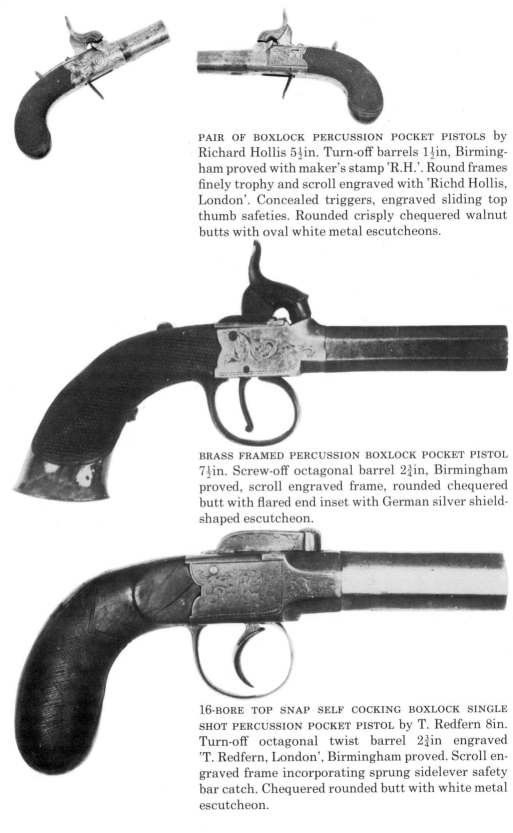

PAIR OF BOXLOCK PERCUSSION POCKET PISTOLS by Richard Hollis 5½in. Turn-off barrels 1½in, Birmingham proved with maker's stamp 'R.H.'. Round frames finely trophy and scroll engraved with 'Richd Hollis, London'. Concealed triggers, engraved sliding top thumb safeties. Rounded crisply chequered walnut butts with oval white metal escutcheons.

BRASS FRAMED PERCUSSION BOXLOCK POCKET PISTOL 7½in. Screw-off octagonal barrel 2¾in, Birmingham proved, scroll engraved frame, rounded chequered butt with flared end inset with German silver shield-shaped escutcheon.

16-BORE TOP SNAP SELF COCKING BOXLOCK SINGLE SHOT PERCUSSION POCKET PISTOL by T. Redfern 8in. Turn-off octagonal twist barrel 2¾in engraved 'T. Redfern, London', Birmingham proved. Scroll engraved frame incorporating sprung sidelever safety bar catch. Chequered rounded butt with white metal escutcheon.

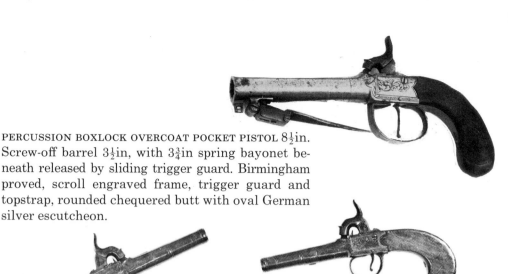

PERCUSSION BOXLOCK OVERCOAT POCKET PISTOL 8½in. Screw-off barrel 3½in, with 3¾in spring bayonet beneath released by sliding trigger guard. Birmingham proved, scroll engraved frame, trigger guard and topstrap, rounded chequered butt with oval German silver escutcheon.

PAIR OF CANNON BARRELLED PERCUSSION BOXLOCK POCKET PISTOLS 7¼in. Screw-off barrels 2¼in by Barbar, London. Tower private proofs, converted from flintlock. Flower and scroll engraved frames, sliding trigger guard safeties (not operative), plain walnut slab butts.

PERCUSSION BOXLOCK SIDEHAMMER POCKET PISTOL 8¾in. Screw-off octagonal twist barrel 3in by 'E. Baker and Sons, London, Maker's to the King'. London and Baker's private proofs, scroll engraving at breech, the frame bearing maker's name in scrolls surrounded by unusually profuse trophy of arms. Expertly converted from flintlock by breech drum method, the entire sideplate to forward of the breech drum is removable, and would originally have had the pan and frizzen spring attached as in a conventional sidelock. Hidden trigger, finely chequered rounded butt with rectangular silver escutcheon.

PAIR OF BOXLOCK PERCUSSION 'TOP HAT' POCKET PISTOLS 6in. Turn-off barrels 1½in, fern tip engraved muzzles, Birmingham proved. Scroll engraved rounded brass frames with 'E. Gill'. Barrels stamped 'CB 413/4'. Sliding top thumb safeties, concealed triggers, tension sprung cap retainers. Rounded chequered butts with foliate engraved butt plates, escutcheons engraved with family crest.

PERCUSSION BOXLOCK 'TOP HAT' POCKET PISTOL by Calderwood of Dublin 6½in. Turn-off barrel 1¾in, Birmingham proved, scroll engraved frame with 'Calderwood, Dublin' within bands. Sliding top thumb safety, tension sprung top hat retainer, concealed trigger, slab wooden butt, oval white metal escutcheon.

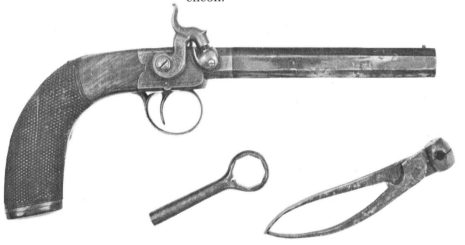

·36 PERCUSSION BOXLOCK SIDEHAMMER PISTOL 10in. Octagonal barrel 4¾in, with Birmingham proofs. Scroll engraved trigger guard, hammer, and frame, the latter with feather border. Rounded chequered walnut butt with horn buttcap. Oval silver escutcheon with owner's initials.

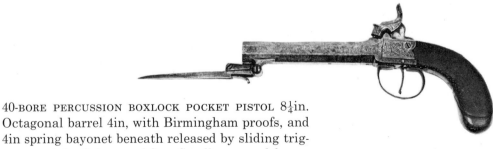

40-BORE PERCUSSION BOXLOCK POCKET PISTOL 8¼in. Octagonal barrel 4in, with Birmingham proofs, and 4in spring bayonet beneath released by sliding trigger guard, by Colgan and Son. Scroll engraved frame, trigger guard and topstrap, rounded chequered butt with rectangular German silver escutcheon.

PAIR OF PERCUSSION BOXLOCK POCKET PISTOLS by B. Cogswell 7¼in. Turn-off fluted blued barrels 3in, London proved. Scroll engraved frames, top plates engraved 'B. Cogswell, 224 Strand, London', concealed blued triggers. Butts inlaid with foliate white metal pique work, oval escutcheons, lion's head butt masks. Contained in their green baize lined fitted mahogany cased with illustrated yellow trade label, containing white metal three way flask, ball mould, barrel key, oil bottle, ebony handled nipple key, bone cap and nipple boxes. Also some lead balls in corner compartment.

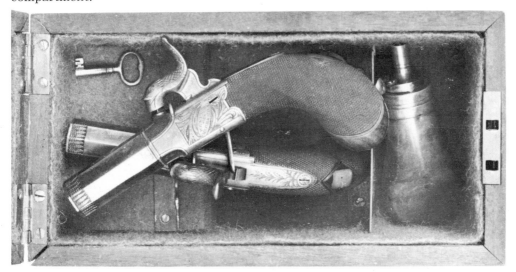

PAIR OF PERCUSSION BOXLOCK POCKET PISTOLS 5in. Octagonal barrels 1½in, engraved with foliage at muzzles, by Westly Richards, London. Rounded frames well chiselled with foliage, dolphin head hammers, Birmingham proved, folding triggers, backstraps well chiselled with floral sprays, diced wood butts inset with blank silver escutcheons.

19-BORE IRISH BACK-ACTION PERCUSSION OVERCOAT PISTOL by Trulock of Dublin, 10in. Barrel 5in engraved Dublin on top flat, breech tapped with nipple lug plug. Full stocked, finely scroll engraved breech and lock with 'Trulock'. Engraved pineapple finialed trigger guard, horn tipped wooden ramrod, chequered fishtail walnut butt, silver barrel wedgeplates, white metal escutcheon.

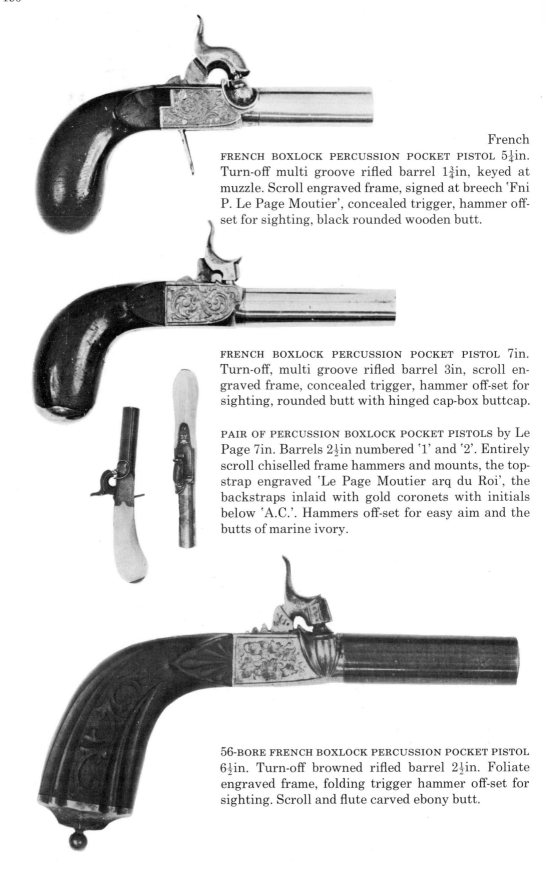

French

FRENCH BOXLOCK PERCUSSION POCKET PISTOL 5¼in.
Turn-off multi groove rifled barrel 1¾in, keyed at
muzzle. Scroll engraved frame, signed at breech 'Fni
P. Le Page Moutier', concealed trigger, hammer off-
set for sighting, black rounded wooden butt.

FRENCH BOXLOCK PERCUSSION POCKET PISTOL 7in.
Turn-off, multi groove rifled barrel 3in, scroll engraved frame, concealed trigger, hammer off-set for
sighting, rounded butt with hinged cap-box buttcap.

PAIR OF PERCUSSION BOXLOCK POCKET PISTOLS by Le
Page 7in. Barrels 2½in numbered '1' and '2'. Entirely
scroll chiselled frame hammers and mounts, the topstrap engraved 'Le Page Moutier arq du Roi', the
backstraps inlaid with gold coronets with initials
below 'A.C.'. Hammers off-set for easy aim and the
butts of marine ivory.

56-BORE FRENCH BOXLOCK PERCUSSION POCKET PISTOL
6½in. Turn-off browned rifled barrel 2½in. Foliate
engraved frame, folding trigger hammer off-set for
sighting. Scroll and flute carved ebony butt.

BELGIAN 36-BORE PERCUSSION BOXLOCK POCKET PIS-
TOL 8½in. Octagonal barrel 4in, with 4in spring
bayonet beneath released by sliding trigger guard,
pineapple and foliage engraved frame, slight
rounded chequered butt.

BELGIAN PERCUSSION BOXLOCK POCKET PISTOL 7in.
Fluted barrel 3in of damascus steel with multi groove
rifling, Liege proved. Finely chiselled foliate decoration to frame and topstrap and mounts, single
blade rearsight, foliate chiselled hammer off-set for
sighting. Finely chequered ebony butt carved with
some foliage, folding trigger. In its original velvet
lined imitation leather paper-covered fitted case.

PAIR OF BELGIAN PERCUSSION BOXLOCK POCKET PIS-
TOLS 7in. Octagonal barrels 2½in, rounded frames engraved with foliage, Liege proved, folding triggers,
diced wood butts with German silver mounts.

192

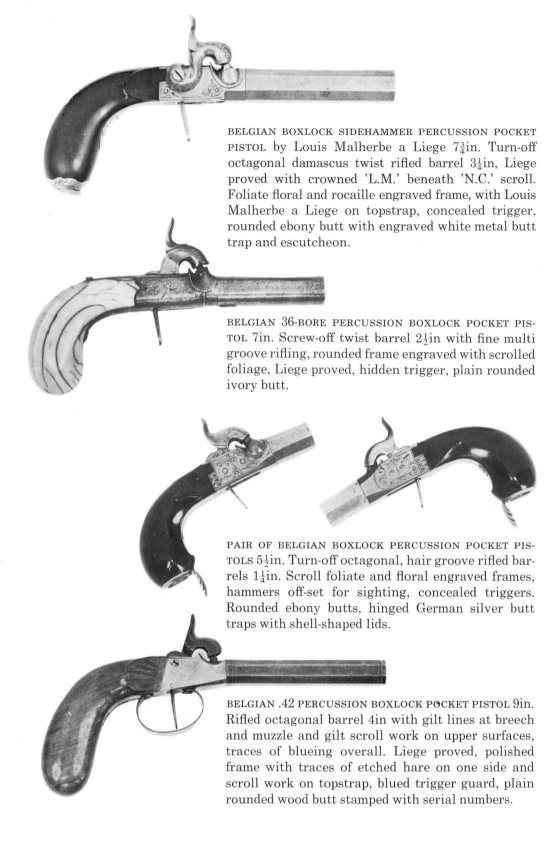

BELGIAN BOXLOCK SIDEHAMMER PERCUSSION POCKET PISTOL by Louis Malherbe a Liege 7¾in. Turn-off octagonal damascus twist rifled barrel 3¼in, Liege proved with crowned 'L.M.' beneath 'N.C.' scroll. Foliate floral and rocaille engraved frame, with Louis Malherbe a Liege on topstrap, concealed trigger, rounded ebony butt with engraved white metal butt trap and escutcheon.

BELGIAN 36-BORE PERCUSSION BOXLOCK POCKET PISTOL 7in. Screw-off twist barrel 2½in with fine multi groove rifling, rounded frame engraved with scrolled foliage, Liege proved, hidden trigger, plain rounded ivory butt.

PAIR OF BELGIAN BOXLOCK PERCUSSION POCKET PISTOLS 5½in. Turn-off octagonal, hair groove rifled barrels 1¼in. Scroll foliate and floral engraved frames, hammers off-set for sighting, concealed triggers. Rounded ebony butts, hinged German silver butt traps with shell-shaped lids.

BELGIAN .42 PERCUSSION BOXLOCK POCKET PISTOL 9in. Rifled octagonal barrel 4in with gilt lines at breech and muzzle and gilt scroll work on upper surfaces, traces of blueing overall. Liege proved, polished frame with traces of etched hare on one side and scroll work on topstrap, blued trigger guard, plain rounded wood butt stamped with serial numbers.

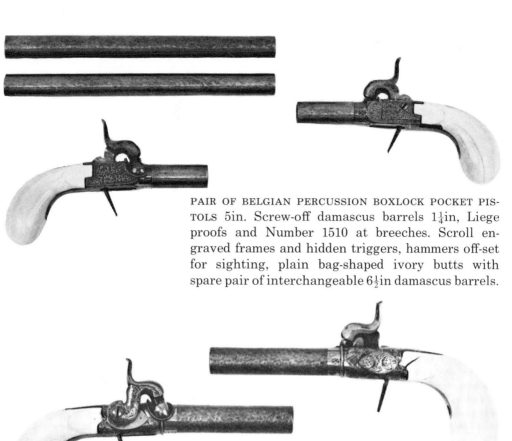

PAIR OF BELGIAN PERCUSSION BOXLOCK POCKET PIS-
TOLS 5in. Screw-off damascus barrels 1¼in, Liege
proofs and Number 1510 at breeches. Scroll engraved frames and hidden triggers, hammers off-set
for sighting, plain bag-shaped ivory butts with
spare pair of interchangeable 6½in damascus barrels.

PAIR OF BELGIAN 40-BORE PERCUSSION BOXLOCK SIDE-
HAMMER PISTOLS 7in. Screw-off damascus barrels
2¾in with multi groove rifling, finely engraved rounded frames and hammers. Liege proofs and Number
2291 at breeches, hidden triggers, plain rounded
ivory butts with hinged traps in engraved steel caps.

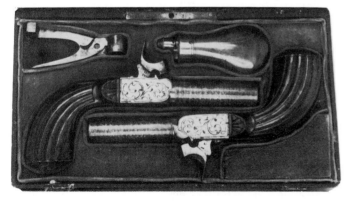

PAIR OF CONTINENTAL PERCUSSION BOXLOCK POCKET
PISTOLS 6½in. Damascus steel barrels 2½in, scroll engraved frames, part off-set hammers, folding triggers,
fluted wood butts.

PAIR OF CONTINENTAL DOUBLE BARRELLED PER-
CUSSION BOXLOCK POCKET PISTOLS, circa 1750, converted from flintlock, 6in. Turn-off rifled cannon
barrels 1¼in, trophy, scroll and linear engraved
frames and trigger guard bows. Sliding trigger guard,
safeties, silver wire inlaid butts, with rocaille and
scroll chiselled silver buttcaps.

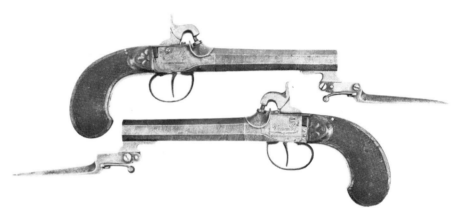

PAIR OF CONTINENTAL PERCUSSION BOXLOCK POCKET
PISTOLS 8¼in. Octagonal barrels 4¼in, fitted with
spring bayonets beneath, barrels 3in and of imitation twist steel, stamped '44 AF' beneath breeches.
Lockplates engraved 'Butet a Versailles'. Some carving to back of frames, finely diced wood butts.

American
88-BORE SELF COCKING UNITED STATES BAR HAMMER
BOXLOCK PERCUSSION POCKET PISTOL 6½in. Half octagonal deeply rifled turn-off barrel 3in stamped 'Allen
and Thur. . . . . . 626', scroll engraved round frame,
hammer stamped 'Allens Patent'. Two piece wooden
grips.

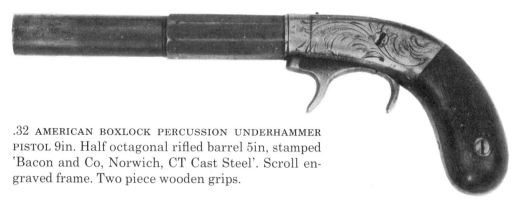

.32 AMERICAN BOXLOCK PERCUSSION UNDERHAMMER
PISTOL 9in. Half octagonal rifled barrel 5in, stamped
'Bacon and Co, Norwich, CT Cast Steel'. Scroll en-
graved frame. Two piece wooden grips.

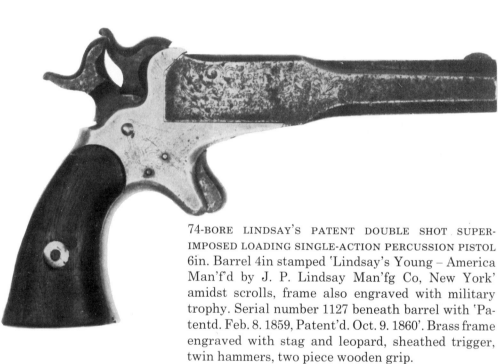

74-BORE LINDSAY'S PATENT DOUBLE SHOT SUPER-
IMPOSED LOADING SINGLE-ACTION PERCUSSION PISTOL
6in. Barrel 4in stamped 'Lindsay's Young – America
Man'f'd by J. P. Lindsay Man'fg Co, New York'
amidst scrolls, frame also engraved with military
trophy. Serial number 1127 beneath barrel with 'Pa-
tentd. Feb. 8. 1859, Patent'd. Oct. 9. 1860'. Brass frame
engraved with stag and leopard, sheathed trigger,
twin hammers, two piece wooden grip.

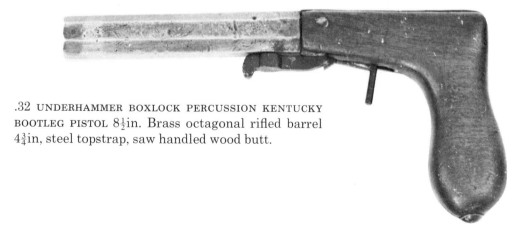

.32 UNDERHAMMER BOXLOCK PERCUSSION KENTUCKY
BOOTLEG PISTOL 8½in. Brass octagonal rifled barrel
4¾in, steel topstrap, saw handled wood butt.

196

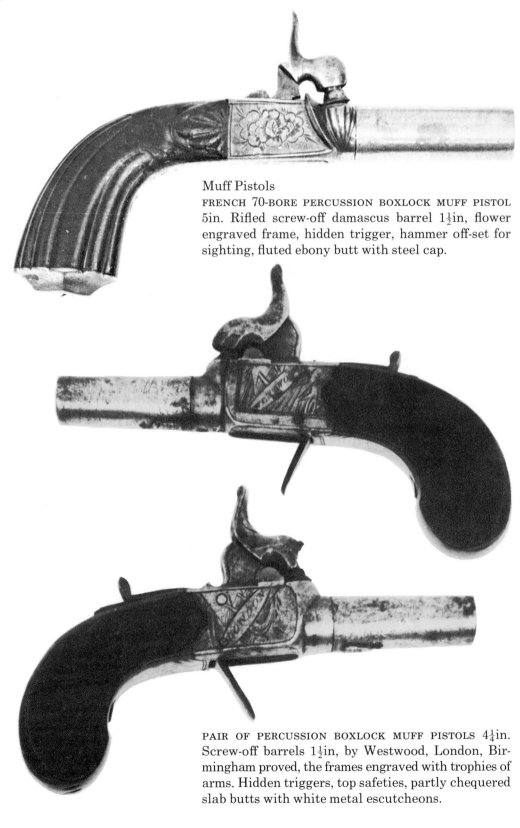

Muff Pistols
FRENCH 70-BORE PERCUSSION BOXLOCK MUFF PISTOL
5in. Rifled screw-off damascus barrel 1½in, flower
engraved frame, hidden trigger, hammer off-set for
sighting, fluted ebony butt with steel cap.

PAIR OF PERCUSSION BOXLOCK MUFF PISTOLS 4¼in.
Screw-off barrels 1½in, by Westwood, London, Birmingham proved, the frames engraved with trophies of
arms. Hidden triggers, top safeties, partly chequered
slab butts with white metal escutcheons.

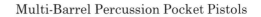

DOUBLE BARRELLED OVER AND UNDER TURNOVER PER-
CUSSION BOXLOCK PISTOL 6¼in. Screw-off barrels 2¼in,
by T. Wilson and Co, Liverpool, Birmingham proved,
hidden trigger top thumb safety, rounded chequered
butt.

UNUSUAL DOUBLE BARRELLED SIDE BY SIDE PER-
CUSSION BOXLOCK POCKET PISTOL 6½in. Round screw-
off barrels 2in with engraved muzzles, by Ward, Birmingham proved. Scroll engraved frame, single hammer with sliding selector catch operating on separate
in-line nipples, hidden trigger, top thumb safety
catch, rounded chequered butt, with oval silver escutcheon.

DOUBLE BARRELLED BOXLOCK PERCUSSION TURNOVER
POCKET PISTOL 7¼in. Birmingham proved, octagonal
barrels 3in, scroll engraved around nipples, fern tip
engraved muzzles side steel ramrod. Well linear and
scroll engraved frame with 'D. Mortimer, London'.
Dolphin hammer, sliding top safety catch, concealed
trigger. Chequered butt with white metal oval escutcheon and lions head buttcap.

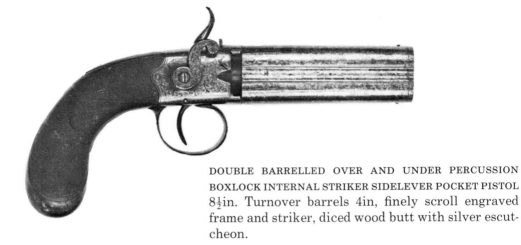

DOUBLE BARRELLED OVER AND UNDER PERCUSSION
BOXLOCK INTERNAL STRIKER SIDELEVER POCKET PISTOL
8½in. Turnover barrels 4in, finely scroll engraved
frame and striker, diced wood butt with silver escutcheon.

DOUBLE BARRELLED 36-BORE SIDE BY SIDE PERCUSSION
BOXLOCK SIDEHAMMER PISTOL 9½in. Octagonal barrels
4½in, Birmingham proved, swivel ramrod in ramp
beneath barrels. The frame, top-strap and trigger
guard profusely scroll engraved, engraved rounded
hammers, safety bolts, rounded chequered butt with
shield-shaped silver escutcheon.

OVER AND UNDER PERCUSSION BOXLOCK POCKET PIS-
TOL 6in. Short turnover barrels 1½in, by 'Kavanagh,
Dublin', finely chiselled scroll decorated lockplate,
breech, hammer and mounts, wooden butt insert with
silver escutcheon.

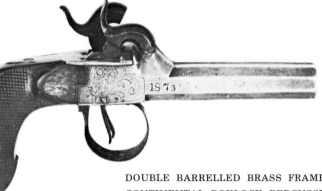

54-BORE DOUBLE BARRELLED OVER AND UNDER BOX-
LOCK SIDEHAMMER REVOLVING HAMMER NOSE PER-
CUSSION TRAVELLING PISTOL, by Essex of London, fitted with spring bayonet, 7in. Octagonal barrels 2½in,
London proved, engraved 'Essex, London' on top flat,
fern tip engraved muzzles. Swivel ramrod, 2½in hollow ground spring bayonet with ramp and roller bearing released by scroll engraved catch on frame side.
Finely scroll and border engraved frame and hammer
with revolving nose, two nipples in longitudinal
array. Rounded chequered walnut butt with rectangular silver escutcheon.

DOUBLE BARRELLED BRASS FRAMED AND BARRELLED
CONTINENTAL BOXLOCK PERCUSSION POCKET PISTOL
7½in. Octagonal barrels 3½in. Liege proved, stamped
'RBSHS 1873'. Scroll engraved frame, broad chequered butt.

DOUBLE BARRELLED OVER AND UNDER PERCUSSION
BOXLOCK POCKET PISTOL by H. W. Mortimer and Co,
7in. Barrels 3in, converted from flintlock, frame engraved with trophies of arms 'H. W. Mortimer and
Co, London, Gun Makers to His Majesty' the hammer
adapted by adding turnover striker. Sliding bar top
safety, slab sided wood butt, folding trigger.

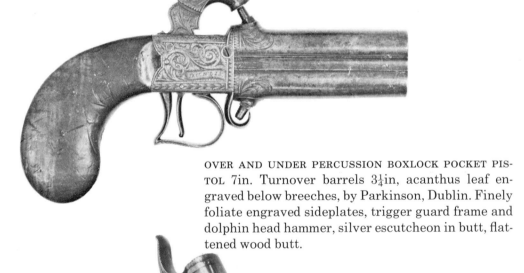

THREE BARRELLED PERCUSSION BOXLOCK POCKET PIS-
TOL 6in. Screw-off barrels 2in, Birmingham proved,
scroll engraved frame engraved 'Ward, London',
single hammer with spring loaded revolving circular
turret nose to fire each barrel in turn. Hidden trigger,
top thumb safety, rounded chequered butt with oval
silver escutcheon and engraved steel cap with trap.

OVER AND UNDER PERCUSSION BOXLOCK POCKET PIS-
TOL 7in. Turnover barrels $3\frac{1}{4}$in, acanthus leaf engraved below breeches, by Parkinson, Dublin. Finely
foliate engraved sideplates, trigger guard frame and
dolphin head hammer, silver escutcheon in butt, flattened wood butt.

RIGBY ALL METAL THREE BARRELLED PERCUSSION POC-
KET KNUCKLEDUSTER PISTOL $5\frac{1}{2}$in. Turn-off barrels
$1\frac{1}{2}$in, stamped 'AR 7237', by William and J. N. Rigby,
Dublin. Foliate engraved slab sided curved frame,
finger ring in butt, finely engraved hammer with circular hand rotated striker, folding trigger.

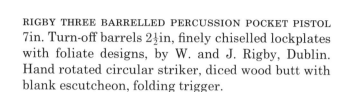

RIGBY THREE BARRELLED PERCUSSION POCKET PISTOL
7in. Turn-off barrels 2½in, finely chiselled lockplates
with foliate designs, by W. and J. Rigby, Dublin.
Hand rotated circular striker, diced wood butt with
blank escutcheon, folding trigger.

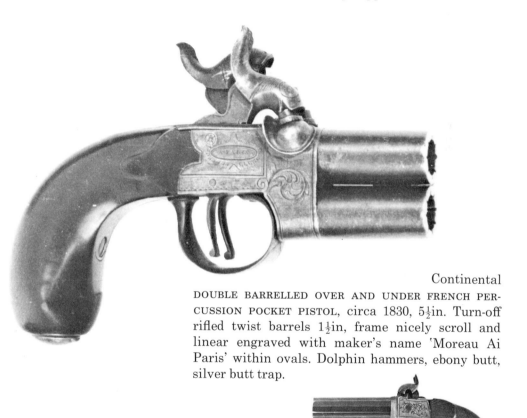

Continental
DOUBLE BARRELLED OVER AND UNDER FRENCH PER-
CUSSION POCKET PISTOL, circa 1830, 5½in. Turn-off
rifled twist barrels 1½in, frame nicely scroll and
linear engraved with maker's name 'Moreau Ai
Paris' within ovals. Dolphin hammers, ebony butt,
silver butt trap.

PAIR OF CONTINENTAL DOUBLE BARRELLED OVER AND
UNDER PERCUSSION BOXLOCK PISTOLS 8¾in. Screw-off
octagonal barrels 3½in, the upper barrels with silver
scroll inlay, scroll engraved frames and topstraps,
plain rounded butts with light shell carving to rear of
frames, steel buttcaps.

DERRINGERS

While the British gunmakers had a lean time in the production of pistols, there was a boom in the American market. Most flintlock pistols up to this time had been imported from Britain or France. Much confusion surrounded this as the name of the lock-plate was quite often that of the importer rather than the manufacturer. The main production of the American gunsmiths was fowling pieces or long rifles.

A German immigrant to Philadelphia, Henry Deringer, saw the possibilities of the new percussion system and in 1825 he started to manufacture percussion pistols. At the beginning they were the same type as English duelling pistols, about the same weight and size and with the extra rigid trigger. However, Deringer's business sense told him that the main need in America at that time was for a small weapon which could be concealed and used in a personal defence situation. Deringer supplied it. The secret weapon that he designed could be as little as 4in long with a bore of $\frac{1}{2}$in. It was an infallible killer at short range. There was no pretence that this weapon was meant to be used in a fight with equal weapons – one carried a Deringer in order to use it in a surprise situation to kill your opponent.

There grew up a situation in the States when everyone carried a pocket pistol as no one knew when they might be attacked. The most famous examples of the Deringer fights were, of course, in the gambling saloons and it was literally essential to have a small concealed gun on your person.

There were, of course, many imitations often called Derringers or Beringers. They were quite literally direct replicas of the earlier Deringer although were not of the same quality and workmanship. So numerous were these imitations that the term Derringer became standard for any small, short pocket pistol.

All Derringer pistols are eagerly sought after especially the genuine Deringer with the mark PHILADEL DERINGER on the lock plate. Many were exported as the European gunsmiths did not really specialise in this type of pistol.

Most Derringers have very little decoration as this was hardly thought necessary. It was a small, cheap pistol purely designed for killing.

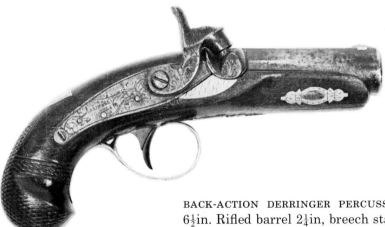

BACK-ACTION DERRINGER PERCUSSION .44in PISTOL 6½in. Rifled barrel 2¼in, breech stamped 'Derringer, Philadel' and 'P', white metal line inlay and foresight. Scroll engraved backaction lock and hammer stamped 'Derringer, Philadel'. Full stocked, scroll engraved white metal trigger guard, sidenail plates, escutcheon and inlaid plates. Chequered butt.

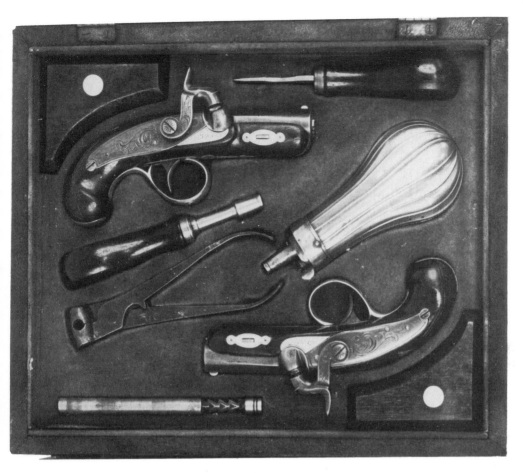

PAIR OF 52-BORE DERRINGER TYPE PERCUSSION POCKET
PISTOLS by John Krider, 1839–70, at 2nd and Walnut
Streets, Philadelphia, Pennsylvania, 5in. Six groove
rifled barrel 2in, white metal foresight and lines at
breech with scrolls stamped with maker's name on
top flats. Scroll engraved back-action lockplates and
hammer. White metal engraved trigger guards, fore
end caps, buttcaps, escutcheons, sidenail plates. Full
stocked with chequered butt heels. Contained in
their dull red velvet lined close fitted black leather-
covered wooden case, containing fluted copper flask,
turn-screw, nipple key, ramrod with worm, a pincer
type bullet mould.

THE PEPPERBOX

The introduction of the copper percussion cap started a new wave of repeating weapons. The cap made the lock construction very simple especially in the field of repeating weapons. There had been flintlock revolvers but their mechanisms were too complex and the constantly moving frizzens caused too many problems.

As soon as the percussion cap system was perfected, around the middle of the 19th century, the first simple percussion revolver was introduced. It was called the pepperbox.

Five or six barrels were driven into a block of metal and arranged concentrically round an axis. Each barrel had a small percussion mechanism, with its own nipple and was loaded and capped separately. This mechanism was not as simple as those developed later but it was the first step to the percussion revolver.

Pepperboxes may not have been perfect but they certainly were popular. They were produced in large quantities as they were particularly good for personal defence although not particularly accurate. A few accurate pepperbox longarms were made but they were singularly unsuccessful. They were too heavy and lacked balance and so they were essentially a short gun design.

There were manually operated pepperboxes, which one rotated after firing but most were rotated by pulling back the trigger which lined up the next unfired barrel.

The main disadvantage of the pepperbox was that it was extremely top heavy, hence its tendency to be inaccurate and many gunsmiths did not produce it at all. These gunsmiths went instead for the transitional revolver. This had one barrel and a short cylinder. There was an art of workmanship in the design and manufacture of this weapon and some very fine, high quality firearms were made.

Although the pepperbox did have these various disadvantages and was much inferior to its successor, the Colt revolver, it was still produced long after Colt was granted his patent.

English
5-SHOT .30in BUDDING PERCUSSION PEPPERBOX RE-VOLVER 8in. Bronze barrels 3¼in with Birmingham proofs and secured by square headed screw incorporating a pricker, bronze frame engraved on topstrap 'Budding, Maker' within simply decorated oval. Combined coil spring operated trigger and hammer beneath, plain rounded walnut grips secured by three large brass headed screws.

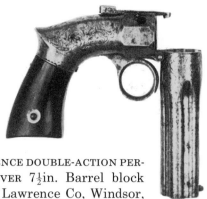

5-SHOT 28 ROBBIN AND LAWRENCE DOUBLE-ACTION PER-
CUSSION PEPPERBOX REVOLVER 7½in. Barrel block
3½in stamped 'Robbins and Lawrence Co, Windsor,
Vt Patent 1849', number 2076. The front 2¼in of the
barrels unscrew and slide forwards to facilitate loading the chambers, the entire barrel block hinging
downwards for capping the nipples. The action is
operated by a ring trigger and is entirely enclosed,
with revolving striker nose firing each barrel in turn,
scroll engraved breech and rounded frame, plain
rosewood grips.

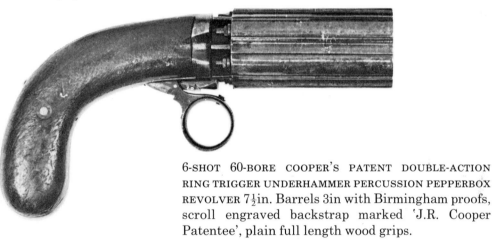

6-SHOT 60-BORE COOPER'S PATENT DOUBLE-ACTION
RING TRIGGER UNDERHAMMER PERCUSSION PEPPERBOX
REVOLVER 7½in. Barrels 3in with Birmingham proofs,
scroll engraved backstrap marked 'J.R. Cooper
Patentee', plain full length wood grips.

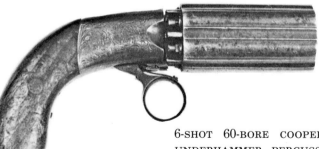

6-SHOT 60-BORE COOPER'S PATENT RING TRIGGER
UNDERHAMMER PERCUSSION PEPPERBOX REVOLVER
7½in. Barrels 3½in, Birmingham proved, rounded
scroll engraved frame and backstrap, the frame engraved 'J.R. Cooper Patentee', plain bag-shaped
grips.

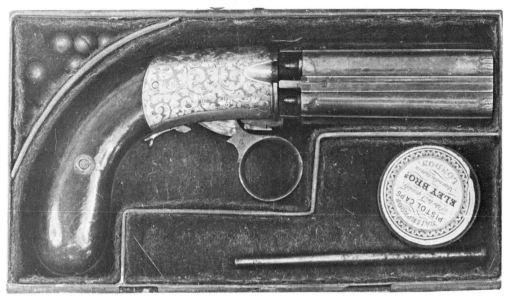

6-SHOT 60-BORE COOPER'S PATENT UNDERHAMMER PER-
CUSSION PEPPERBOX REVOLVER 7¼in. Fluted cylinder
3¼in, Birmingham proved, retaining nearly all original colour hardened finish, fern tip engraved muz
zle. Finely scroll engraved white metal frame with
'J. R. Cooper's Patent' within bands, and 'O. Harold
Dundalk' on scroll engraved backstrap. Ring trigger
with sliding safety catch both retain some original
blued finish. Two piece varnished walnut bag-shaped
grips.

6-SHOT TOP SNAP SELF COCKING PERCUSSION PEP-
PERBOX REVOLVER 7½in. Fluted cylinder 3in, London
proved. Scroll and border engraved white metal rounded frame, nipple shield and backstrap with retailer's
name 'C. and H. Egg, 1 Piccadilly, London'. Thunderburst and strap engraved bar hammer. Two piece
polished wooden grips.

6-SHOT 80-BORE BAR HAMMER SELF COCKING PER-
CUSSION PEPPERBOX REVOLVER 8in. Barrel 2¾in, foliate engraved, rounded frame, Birmingham proved,
plain wood grips.

6-SHOT 48-BORE BAR HAMMER PERCUSSION PEPPERBOX
REVOLVER 8½in. Barrels 3½in, by Westley Richards,
London, foliate engraved frame and hammer, barrels
numbered one to six. Birmingham proved, engraved
on right of frame 'Improved revolving pistol', sliding
bar top safety, diced wood butt with silver escutcheon, hinged butt trap with foliate engraving.

LARGE 6-SHOT 38-BORE BAR HAMMER PERCUSSION PEP-
PERBOX REVOLVER 9in. Barrels 4in with Birmingham
proofs and numbered one to six, scroll engraved
rounded frame with maker's name 'W. Kimberley'
and 'Improved Revolving Pistol' in panels. Scroll engraved topstrap, hammer and trigger guard, hinged
trap in buttcap, rounded chequered butt with oval
silver escutcheon. In its fitted green baize lined oak
case, with brass lid escutcheon, complete with three
way cylindrical copper flask stamped 'Sykes' on the
body, steel pincer mould, and cleaning rod.

American

6-SHOT .32 TOP SNAP ALLEN'S PATENT BAR HAMMER
PERCUSSION PEPPERBOX REVOLVER 7¼in. Fluted bar-
rels 3½in stamped 'Allen and Wheelock, Worcester,
Patented April 15'. Scroll engraved rounded frame
and nipple shield. Bar hammer stamped 'Allen's
Patent 1845'. Two piece rounded wood grips.

5-SHOT TOP SNAP ALLEN AND WHEELOCK PERCUSSION PEPPERBOX REVOLVER 6in. Barrels 3in stamped 'Allen and Wheelock, number 215', bar hammer stamped 'Patented April 14, 1845'. Rounded frame, two piece wooden grips.

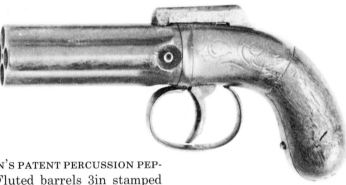

4-SHOT .30 TOP SNAP ALLEN'S PATENT PERCUSSION PEPPERBOX REVOLVER 6in. Fluted barrels 3in stamped 'Allen and Wheelock, Patented 1845, number 532'. Scroll engraved rounded frame, bar hammer stamped 'Allen's Patent Jan 13, 1857'. Two piece wood grips.

UNUSUALLY LONG BARRELLED .31 ALLEN AND THURBER SELF COCKING BAR HAMMER PERCUSSION PEPPERBOX REVOLVER 8½in. Barrels 5in stamped 'Allen and Thurber, Worcester, Patented 1837, Cast Steel', the hammer stamped 'Allen's Patent'. Rounded scroll engraved frame, plain bag-shaped wooden grips.

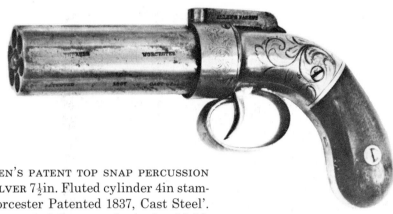

6-SHOT .32in ALLEN'S PATENT TOP SNAP PERCUSSION PEPPERBOX REVOLVER 7½in. Fluted cylinder 4in stamped 'Thurber Worcester Patented 1837, Cast Steel'. Scroll engraved rounded frame and nipple shield, hammer stamped 'Allen's Patent'. Two piece bag-shaped wooden grips.

3-SHOT 31 HAND ROTATED DOUBLE-ACTION BAR HAMMER PERCUSSION PEPPERBOX REVOLVER 6¼in. Barrels 3in, numbered 420 and stamped 'Cast Steel', the hammer stamped 'Manhattan F.A. Mfg. Co, New York'. Rounded scroll engraved frame, bag-shaped butt with plain wood grips.

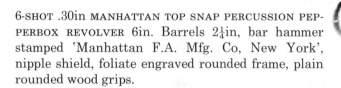

6-SHOT .30in MANHATTAN TOP SNAP PERCUSSION PEPPERBOX REVOLVER 6in. Barrels 2¼in, bar hammer stamped 'Manhattan F.A. Mfg. Co, New York', nipple shield, foliate engraved rounded frame, plain rounded wood grips.

6-SHOT TOP SNAP MANHATTAN PERCUSSION PEPPERBOX REVOLVER 7½in. Fluted barrels 4in stamped 'Cast Steel'. Scroll engraved rounded frame, bar hammer stamped 'Manhattan F.A. Mfg. Co, New York'. Two piece bag-shaped wooden grips.

210

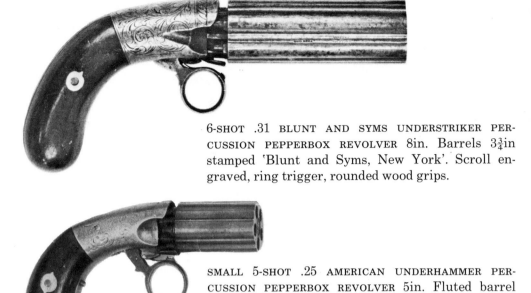

6-SHOT .31 BLUNT AND SYMS UNDERSTRIKER PER-
CUSSION PEPPERBOX REVOLVER 8in. Barrels 3¾in
stamped 'Blunt and Syms, New York'. Scroll engraved, ring trigger, rounded wood grips.

SMALL 5-SHOT .25 AMERICAN UNDERHAMMER PER-
CUSSION PEPPERBOX REVOLVER 5in. Fluted barrel
2in, the muzzle stamped 'R.C. 56'. Scroll engraved
rounded frame, ring trigger, two piece wooden grips.

FOUR BARRELLED 12-BORE PHILADELPHIA HAND ROT-
ATED SINGLE ACTION PERCUSSION PEPPERBOX RE-
VOLVER 12½in. Barrels 7¼in, rounded frame with
simple long curved hammer, rounded cast brass butt
with slight flared cap.

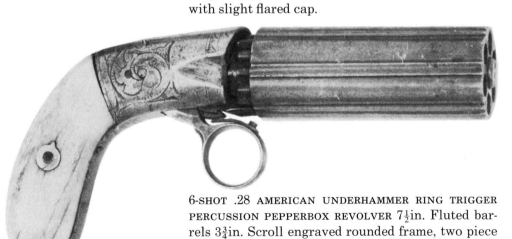

6-SHOT .28 AMERICAN UNDERHAMMER RING TRIGGER
PERCUSSION PEPPERBOX REVOLVER 7½in. Fluted barrels 3¾in. Scroll engraved rounded frame, two piece
round ivory grips.

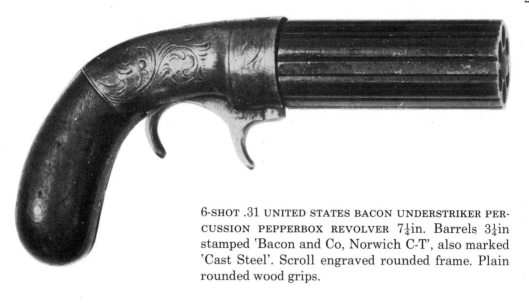

6-SHOT .31 UNITED STATES BACON UNDERSTRIKER PER-
CUSSION PEPPERBOX REVOLVER 7¼in. Barrels 3¼in
stamped 'Bacon and Co, Norwich C-T', also marked
'Cast Steel'. Scroll engraved rounded frame. Plain
rounded wood grips.

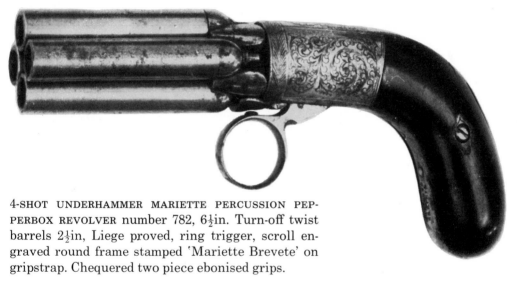

4-SHOT UNDERHAMMER MARIETTE PERCUSSION PEP-
PERBOX REVOLVER number 782, 6½in. Turn-off twist
barrels 2½in, Liege proved, ring trigger, scroll engraved round frame stamped 'Mariette Brevete' on
gripstrap. Chequered two piece ebonised grips.

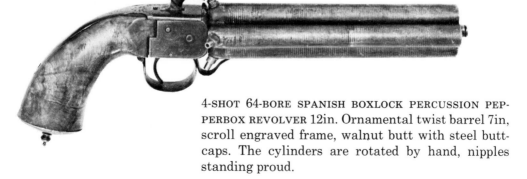

4-SHOT 64-BORE SPANISH BOXLOCK PERCUSSION PEP-
PERBOX REVOLVER 12in. Ornamental twist barrel 7in,
scroll engraved frame, walnut butt with steel buttcaps. The cylinders are rotated by hand, nipples
standing proud.

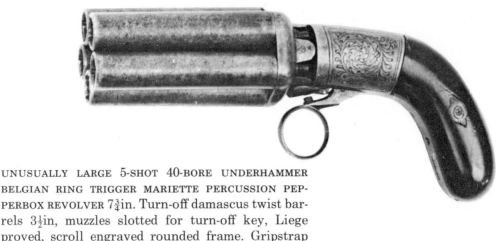

UNUSUALLY LARGE 5-SHOT 40-BORE UNDERHAMMER BELGIAN RING TRIGGER MARIETTE PERCUSSION PEP-PERBOX REVOLVER 7¾in. Turn-off damascus twist barrels 3½in, muzzles slotted for turn-off key, Liege proved, scroll engraved rounded frame. Gripstrap stamped 'Mariette Bte', two piece rounded ebony grips.

6-SHOT 90-BORE UNDERHAMMER SELF COCKING BELGIAN RING TRIGGER MARIETTE PERCUSSION PEPPERBOX RE-VOLVER 7½in. Fluted barrels 3½in, Liege proved, round scroll engraved frame inlaid with silver scrolls. Two piece rounded ebony grips.

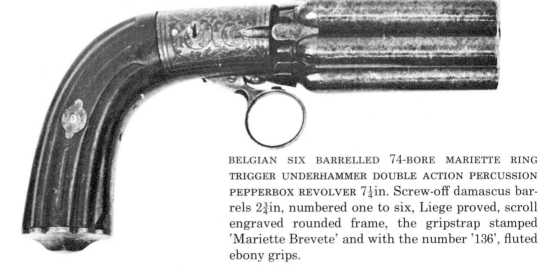

BELGIAN SIX BARRELLED 74-BORE MARIETTE RING TRIGGER UNDERHAMMER DOUBLE ACTION PERCUSSION PEPPERBOX REVOLVER 7¼in. Screw-off damascus barrels 2¾in, numbered one to six, Liege proved, scroll engraved rounded frame, the gripstrap stamped 'Mariette Brevete' and with the number '136', fluted ebony grips.

PERCUSSION RIFLES AND SPORTING GUNS

The percussion cap really opened a floodgate for the introduction of new weapons from the revolver to the magazine rifle and the breech-loader. This was not to say that immediately the percussion cap was discovered that all weapons were converted or thrown out. The Ordnance were always slow in adopting any new system and that was particularly true for percussion. One of the reasons was the enormous expense of equipping the army and navy with new weapons especially as there were vast stocks of adequate flintlocks around. In stock or on issue there were a hundred thousand rifles and nearly two million muskets, all very dependable and liked by the troops as they had proved their value throughout the Napoleonic struggle.

However, despite the natural conservation of some of the higher ranks between 1834–38 the Ordnance were quietly selling off their out-of-date flintlocks. Perhaps it was the realisation that if European peace did not last England would be left in a very embarrassing situation.

The first rifle of the new kind to be used was the Brunswick rifle. It was adopted in 1837 and was, in shape and appearance, very similar to the Baker rifle. The idea behind the weapon was to give the advantages of the rifle along with the quick loading of the musket. Its most noticeable feature was the two very deep grooves, giving a whole turn. A bullet was designed to fit. This gun was an unfortunate choice as the deep grooves tended to lead up, it was difficult to load and hence very unpopular with the troops. It was fortunate there was no need to use this weapon in active service and it was soon palmed off to the Navy.

Another rifle which was produced at this time was the Jacobs rifle. It was called after a Major Jacob who was with the East India Company. He seemed to spend his time designing firearms and sending his prolific designs back to London to be made by English gunsmiths. His final design was this rifle which was double-barrelled and sighted up to 2,000 yards, although it had a short barrel about twenty-four inches long and four deep grooves. He also designed a bullet for his weapon which was cylindrical with a conical nose. Major Jacob ordered 1,000 of these rifles to be sent back to him but the consignment took three years to reach India and by that time he was dead.

Another rifle which was quite common at this time was the Minié rifle. Its main notoriety was the addition of a hollow iron core which was forced by the explosion into the base of the bullet. This was the rifle which was used for most of the Crimean War and was considered a good rifle.

In 1852 it looked as though Britain would soon be at war again in Europe and the Select Committee on Small Arms asked for designs to enable them to produce an all British rifle. They lifted what they thought were the best points of all the designs submitted and produced a long-arm with the following specifications; it was to have a percussion lock, to be muzzle-loading and have a barrel length of thirty-nine inches. The bullet for this new weapon was designed by Pritchett. The rifle was made at the Government's arsenal at Enfield and when tested it was found to be accurate up to 800 yards. The Enfield Rifle of Patt '53 was given to the Army in time for the end of the Crimean War. It was a fine weapon, certainly the best of the muzzle-loaders and was of the conventional type with shallow grooves cut on the inside of the barrel. It is a tribute to the gun that many Enfields are still fired by muzzle-loading enthusiasts.

Conversions were very common at this period and many flintlock longarms were converted to the percussion system. Many flintlock blunderbusses were converted but only a few percussion blunderbusses were actually made. This was probably due to the development which was to render the blunderbuss obsolete as a weapon of personal defence – the percussion revolver.

17-BORE PAGET PERCUSSION CARBINE 31½in. Tower proved sighted barrel 15¾in. Full stocked, stepped lockplate engraved 'Tower', with crowned 'GR'. Adapted flintlock lockplate. Brass mounts, buttplate engraved 'RCH 380'. Swivel ramrod.

10-BORE 1842 PATTERN LOVELL'S PERCUSSION MUSKET 55in. London proved, barrel 39in engraved 'Bank of England' behind rear-sight. Full stocked, linear engraved lockplate with 'Lacy and Co'. Brass mounts, steel ramrod, bayonet clip and sling mounts.

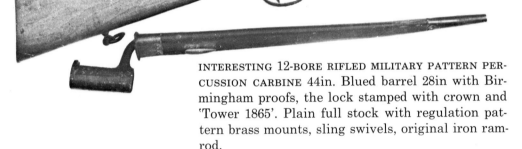

INTERESTING 12-BORE RIFLED MILITARY PATTERN PERCUSSION CARBINE 44in. Blued barrel 28in with Birmingham proofs, the lock stamped with crown and 'Tower 1865'. Plain full stock with regulation pattern brass mounts, sling swivels, original iron ramrod.

.577 ENFIELD TYPE THREE BAND VOLUNTEER PERCUSSION RIFLE 55in. Barrel 39in, Birmingham proved, engraved 'Reilly, 315 and 502 Oxford Street, London'. Full stocked, lockplate engraved 'Reilly London', regulation brass mounts, steel barrel bands, fore stock partly chequered, steel ramrod leather sling, with Enfield socket bayonet. In its brass mounted leather sheath.

.653 TOWER CONSTABULARY PERCUSSION CARBINE 42in. Barrel 26in, full stocked, brass mounts, lock engraved with crown and 'VR Tower 1843', butt stamped 'BO', '1843', butt engraved 'C.3962', ramrod numbered 'C.2619'. With its original triangular socket bayonet, engraved 'C.7895' and its brass mounted leather scabbard with spring catch.

PRINCE'S PATENT BREECH LOADING PERCUSSION .577in RIFLE, by Cogswell, 46½in. Browned twist barrel 30in, engraved 'Prince's Patent' at breech, ladder sights to seven hundred yards, back-action lock engraved 'B. Cogswell, 224 Strand, London'. Plain steel furniture and sling swivels, the breech is opened at half cock by sliding the locking bolt backwards along trigger guard. This allows the ball-ended lever to be rotated and the barrel to be slid forward. Chequered walnut stock, oval silver escutcheon.

Continental and Indian

SWEDISH M.1840 13-BORE MILITARY PERCUSSION MUSKET 50in. Barrel 33½in. Full stocked, brass mounts, three brass spring clip retained barrel bands, lock stamped 'Carl Gustaf Maa' and dated '1855', dog catch. Butt, lockplate and barrel numbered '727'.

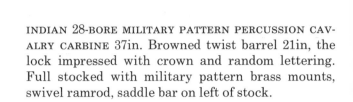

INDIAN 28-BORE MILITARY PATTERN PERCUSSION CAV-
ALRY CARBINE 37in. Browned twist barrel 21in, the
lock impressed with crown and random lettering.
Full stocked with military pattern brass mounts,
swivel ramrod, saddle bar on left of stock.

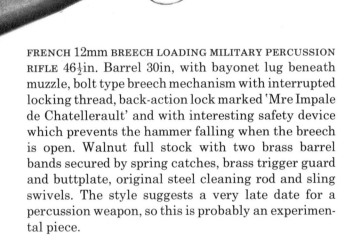

FRENCH 12mm BREECH LOADING MILITARY PERCUSSION
RIFLE 46½in. Barrel 30in, with bayonet lug beneath
muzzle, bolt type breech mechanism with interrupted
locking thread, back-action lock marked 'Mre Impale
de Chatellerault' and with interesting safety device
which prevents the hammer falling when the breech
is open. Walnut full stock with two brass barrel
bands secured by spring catches, brass trigger guard
and buttplate, original steel cleaning rod and sling
swivels. The style suggests a very late date for a
percussion weapon, so this is probably an experimen-
tal piece.

30-BORE BURNSIDE PATENT MODEL 1864 BREECH LOAD-
ING PERCUSSION CARBINE 40in. Round rifled barrel
21in with flip-up sight, half stocked, back-action lock,
action stamped 'Burnside Patent Model 1864'. Spring
trigger guard releases hinged falling breech block,
wooden butt, steel buttcap.

CIVIL WAR PERIOD BREECH LOADING RIFLED PER-
CUSSION .54in CARBINE 39in. Barrel 21in, with octagonal breech engraved 'Gilbert Smith's Patent, 1857',
address 'Poultney and Trimble, Baltimore, Md.'. Two
folding leaf rearsights, the hinged barrel released by
thumb catch in large trigger guard boxlock-action
with side hammer. Plain polished butt and half stock,
the latter secured by single barrel band.

AMERICAN 48-BORE UNDERHAMMER PERCUSSION CAR-
BINE OR BUGGY RIFLE 39½in. Heavy octagonal barrel
22¾in, stamped at breech 'N. Kendall, Windsor, Vt.,
Patent', the breech plug being directly attached to
the butt which is of Kentucky style in birds eye
maple. The breech plug tang stamped 'Smith's Improved Patent Stud Lock'. Brass mounts including
scrolled trigger guard, oblong copper escutcheon in
side of butt. A curious feature of this weapon is that
the breech bears British Government surplus stamps.
These weapons were made between 1835 and 1842 in
the workshops of the Vermont State Prison, under
convict labour.

AMERICAN 60-BORE UNDERHAMMER PERCUSSION
TARGET RIFLE 45¼in. Heavy octagonal barrel 29¼in
with narrow band at muzzle, the breech stamped
'Hitchcock and Muzzy, Cast Steel' and 'D.H. Hil-
liard, Comish, N.H.'. Adjustable 'V' and aperture
rearsights, fine pedestal foresight within tubular
protector, rammer carried in four pipes beneath barrel, the sweeping mahogany Kentucky type butt
fixed directly to the breech plug. Brass mounts including scrolled trigger guard, cheek piece inset
with German silver star, the other side of the butt
inset with German silver plaque.

Sporting Guns

80-BORE SINGLE BARRELLED BREECH LOADING TAP-
ACTION PERCUSSION SPORTING RIFLE 49in. Half octagonal tapering barrel 30in, silver line inlaid at
breech, thunderburst engraved around loading port,
scroll engraved back-action lock with 'Mapplebeck
and Lowe'. Half stocked, scroll engraved steel furniture, silver forecap, barrel wedgeplates and escutcheon, chequered small of stock, steel ramrod on
lower rib.

40-OVAL-BORE PERCUSSION RIFLE 45½in. Heavy octagonal damascus steel barrel 30in, marked 'Charles
Lancaster, 151 New Bond Street, London' and
'Patent Smooth Bore Rifle', by 'W. Watmough, London'. Half stocked, finely foliate engraved lockplate
and mounts, dolphin head hammer, set trigger, semi-
spurred large trigger guard, plat vent at breech. Horn
fore-end tip, adjustable horizontal peepsight in small
of stock, window rearsight, four folding leafsights
with gold lines.

HEAVY SINGLE BARRELLED 26-BORE JACOB'S RIFLED
PERCUSSION SPORTING RIFLE by G. H. Daw, 40½in.
Twist barrel 24in, London proved, deep four groove
rifling, flattened top engraved 'George H. Daw, 57
Threadneedle Street, London', gold lined ladder
rearsight to one thousand two hundred yards. Half
stocked, scroll engraved lockplate and hammer with
maker's name. Deeply scroll engraved steel furniture, sprung patch box (roller on spring). Walnut
stock, chequered at small and fore. Brass tipped
wooden ramrod.

DOUBLE BARRELLED 14-BORE BACK-ACTION PERCUSSION
SPORTING GUN by Samuel Nock, 45½in. Barrels 26¼in,
engraved 'Samuel Nock, Regent Circus, Piccadilly,
London, Gun Maker to Her Majesty'. Quarter
stocked, very finely scroll and game engraved locks
and dolphin hammers with 'Samuel Nock Invenit' on
raised plinths below hammers. Finely scrolled, dog
and game engraved furniture, grip safety, silver sidenail plates and safety vents. Brass tipped ebony
ramrod with capped worm. Chequered grip of stock.

24-BORE PERCUSSION MUSKET DECORATED IN JAPAN
45in. Barrel 31½in, decorated overall with inlaid
brass foliate patterns and with standing figure,
panel, etc. Half stocked, by Parker Field and Sons,
London. Enfield type lock. Brass trigger guard. Stock
inlaid with gilt metal decoration of fish, floral and
other patterns.

WESTLEY RICHARDS MONKEYTAIL BREECH LOADING PRE-
SENTATION .450 PERCUSSION TARGET RIFLE 52½in. Barrel 35½in, with Birmingham proofs, serial number 790
and 'Whitworth Patent' at breech, fitted with sliding
ramp rearsight and pillar foresight with guard, the
bolted lock stamped 'Westley Richards and Co, 1866'.
Walnut full stock with chequered wrist and fore end
grip, steel mounts including two barrel bands, sling
swivels, steel ramrod, the butt with inlaid German
silver plaque engraved '19th Middlesex R.V. Pre-
sented by Captain Williams, won by Private C. Bur-
ley, 1866'.

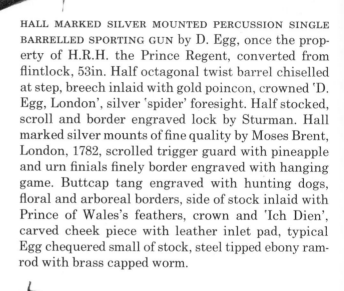

HALL MARKED SILVER MOUNTED PERCUSSION SINGLE BARRELLED SPORTING GUN by D. Egg, once the property of H.R.H. the Prince Regent, converted from flintlock, 53in. Half octagonal twist barrel chiselled at step, breech inlaid with gold poincon, crowned 'D. Egg, London', silver 'spider' foresight. Half stocked, scroll and border engraved lock by Sturman. Hall marked silver mounts of fine quality by Moses Brent, London, 1782, scrolled trigger guard with pineapple and urn finials finely border engraved with hanging game. Buttcap tang engraved with hunting dogs, floral and arboreal borders, side of stock inlaid with Prince of Wales's feathers, crown and 'Ich Dien', carved cheek piece with leather inlet pad, typical Egg chequered small of stock, steel tipped ebony ramrod with brass capped worm.

SINGLE BARRELLED 13-BORE SILVER MOUNTED PERCUSSION SPORTING GUN by Rigby 49in. Half octagonal twist barrel $32\frac{1}{2}$in engraved 'J. Rigby, Dublin'. Half stocked, scroll engraved stepped lock hammer with blank gold escutcheon. Floral and border engraved acorn finialed trigger guard, large buttcap. Chequered small of stock. Horn tipped wooden ramrod.

HEAVY 8-BORE PERCUSSION DUCK GUN 57in. Half octagonal twist barrel $41\frac{1}{2}$in, with plat line at breech and maker's name 'C. Moore, Regent Circus, London', flat scroll engraved hammer and bolted lock, the latter also engraved 'C. Moore, London'. Half stocked with horn fore-end cap and chequered wrist, steel mounts, brass tipped wooden ramrod on ramp beneath barrel.

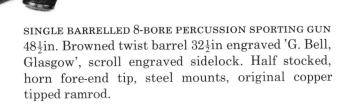

SINGLE BARRELLED 8-BORE PERCUSSION SPORTING GUN
48½in. Browned twist barrel 32½in engraved 'G. Bell,
Glasgow', scroll engraved sidelock. Half stocked,
horn fore-end tip, steel mounts, original copper
tipped ramrod.

24-BORE UNDERHAMMER PERCUSSION SPORTING GUN
46in. Barrel 27½in, plain steel mounts, silver escutcheon, walnut butt, boxlock-action with folding trigger and hammer contained within tubular breech
extension, steel ramrod, brass pipes.

DOUBLE BARRELLED 13-BORE PERCUSSION SPORTING
GUN 45in. Barrels 29in, gold inlaid at breech with a
game dog, the barrel rib gold inlaid 'J. Blanch, London', flat locks with herringbone borders and engraved with maker's name, game birds, dogs, etc.
Burr-maple half stock and semi-pistol grip, small engraved silver throat pipe and plain silver barrel
wedgeplates, large steel trigger guard engraved with
game dog, brass tipped ebony ramrod.

DOUBLE BARRELLED 12-BORE PERCUSSION SPORTING
GUN 44in. Barrels 28in, engraved at breech 'Goldings
Improvement', flat hammers and lockplates engraved
with scroll work and game birds. Walnut half stock
with engraved steel mounts including large trigger
guard with pineapple finial, brass tipped wooden
ramrod.

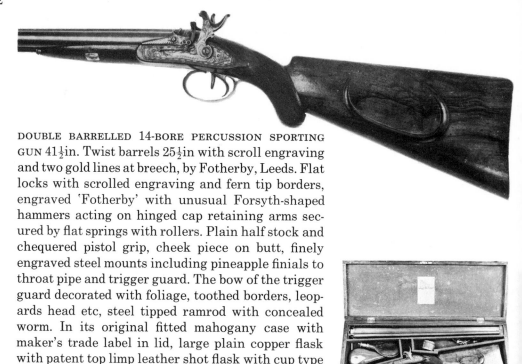

DOUBLE BARRELLED 14-BORE PERCUSSION SPORTING GUN 41½in. Twist barrels 25½in with scroll engraving and two gold lines at breech, by Fotherby, Leeds. Flat locks with scrolled engraving and fern tip borders, engraved 'Fotherby' with unusual Forsyth-shaped hammers acting on hinged cap retaining arms secured by flat springs with rollers. Plain half stock and chequered pistol grip, cheek piece on butt, finely engraved steel mounts including pineapple finials to throat pipe and trigger guard. The bow of the trigger guard decorated with foliage, toothed borders, leopards head etc, steel tipped ramrod with concealed worm. In its original fitted mahogany case with maker's trade label in lid, large plain copper flask with patent top limp leather shot flask with cup type charger, wad punch mainspring and an original tin of caps.

13-BORE DOUBLE BARRELLED CONTINENTAL PERCUSSION SPORTING GUN 44½in. Browned damascus twist barrels 28¾in. Half stocked, locks gold inlaid 'Lavand A Bourg', steel furniture, some gold inlay to screw heads, brass tipped ebony ramrod with steel worm.

Gun on p.223 viewed from underneath.

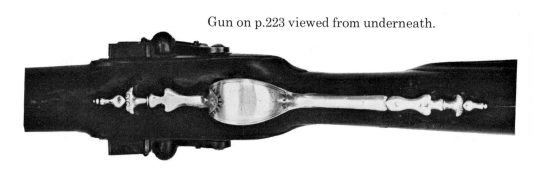

INTERESTING CONTINENTAL SILVER MOUNTED DOUBLE
BARRELLED 18-BORE SPORTING GUN with contemporary conversion to Forsyth sliding magazine
primer, 49in. Twist barrels 33in, by Lambert a Liege.
Plain rounded locks retaining original flintlock pans
and frizzen springs, scroll engraved flattened hammers, the conversion carried out by Patrick of Liverpool and bearing his silver poincons. The sliding
primers engraved 'percussion'. The butt and half
stock lightly carved with flowers, etc around mounts.
All mounts of silver with some chiselled and engraved decoration, the trigger guard and buttplate
hall marked and dated 1771. Silver wire inlay in small
of stock, brass tipped wooden ramrod. A most interesting Forsyth conversion that was presumably
made by Patrick under licence.

CONTINENTAL DOUBLE BARRELLED 16-BORE PER-
CUSSION SPORTING GUN 50½in. Finely twisted ribbed
barrels 34in, gold damascened on rib 'Damas Fin' and
some scroll work, the flat elaborately-shaped hammers and locks engraved with scroll work and game
birds. Half stocked, with large rosette on butt and
deeply carved with dragon at wrist and beneath butt,
deeply chiselled gilt brass mounts decorated with
dogs, classical figure, caduceus, etc, with sling swivels and German silver tipped ebony ramrod with iron
worm. In its original close fitted velvet lined ebonised
case with good quality brass mounted, horn flask
with sight glass charger, three piece ebony cleaning
rod, and small adjustable powder measure.

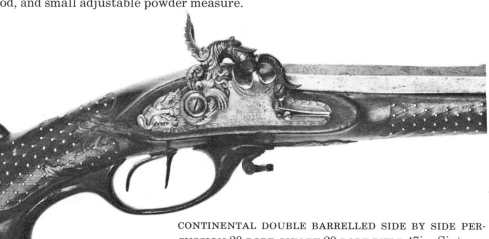

CONTINENTAL DOUBLE BARRELLED SIDE BY SIDE PER-
CUSSION 23-BORE GUN BY 20-BORE RIFLE 47in. Sixteen-
sided barrels 31in with octagonal breeches, the barrel rib silver inlaid 'F. Margenroth in Gernrode', flat
lockplates gold inlaid 'Sihauer in Ballenstedt', with
leaf engraved borders, the tails intricately chiselled
with boar's heads, the eyes, tongues and teeth inlaid
in silver and gold, the hammers also intricately chiselled in the form of monsters with some silver inlay,
hinged nipple protector safeties. Half stocked with
animals head carving, the open mouth forming the
ramrod throat pipe, cheek piece on butt, the fore-end
grip and small of stock chequered, carved and inset
with silver pique studs, black polished horn trigger
guard with scrolled grip, and heelplate, plain horn
tipped wooden ramrod supported by two white metal
pipes.

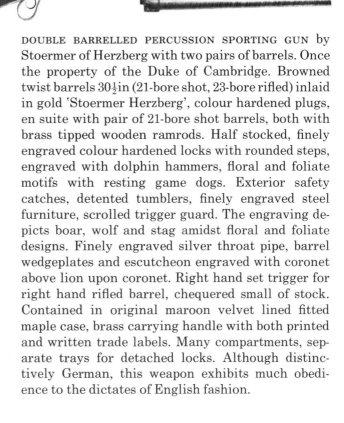

DOUBLE BARRELLED PERCUSSION SPORTING GUN by Stoermer of Herzberg with two pairs of barrels. Once the property of the Duke of Cambridge. Browned twist barrels 30½in (21-bore shot, 23-bore rifled) inlaid in gold 'Stoermer Herzberg', colour hardened plugs, en suite with pair of 21-bore shot barrels, both with brass tipped wooden ramrods. Half stocked, finely engraved colour hardened locks with rounded steps, engraved with dolphin hammers, floral and foliate motifs with resting game dogs. Exterior safety catches, detented tumblers, finely engraved steel furniture, scrolled trigger guard. The engraving depicts boar, wolf and stag amidst floral and foliate designs. Finely engraved silver throat pipe, barrel wedgeplates and escutcheon engraved with coronet above lion upon coronet. Right hand set trigger for right hand rifled barrel, chequered small of stock. Contained in original maroon velvet lined fitted maple case, brass carrying handle with both printed and written trade labels. Many compartments, separate trays for detached locks. Although distinctively German, this weapon exhibits much obedience to the dictates of English fashion.

18-BORE DOUBLE BARRELLED BACK-ACTION GERMAN PERCUSSION SPORTING GUN 48in. Lightly browned damascus twist barrels 32in. Half stocked, scroll engraved back-action locks with 'Blanck Mainz', C-shaped hammer, hinged safety levers, finely scroll and foliate engraved steel furniture. Scrolled trigger guard, carved cheek piece, chequered small of stock, white metal barrel wedgeplates, white metal tipped wooden ramrod.

UNUSUAL 34-BORE SILVER MOUNTED SPANISH COL-
ONIAL MIQUELET PERCUSSION SPORTING GUN 60in.
Octagonal barrel 42in, foliate chiselled at breech,
gold inlaid 'El Rallo', with gold poincons, gold inlaid
borders and gold inlaid fluted breech section. Full
stocked, foliate and floral engraved with silver inlaid
border, hammer finely chiselled in the round as a
male monkey holding gold inlaid cap (hammer nose),
engraved serpent bridle, engraved silver furniture
comprising foliate finialed trigger guard, butterfly on
bow, foliate finialed buttcap, 'fish' shaped and engraved sideplate. Forestock inlaid with foliate and
floral engraved strips, plaques, 'monkey tails', and
the throatplate with Mexican eagle and 'A de J',
silver patch box, lower part of butt carved as the head
of a stag, wooden rammer.

30-BORE CZECHOSLOVAKIAN PERCUSSION TARGET RIFLE
54in. Heavy octagonal barrel 36in, half stocked, lock stamped 'J. Burda', double set triggers, scrolled trigger guard, recurved buttcap, chequered small of stock, carved cheek piece.

MAYNARD'S PATENT 30-BORE PERCUSSION SPORTING GUN, with interchangeable 30-bore shot barrel and a .36 calibre rifle barrel. Stock and action 20¼in overall, number 4789 with Maynard's Patent tape primer built into steel breech. Frame stamped 'Maynard Arms Co, Washington', 'Manufactured by Mass Arms Co, Chicopee Falls'. Ladder rearsight, Maynard's Patent steel butt trap for holding spare cap reels, flattened polished walnut butt, round shot barrel, 26in octagonal at breech. Round rifled barrel 20in octagonal at breech.

36-BORE AMERICAN PERCUSSION SPORTING GUN OF KENTUCKY FORM 41in. Round barrel 25½in, scroll engraved breech with 'New York', twin brass inlaid lines, fixed sights. Half stocked, scroll engraved lock stamped 'Warranted', scroll engraved scrolled trigger guard, iron buttcap with engraved brass spur. White metal forecap, barrel wedgeplates and escutcheon, carved cheek piece, the butt inlaid with engraved white metal plaques for fox, game dog, star, hunter and dog, and stag. Brass tipped wooden ramrod, steel worm.

PERCUSSION REVOLVERS

Matchlock, wheellock and flintlock revolvers had been manufactured but had not been successful. A flintlock revolver was patented by Collier in Britain in 1818. This had a manually operated cylinder and was tested by Ordnance but it was found too complex. Another company, Mortimer of London, made repeating pistols in the Lorenzoni principle but these again were extremely complicated and quite dangerous as flash-back was common.

Pepperboxes were rather heavy and cumbersome and were also prone to the 'Roman Candle' effect.

Then in 1835, Samuel Colt obtained patents for his revolver action in Britain and America. A revolver is basically a hand gun with a cylinder which has a number of charges which ran by firing separately. His action was simple and reliable and he set up in business in Paterson, New Jersey. Colt went bankrupt after three years but had produced enough Paterson Colts to make an impact on the market and in 1847, when the Mexican war started, he was in business again.

Samuel Colt is probably best thought of as a great collator rather than inventor but most of all he was a great salesman. The mechanism was simplicity itself, the hammer was pulled back with the thumb, the cylinder rotated at locked-in position at full cock. Pressure on the trigger now released the hammer which flew forward to strike the cap on a nipple. These early Colts were engraved with set scenes; the pocket Colts showed a stage-coach hold-up, the Dragoon model showed a battle with Indians and the Navy Colts showed ships engaged in battle.

Colt had taken a stand at the Great Exhibition of 1851 as he sensed the warlike situation in Europe. Such was the response that he set up a factory in Pimlico. He could not find skilled British gunmakers who would work for him and so he installed machines which could be worked by machine-operators. This was the beginning of mass production in the manufacture of weapons. Scares about the Russian Navy being armed with revolvers (quite possibly emanating from Colt!) meant that by 1853 Colt was producing 1,000 revolvers per week for the British Navy.

Many of Colt's revolvers were sold cased with all their accessories and such sets are highly prized.

In 1851, Robert Adam patented a true rival to Colt's supremacy – the double-action revolver. Adam had realised that one of the main disadvantages of Colt's Navy was that it had to be cocked between each shot. Adam's revolver was self-cocking and continued pressure on the trigger caused the weapon to fire again.

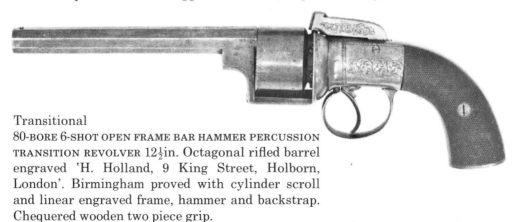

Transitional
80-BORE 6-SHOT OPEN FRAME BAR HAMMER PERCUSSION TRANSITION REVOLVER 12½in. Octagonal rifled barrel engraved 'H. Holland, 9 King Street, Holborn, London'. Birmingham proved with cylinder scroll and linear engraved frame, hammer and backstrap. Chequered wooden two piece grip.

The single-action Colt was better for accuracy and careful shooting. The double-action was made for fast shooting which was so vital in war. Adam's revolver had nothing like the range of a Colt but was a sure stopper in close quarters. The Adam revolver was made even more effective by the addition of Frederick Beaumont's cocking mechanism, which allowed separate cocking if desired. The Beaumont Adams revolver was the choice of the Army in 1856 and also the East India Company. Colt decided on a tactical withdrawal and returned to America, closing his Pimlico factory.

In 1853, a William Tranter patented an idea for an improved version of the Adam revolver. Tranter's introduction was a double trigger. One trigger projected down below the trigger guard and when pressed it rotated the cylinder but did not fire. In order to fire a second small trigger had to be pressed. This meant it was possible to bring the revolver to firing position and then aim. It was also possible to make the weapon function like a conventional double-action revolver by pressing both triggers at once.

Another famous revolver was the Webley revolver. In 1833, the Webleys were producing a revolver with a Colt-style frame but with a very distinctive projection from the top of the hammer. This earned its name of Longspur.

All these percussion revolvers were basically plain, serviceable guns and were only replaced by an idea which Samuel Colt turned down: a cartridge-loading revolver by Rollin White. This patent was acquired by Smith & Wesson and by 1857 they were producing a cartridge breech-loading revolver.

6-SHOT 52-BORE DOUBLE-ACTION BAR HAMMER TRANSITION PERCUSSION REVOLVER 12in. Octagonal barrel 5¾in with engraved band round muzzle, Birmingham proved, plain cylinder with engraved numbers one to six on chambers. Scroll engraved rounded frame, trigger guard, etc, rounded chequered wood grips.

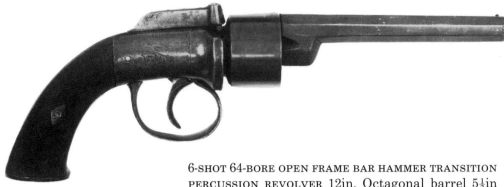

6-SHOT 64-BORE OPEN FRAME BAR HAMMER TRANSITION PERCUSSION REVOLVER 12in. Octagonal barrel 5½in engraved 'Improved Revolver', Birmingham proved, scroll engraved rounded frame, trigger guard, etc. Two piece chequered wood grips.

6-SHOT 52-BORE TRANSITION PERCUSSION REVOLVER 12in. Octagonal barrel 5½in, Birmingham proved, plain cylinder, scroll engraved rounded frame, hammer, trigger guard, etc. The hammer slotted for sighting, rounded chequered grips.

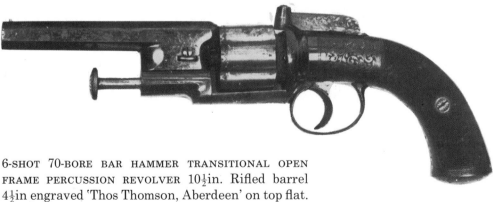

6-SHOT 70-BORE BAR HAMMER TRANSITIONAL OPEN FRAME PERCUSSION REVOLVER 10½in. Rifled barrel 4½in engraved 'Thos Thomson, Aberdeen' on top flat. Birmingham proved, rosette sectioned cylinder scroll engraved round frame and bar hammer, finely chequered two piece wooden grips, hinged cap trap in butt, coil spring loaded mono axial ramrod of unusual type.

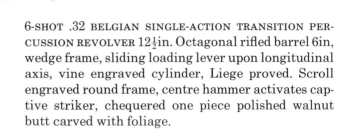

6-SHOT .32 BELGIAN SINGLE-ACTION TRANSITION PERCUSSION REVOLVER 12½in. Octagonal rifled barrel 6in, wedge frame, sliding loading lever upon longitudinal axis, vine engraved cylinder, Liege proved. Scroll engraved round frame, centre hammer activates captive striker, chequered one piece polished walnut butt carved with foliage.

6-SHOT 60-BORE BAR HAMMER TYPE TRANSITION PERCUSSION REVOLVER, by T. R. James, 12in. Part octagonal, part round barrel 5¾in, Birmingham proved with deep eleven groove rifling, integral white metal frame, nipple shield and backstrap scroll and border engraved with maker's name, two piece polished wood grips.

6-SHOT 52-BORE OPEN FRAME BAR HAMMER TRANSITION PERCUSSION REVOLVER 12in. Octagonal barrel 5½in by Reilly, 502 New Oxford Street, London. Plain cylinder with London proofs, rounded engraved frame, trigger guard, buttcap, etc. Finely chequered rounded grips.

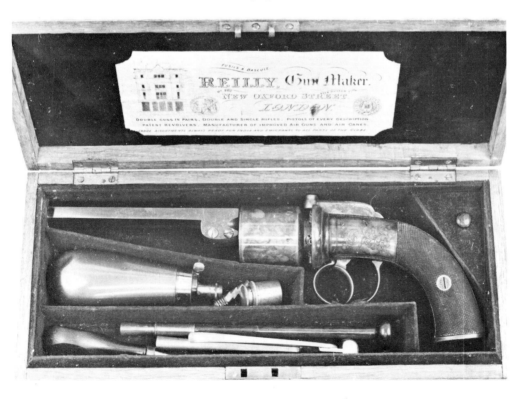

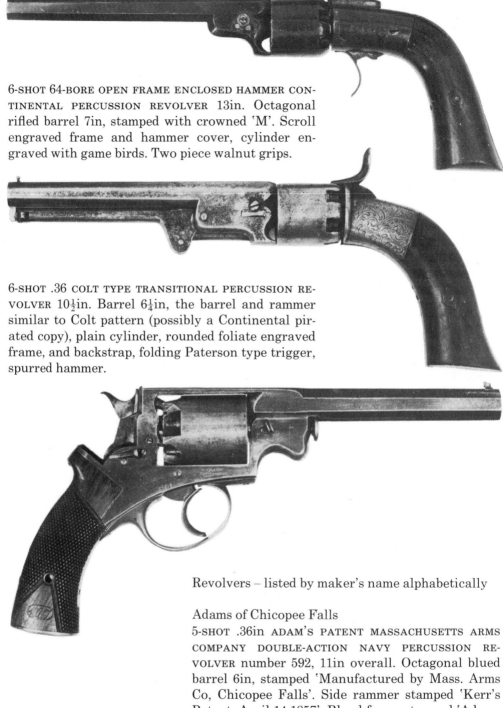

6-SHOT 64-BORE OPEN FRAME ENCLOSED HAMMER CON-
TINENTAL PERCUSSION REVOLVER 13in. Octagonal
rifled barrel 7in, stamped with crowned 'M'. Scroll
engraved frame and hammer cover, cylinder engraved with game birds. Two piece walnut grips.

6-SHOT .36 COLT TYPE TRANSITIONAL PERCUSSION RE-
VOLVER 10½in. Barrel 6¼in, the barrel and rammer
similar to Colt pattern (possibly a Continental pir-
ated copy), plain cylinder, rounded foliate engraved
frame, and backstrap, folding Paterson type trigger,
spurred hammer.

Revolvers – listed by maker's name alphabetically

Adams of Chicopee Falls
5-SHOT .36in ADAM'S PATENT MASSACHUSETTS ARMS
COMPANY DOUBLE-ACTION NAVY PERCUSSION RE-
VOLVER number 592, 11in overall. Octagonal blued
barrel 6in, stamped 'Manufactured by Mass. Arms
Co, Chicopee Falls'. Side rammer stamped 'Kerr's
Patent, April 14 1857'. Blued frame stamped 'Adams
Patent, May 3 1863', and 'Patent, June 3 1856'. Sliding
side safety catch locking cylinder. Chequered one
piece grip pierced for lanyard and stamped 'W.A.T.'
(Inspector William A. Thornton) and 'J.T.'.

PAIR OF 5-SHOT 54-BORE MODEL 1851 ADAM'S PATENT SELF-COCKING PERCUSSION REVOLVERS with 'Improved' frames as normally found on the Beaumont Adams, numbers 12963R and 12995R, 12½in. Octagonal rifled barrels 6½in, London proved, twin line border engraved on each flat, fern tip engraved muzzles, topstraps engraved 'Deane Adams and Deane, 30 King William Street, London Bridge'. Scroll engraved frames with 'Adams Patent' and serial numbers, London proved, cylinders with serial numbers and fern tipped borders. Chequered one piece grips, hinged butt traps. Contained in their green beize lined fitted oak case with yellow trade label, containing Dixon flask, ebony turnscrew, nipple key, brass bullet mould, bronze tipped ebony cleaning rod, cap bag and oil bottle. Also a three part bronze loading rod for use with cylinders, removable head, the tip unscrews to reveal steel worm.

5-SHOT .32 ADAMS PATENT DOUBLE-ACTION PERCUSSION REVOLVER 9½in. Barrel 4½in, London proved and stamped 'L.A.C.'. Side lever rammer, frame with sliding safety, engraved Adams patent 21924, 37731. Chequered one piece wood grip.

6-SHOT .442 JOHN ADAMS PATENT IMPROVED DOUBLE-ACTION PERCUSSION REVOLVER 11in. Octagonal barrel 6in, the frame engraved 'Adams's Patent Improved number 107', the top strap engraved 'Adams's Patent, Small Arms Co, 391 Strand, London'. London proved, rammer beneath barrel, one piece chequered walnut grip.

5-SHOT 38-BORE ADAMS MODEL 1851 SELF COCKING
'DRAGOON' PERCUSSION REVOLVER 10½in. Barrel 4¾in,
by Deane, Adams and Deane, 30 King William Street,
London Bridge, number 12127R. London proved,
chequered walnut butt with plain cap containing
hinged trap. In a fitted oak case with trade label of
Thomas W. Watson.

5-SHOT 48-BORE 1851 MODEL ADAMS SELF COCKING PER-
CUSSION REVOLVER 12in. Barrel 6¾in, London proved,
engraved 'Deane, Adams and Deane, 30 King William
Street, London Bridge'. Frame engraved 'Adams
Patent number 12688R'.

Allen & Wheellock of Worcester, Mass.

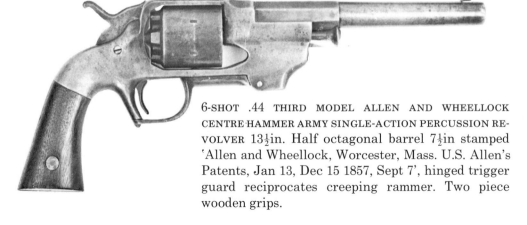

6-SHOT .44 THIRD MODEL ALLEN AND WHEELLOCK
CENTRE HAMMER ARMY SINGLE-ACTION PERCUSSION RE-
VOLVER 13½in. Half octagonal barrel 7½in stamped
'Allen and Wheellock, Worcester, Mass. U.S. Allen's
Patents, Jan 13, Dec 15 1857, Sept 7', hinged trigger
guard reciprocates creeping rammer. Two piece
wooden grips.

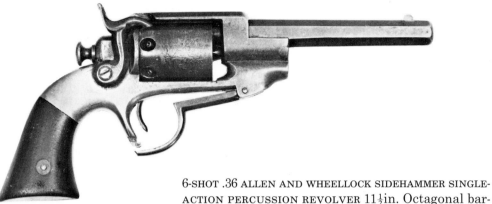

6-SHOT .36 ALLEN AND WHEELLOCK SIDEHAMMER SINGLE-ACTION PERCUSSION REVOLVER 11½in. Octagonal barrel 5¾in stamped 'Allen and Wheellock, Worcester, Mass US, Allen's Patents Jan 13, Dec 15 1857, Sept 7 1858'. Cylinder roll engraved with deer within forest, hinged trigger guard forming level for rammer. Two piece wooden grips.

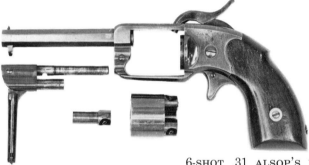

Alsop of Middletown

6-SHOT .31 ALSOP'S PATENT SINGLE-ACTION CLOSED FRAME PERCUSSION POCKET REVOLVER 9½in. Octagonal rifled barrel 4in stamped 'C. R. Alsop, Middletown, Conn, Patented July 17th, August 7th 1860, May 14th 1861' (two lines), under lever rammer, sheathed trigger. Two piece wooden grips.

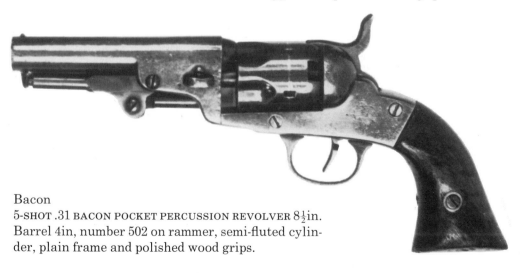

Bacon

5-SHOT .31 BACON POCKET PERCUSSION REVOLVER 8½in. Barrel 4in, number 502 on rammer, semi-fluted cylinder, plain frame and polished wood grips.

236

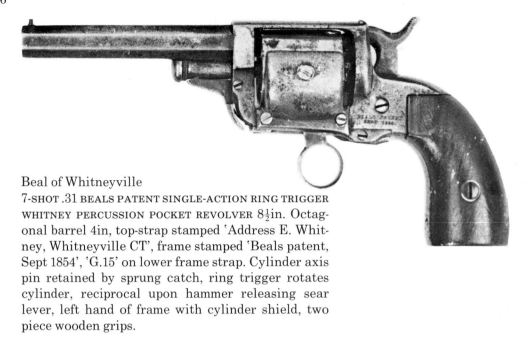

Beal of Whitneyville

7-SHOT .31 BEALS PATENT SINGLE-ACTION RING TRIGGER WHITNEY PERCUSSION POCKET REVOLVER 8½in. Octagonal barrel 4in, top-strap stamped 'Address E. Whitney, Whitneyville CT', frame stamped 'Beals patent, Sept 1854', 'G.15' on lower frame strap. Cylinder axis pin retained by sprung catch, ring trigger rotates cylinder, reciprocal upon hammer releasing sear lever, left hand of frame with cylinder shield, two piece wooden grips.

Beaumont-Adams of London

5-SHOT 54-BORE DOUBLE-ACTION BEAUMONT-ADAMS PERCUSSION REVOLVER 12in. Octagonal rifled barrel 5¾in. London proved, topstrap engraved 'O.R. Middleton Esq, 4th Kings Own'. Frame engraved 'B8624 Adams Patent number 24278R', cylinder numbered '24278R', side loading lever numbered '10966', sliding safety catch, chequered one piece wooden grip.

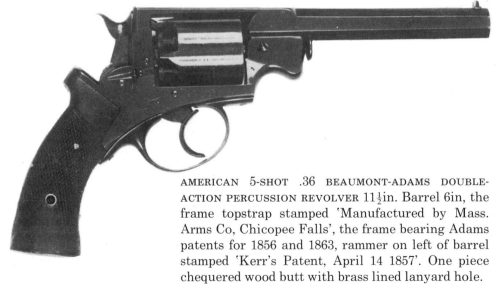

AMERICAN 5-SHOT .36 BEAUMONT-ADAMS DOUBLE-ACTION PERCUSSION REVOLVER 11½in. Barrel 6in, the frame topstrap stamped 'Manufactured by Mass. Arms Co, Chicopee Falls', the frame bearing Adams patents for 1856 and 1863, rammer on left of barrel stamped 'Kerr's Patent, April 14 1857'. One piece chequered wood butt with brass lined lanyard hole.

5-SHOT .31 BEAUMONT-ADAMS SINGLE-ACTION PER-
CUSSION POCKET REVOLVER 9in. Barrel 4in stamped
'LAC', Adams patent B19774, London proved, sliding
bar safety on right of frame, diced wood butt.

Clayton of Southampton
5-SHOT 54 BORE SINGLE-ACTION CLOSED FRAME PER-
CUSSION REVOLVER 11in. Barrel 5in, by Clayton,
Southampton, cylinders numbered one to five, Birmingham proved, side rammer. Plain frame, diced wood
grips.

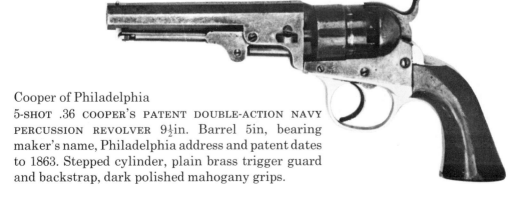

Cooper of Philadelphia
5-SHOT .36 COOPER'S PATENT DOUBLE-ACTION NAVY
PERCUSSION REVOLVER 9½in. Barrel 5in, bearing
maker's name, Philadelphia address and patent dates
to 1863. Stepped cylinder, plain brass trigger guard
and backstrap, dark polished mahogany grips.

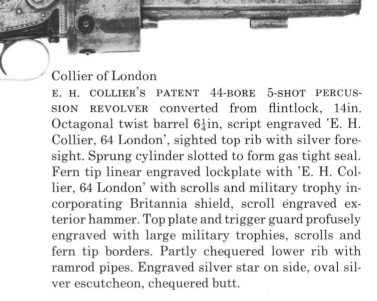

Collier of London

E. H. COLLIER'S PATENT 44-BORE 5-SHOT PERCUS-
SION REVOLVER converted from flintlock, 14in.
Octagonal twist barrel 6¼in, script engraved 'E. H.
Collier, 64 London', sighted top rib with silver foresight. Sprung cylinder slotted to form gas tight seal.
Fern tip linear engraved lockplate with 'E. H. Collier, 64 London' with scrolls and military trophy incorporating Britannia shield, scroll engraved exterior hammer. Top plate and trigger guard profusely
engraved with large military trophies, scrolls and
fern tip borders. Partly chequered lower rib with
ramrod pipes. Engraved silver star on side, oval silver escutcheon, chequered butt.

Colt of New York

5-SHOT .36in COLT MODEL 1853 POCKET PERCUSSION
REVOLVER 11½in. Barrel 6½in, number 683 on most
parts, New York, U.S.A. address. Traces of stage-
coach scene on stepped cylinder, brass trigger guard
and backstrap, plain wood grips.

5-SHOT .31in MODEL 1849 PRESENTATION ENGRAVED
COLT POCKET SINGLE-ACTION PERCUSSION REVOLVER
9¾in overall. Blued octagonal barrel 5in, hand engraved 'Saml Colt' on top flat. Scroll engraved en
suite with colour hardened frame and ramrod, an
eagle's head appears in the midst of scrolls on left of
barrel. Wolf's head engraved hammer, heavily silver
plated rounded trigger guard and backstrap, with
blank for presentation inscription. One piece ivory
grip. Cylinder engraved with stagecoach hold-up
scene.

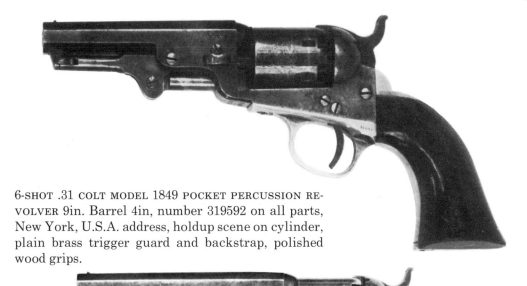

6-SHOT .31 COLT MODEL 1849 POCKET PERCUSSION RE-
VOLVER 9in. Barrel 4in, number 319592 on all parts,
New York, U.S.A. address, holdup scene on cylinder,
plain brass trigger guard and backstrap, polished
wood grips.

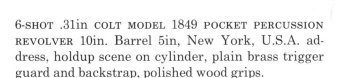

6-SHOT .31in COLT MODEL 1849 POCKET PERCUSSION
REVOLVER 10in. Barrel 5in, New York, U.S.A. address, holdup scene on cylinder, plain brass trigger
guard and backstrap, polished wood grips.

Colt-Navy
6-SHOT .36in COLT MODEL 1861 ROUND BARRELLED NAVY
PERCUSSION REVOLVER 13in. Barrel 7½in, New York,
U.S.A. address, brass trigger guard and backstrap,
polished wood grips. In original flap top leather holster.

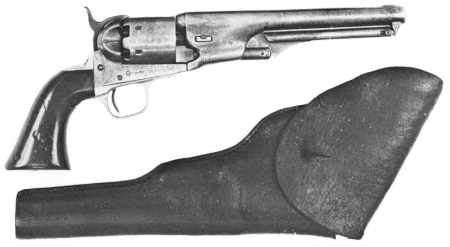

6-SHOT .36in MODEL 1851 THIRD TYPE COLT NAVY SINGLE-ACTION PERCUSSION REVOLVER number 51879, 13in overall. Blued octagonal barrel 7½in stamped 'Address Saml. Colt, New York City – H'. Colour hardened ramrod and frame stamped 'Colt's Patent U.S.'. Roll engraved cylinder with navy scenes and 'Colt's Patent number 51879H'. Brass trigger guard and backstrap, one piece wooden grip stamped 'J.H.' and 'R.H.K.W.'.

Colt – Army
6-SHOT .44in COLT'S PATENT THIRD MODEL HARTFORD DRAGOON SINGLE-ACTION PERCUSSION REVOLVER number 12623, 14in overall. Barrel 7½in stamped 'Address Saml. Colt, New York City'. White metal blade foresight, underlever ramrod. Cylinder roll engraved with Indian fighting scene and 'Model U.S. M.R. 12623. H. Colt's Patent', and 'W. L. Ormsby Sc. N.Y.'. Colour hardened frame stamped 'Colt's Patent U.S.', brass backstrap and round trigger guard. One piece wooden grip stamped 'W.A.T.' (Inspector William A. Thornton) and 'J.H.'.

Deane of London
5-SHOT 54-BORE DEANE HARDING'S PATENT DOUBLE-ACTION PERCUSSION REVOLVER 12in. Octagonal barrel 6in, London proved, engraved 'Deane and Son, London Bridge' on topstrap. Enclosed underlever rammer, frame engraved with patent details. Chequered one piece grip with lanyard ring, back of grip slotted for detachable shoulder stock, hinged side safety catch.

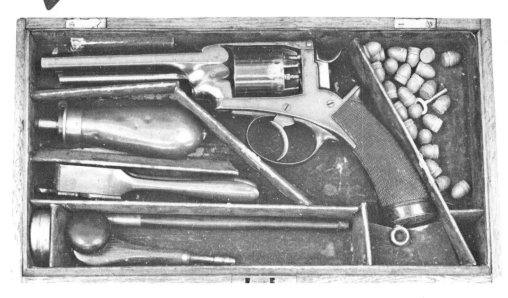

Ells

5-SHOT .31 ELLS PATENT PERCUSSION REVOLVER 9in.
Octagonal barrel 3¾in, foliate engraved barrel top,
cylinder and frame, bar hammer stamped 'Ells patent
April 28 1857, Aug 1 1854', underlever rammer, hammer off-set for sighting, two piece bone grips.

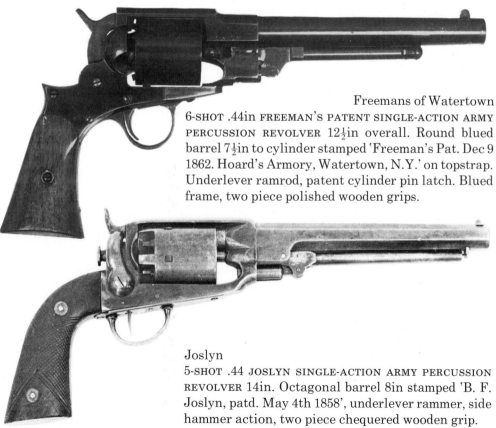

Hart

5-SHOT .30 HART PATTERN SELF COCKING PERCUSSION
POCKET REVOLVER 7in. Octagonal barrel 2½in, foliate
engraved frame, trigger guard and backstrap, swivel
half cock safety arm to right of frame, polished wood
grips.

Freemans of Watertown

6-SHOT .44in FREEMAN'S PATENT SINGLE-ACTION ARMY
PERCUSSION REVOLVER 12½in overall. Round blued
barrel 7½in to cylinder stamped 'Freeman's Pat. Dec 9
1862. Hoard's Armory, Watertown, N.Y.' on topstrap.
Underlever ramrod, patent cylinder pin latch. Blued
frame, two piece polished wooden grips.

Joslyn

5-SHOT .44 JOSLYN SINGLE-ACTION ARMY PERCUSSION
REVOLVER 14in. Octagonal barrel 8in stamped 'B. F.
Joslyn, patd. May 4th 1858', underlever rammer, side
hammer action, two piece chequered wooden grip.

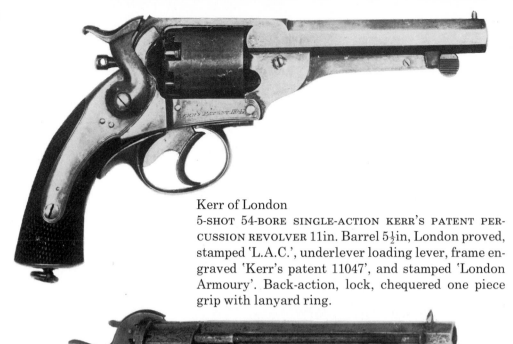

Kerr of London

5-SHOT 54-BORE SINGLE-ACTION KERR'S PATENT PER-
CUSSION REVOLVER 11in. Barrel 5½in, London proved,
stamped 'L.A.C.', underlever loading lever, frame engraved 'Kerr's patent 11047', and stamped 'London
Armoury'. Back-action, lock, chequered one piece
grip with lanyard ring.

9-SHOT 48-BORE SINGLE-ACTION LE-MATT PATTERN PIN-
FIRE REVOLVER with 22-bore central percussion shot
barrel 12in. Octagonal sighted rifled barrel 6½in.
Floral engraved cylinder and frame. Side gate loading, adjustable hammer nose for firing either chamber. Two piece chequered wooden grips.

Manhattan of New York

5-SHOT .36 MANHATTAN NAVY SINGLE-ACTION PER-
CUSSION REVOLVER 11in. Barrel 6½in marked 'Manhattan Firearms Co, Newark, N.J., Patented March
8, 1864'. Brass trigger guard and backstrap with
traces of plating, cylinder bears engraved scenes
within panels polished wood grips.

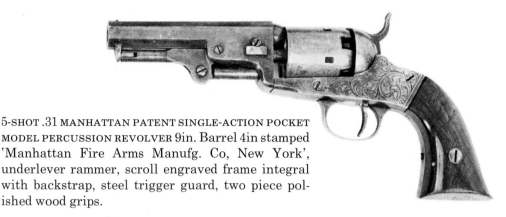

5-SHOT .31 MANHATTAN PATENT SINGLE-ACTION POCKET
MODEL PERCUSSION REVOLVER 9in. Barrel 4in stamped
'Manhattan Fire Arms Manufg. Co, New York',
underlever rammer, scroll engraved frame integral
with backstrap, steel trigger guard, two piece polished wood grips.

Massachusetts Arms Company of Chicopee Falls
6-SHOT .31 MAYNARD TAPE PRIMED MASSACHUSETTS
ARMS COMPANY SINGLE-ACTION PERCUSSION REVOLVER
6¾in. Octagonal barrel 3in stamped 'Mass. Arms Co,
Chicopee Falls', foliate etched cylinder, scroll engraved frame and hinged tape primer cover, stamped
with 'Maynards patent, Sept. 22 1845'. Plated brass
trigger guard, hinged latch upon cylinder axis pin for
barrel tip up, two piece ivory grips.

6-SHOT .31 MASSACHUSETTS ARMS COMPANY SINGLE-
ACTION PERCUSSION REVOLVER 11¾in. Round barrel
6in which hinges upwards to release cylinder for
loading, the topstrap stamped 'Mass. Arms Co,
Chicopee Falls', etched cylinder, engraved back-
action lock with sidehammer, the frame incorporating Maynard's Patent tape primer, stamped with U.S.
eagle and 'Maynard's Patent, Sept 22 1845'. Silver
plated brass buttstrap and trigger guard, plain wood
grips.

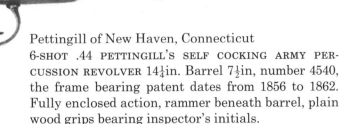

Pettingill of New Haven, Connecticut
6-SHOT .44 PETTINGILL'S SELF COCKING ARMY PER-
CUSSION REVOLVER 14¼in. Barrel 7½in, number 4540,
the frame bearing patent dates from 1856 to 1862.
Fully enclosed action, rammer beneath barrel, plain
wood grips bearing inspector's initials.

Remington-Beals of New York
5-SHOT .32 REMINGTON-BEALS 1ST MODEL SINGLE-
ACTION PERCUSSION POCKET REVOLVER 6½in. Octagonal barrel 3in, stamped 'F. Beals patent, June 24
1856 and May 26 1857', and on topstrap 'Manufactured by Remington Ilion N.Y.', white metal trigger
guard, composition one piece grip.

Remington-Rider of New York
5-SHOT .32 REMINGTON-RIDER 'MUSHROOM CYLINDER'
DOUBLE-ACTION POCKET MODEL PERCUSSION RE-
VOLVER 6½in. Octagonal barrel 3in stamped 'Manufactured by Remington, Ilion, N.Y., Riders Pt, Aug
17 1858, May 3 1859', German silver trigger guard,
composition grips.

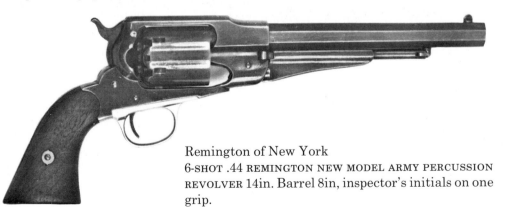

Remington of New York
6-SHOT .44 REMINGTON NEW MODEL ARMY PERCUSSION
REVOLVER 14in. Barrel 8in, inspector's initials on one
grip.

Rogers & Spencer of New York
6-SHOT .44 ROGERS AND SPENCER'S PATENT SINGLE-ACTION ARMY PERCUSSION REVOLVER 12½in. Octagonal barrel 7½in, underlever rammer, topstrap stamped 'Rogers and Spencer, Utica, N.Y.', two piece wooden grips.

Starr of New York
6-SHOT .44in STARR ARMS COMPANY SINGLE-ACTION ARMY PERCUSSION REVOLVER 14in overall. Round barrel 8in, blued en suite with frame, stamped 'Starr's Patent Jan 15 1858' and 'Starr Arms Co, New York'. One piece wooden grip stamped with inspector's initials.

Savage of Middletown
DOUBLE-ACTION RECIPROCATING-ACTION SAVAGE NAVY PERCUSSION .36in REVOLVER 14¼in. Octagonal barrel 7in stamped 'Savage R.F.A. Co, Middletown Ct H.S. North, Patented June 17 1856, January 19 1859, May 15 1860' on topstrap. Underlever rammer, ring cocking trigger, heart-shaped trigger guard, two piece wooden grips.

6-SHOT .44in STARR DOUBLE-ACTION ARMY PERCUSSION REVOLVER 11½in. Barrel 6in, the frame stamped 'Starr Arms Co, New York', and patent dated 1856, plain varnished wood butt with faint traces of inspector's initials, rammer beneath barrel.

Tranter Patent from England
5-SHOT 54-BORE TRANTER SELF-COCKING PERCUSSION REVOLVER 11in. Barrel 6in, by Garden and Son, 200 Piccadilly, London. London proved, rammer on left of barrel, chequered walnut butt, the rammer and trigger stamped 'Tranter's Patent'.

5-SHOT 54-BORE 1ST MODEL SELF COCKING TRANTER SINGLE-ACTION PERCUSSION REVOLVER 12in. Barrel 6¾in, by Deane Adams and Deane, 50 King William Street, London Bridge. London proved. Diced wood butt.

5-SHOT 45-BORE TRANTER SELF COCKING PERCUSSION REVOLVER 13½in. Octagonal barrel 7½in engraved 'Hollis and Sheath, makers to H.M.H. Board of Ordnance'. Birmingham proved, cylinder slight scroll engraved frame, chequered butt.

5-SHOT 100-BORE DOUBLE-ACTION TRANTER'S PATENT PERCUSSION REVOLVER 8¼in. Barrel 3¾in. Birmingham proved, engraved 'J. W. Edge, Manchester', on topstrap, side loading lever stamped 'W. Tranter's patent', en suite with frame stamp. Twin line border engraved frame with sliding side safety catch, one piece chequered wooden grip.

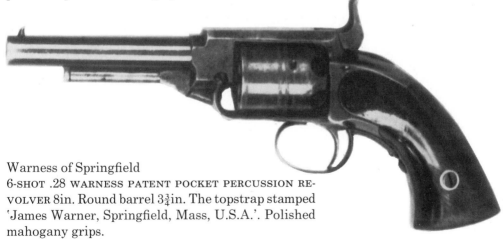

Warness of Springfield
6-SHOT .28 WARNESS PATENT POCKET PERCUSSION RE-VOLVER 8in. Round barrel 3¾in. The topstrap stamped 'James Warner, Springfield, Mass, U.S.A.'. Polished mahogany grips.

248

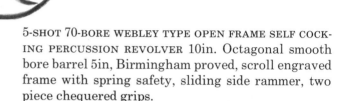

5-SHOT 70-BORE WEBLEY TYPE OPEN FRAME SELF COCK-
ING PERCUSSION REVOLVER 10in. Octagonal smooth
bore barrel 5in, Birmingham proved, scroll engraved
frame with spring safety, sliding side rammer, two
piece chequered grips.

5-SHOT 44-BORE WEBLEY 3RD MODEL LONGSPUR SINGLE-
ACTION PERCUSSION REVOLVER 12in. Octagonal barrel
6in engraved 'Webley's Patent Improved', Birmingham proved, the chambers numbered one to five
within engraved circles surmounted by floral sprays.
Scroll engraved frame, hammer and trigger guard,
rammer on left of barrel, French style fluted wood
butt with panels of scrolls.

Whitney of New Haven, U.S.A.
6-SHOT .36 WHITNEY SINGLE-ACTION 2ND MODEL NAVY
PERCUSSION REVOLVER 12½in. Barrel 7½in, stamped 'E.
Whitney, N'haven', brass trigger guard, traces of
engraved cylinder scene. Number on rammer '419',
polished wood grips.

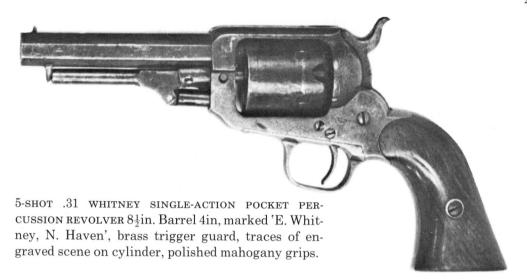

5-SHOT .31 WHITNEY SINGLE-ACTION POCKET PER-
CUSSION REVOLVER 8½in. Barrel 4in, marked 'E. Whitney, N. Haven', brass trigger guard, traces of engraved scene on cylinder, polished mahogany grips.

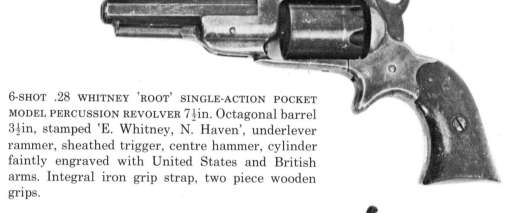

6-SHOT .28 WHITNEY 'ROOT' SINGLE-ACTION POCKET
MODEL PERCUSSION REVOLVER 7½in. Octagonal barrel
3½in, stamped 'E. Whitney, N. Haven', underlever
rammer, sheathed trigger, centre hammer, cylinder
faintly engraved with United States and British
arms. Integral iron grip strap, two piece wooden
grips.

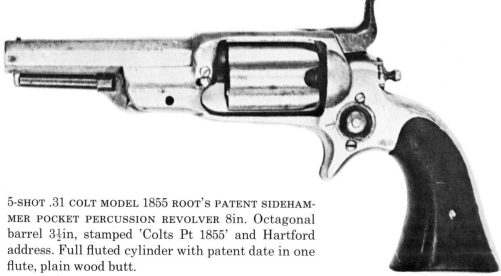

5-SHOT .31 COLT MODEL 1855 ROOT'S PATENT SIDEHAM-
MER POCKET PERCUSSION REVOLVER 8in. Octagonal
barrel 3½in, stamped 'Colts Pt 1855' and Hartford
address. Full fluted cylinder with patent date in one
flute, plain wood butt.

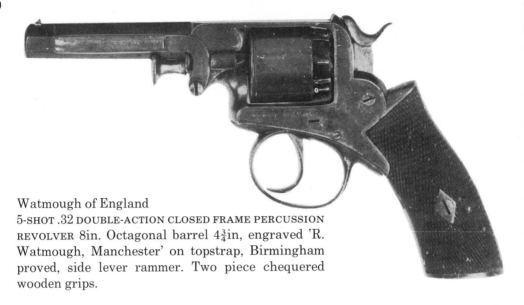

Watmough of England
5-SHOT .32 DOUBLE-ACTION CLOSED FRAME PERCUSSION REVOLVER 8in. Octagonal barrel 4¾in, engraved 'R. Watmough, Manchester' on topstrap, Birmingham proved, side lever rammer. Two piece chequered wooden grips.

Parker Field of England
6-SHOT 40-BORE OPEN WEDGE FRAME SINGLE-ACTION PERCUSSION REVOLVER 12½in. Octagonal barrel 6in with multi groove rifling, fixed front and rearsights and spring loaded plunger type rammer on right side, engraved 'Regisd June 14th 1852 by Parker Field and Sons'. The top flat of the barrel engraved 'Parker Field and Sons, 233 High Holborn, London'. London proved, plain cylinder with reciprocating-action, longspur hammer, scroll engraved rounded frame, finely chequered butt with engraved domed steel cap.

Harvey's of England
HARVEY'S PATENT 50-BORE 6-SHOT PERCUSSION RE-VOLVER 11½in. Octagonal barrel 4¾in engraved 'Harvey's Patent 4147'. Breech loading revolving pistol. Cylinder engraved 'Harvey's Patent 4047', the chambers numbered from one to six. Scroll engraved frame completely enclosing the internal-action and striker, with vertically sliding safety catch. The lever ramrod to this pistol is a removable tool, being a combined nipple wrench and turnscrew. Finely chequered walnut butt with blank silver escutcheon and scroll engraved cap box to steel buttcap.

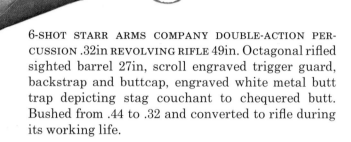

6-SHOT STARR ARMS COMPANY DOUBLE-ACTION PER-
CUSSION .32in REVOLVING RIFLE 49in. Octagonal rifled
sighted barrel 27in, scroll engraved trigger guard,
backstrap and buttcap, engraved white metal butt
trap depicting stag couchant to chequered butt.
Bushed from .44 to .32 and converted to rifle during
its working life.

5-SHOT 24-BORE ADAMS SELF COCKING REVOLVING PER-
CUSSION RIFLE 43½in. Octagonal barrel 25½in, London
proofs and two folding leaf rearsights, by Brooks and
Son, Birmingham, scroll engraved frame. Safety bolt
on right of frame, hinged rammer on left, detachable cover over hammer, large square fronted trigger guard, scroll end hand grip walnut butt with
chequered wrist.

5-SHOT .32-BORE RUSSIAN DOUBLE TRIGGER PER-
CUSSION REVOLVING CARBINE with detachable barrel,
37in. Barrel 20¼in, 12½in unscrewing for travelling
purposes and made from a Persian true damascus
twist barrel, last 7½in of octagonal false damascus
steel, etched with Russian inscription. Frame and
cylinder etched with scrolling vine foliage and
mounted Cossacks, hunting stags and dogs. Sprung
side safety catch, lever cranked creeping rammer,
polished wood butt with chequered small of stock.

5-SHOT ADAMS PATENT 30-BORE SELF COCKING REVOLV-
ING PERCUSSION RIFLE 40½in. Octagonal barrel 22½in,
folding leaf rearsights to two hundred and three
hundred yards, engraved on closed frame 'Deane
Adams and Deane, 30 King William Street, London
Bridge', foliate engraved frame. London proved,
numbered '52' at breech, foliate engraved German
silver hammer cover, steel buttplate.

44-BORE 7-SHOT PERCUSSION REVOLVING RIFLE by
Billinghurst on the Miller patent, 48in. Octagonal
sighted rifled barrel 29in, stamped 'W. Billinghurst, Rochester, N.Y.'. Forward cylinder locking
catch, back-action lock, scrolled brass trigger guard,
pointed buttcap, white metal fore cap, wooden
ramrod, chequered small of stock.

.38 6-SHOT SINGLE-ACTION REMINGTON'S PATENT PER-
CUSSION REVOLVING RIFLE 45½in. Octagonal rifled
barrel 28in with adjustable ramp rearsight. Underlever ramrod. Scrolled trigger guard. Engraved white
metal butt trap depicting bird on branch.

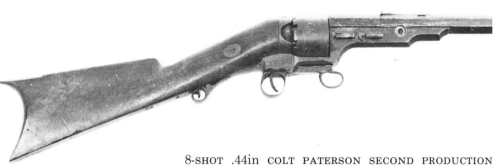

8-SHOT .44in COLT PATERSON SECOND PRODUCTION
MODEL PERCUSSION REVOLVING RIFLE 47in. Eleven
groove rifled octagonal barrel 28½in, engraved
'Patent Arms Mg . . . . .' on top flat, the rest of the
engraving is concealed beneath the ramp adjustable
rearsight, which has been moved back 6in from its
origional position. Side loading lever gear removed,
ring bar cocking lever, finely figured carved walnut
butt with iron buttcap.

Air weapons

Air guns fall into two distinct types – those that create air pressure just before being used to propel the bullet and those that use air compressed in a type of reservoir. The very early air guns used the first principle when pressing the trigger produced a fierce blast of air. This was extremely limited as the pressure was small and hence the size of the bullet was restricted.

In the late 17th century the reservoir system was introduced in the double-walled barrel style. This relied on a space between the inner and outer barrel being the reservoir and the pressure was built up by a pumping action. As one pressed the trigger a valve opened and a blast of this pressurised air burst out and freed the bullet.

This system was later superseded by a ball-like reservoir positioned under the barrel. This was quite successful although certainly could not take too much hard usage.

A later development involved having a detachable butt reservoir and spares were carried. In shape, these guns closely resembled the conventional flintlock mechanism, the cock opening the valve.

The most serious drawback of air guns of this period was that efficiency of air decreased with rapidity of fire.

40-BORE AIR RIFLE WITH BALL RESERVOIR DISGUISED AS PERCUSSION, by Shaw of Manchester, circa 1830, 47in. Part octagonal, polygonal and round twist barrel. Half stocked, stepped lockplate engraved with maker's name, flowers and sunburst, engraved steel furniture, Britannia shield trophy engraved trigger guard, and buttcap. Full stocked, silver forecap, sidenail plates and escutcheon, brass tipped wooden ramrod. Chequered grip, butt carved with cheek piece.

64-BORE BALL RESERVOIR HALL MARKED SILVER MOUN-
TED (1775) AIR GUN, disguised as a flintlock fowling
piece by Bate, 49in. Half octagonal barrel 34in, silver
inlaid at breech with plaque engraved 'Bate, London'. Full stocked, stepped scroll and floral engraved
slab lockplate and throat hole cock with maker's
name. Engraved hall marked silver. Unusual pierced
buttplate, oval escutcheon, silver rosette sidenail
cups, three silver ramrod pipes. Original screw-in
copper ball reservoir with brass mount. Egg type
chequered small and fore of stock. Skeleton butt,
original wooden ramrod.

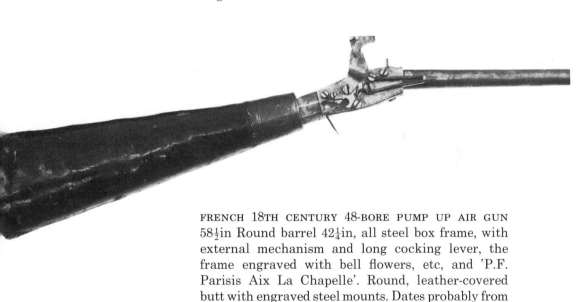

FRENCH 18TH CENTURY 48-BORE PUMP UP AIR GUN
58½in Round barrel 42¼in, all steel box frame, with
external mechanism and long cocking lever, the
frame engraved with bell flowers, etc, and 'P.F.
Parisis Aix La Chapelle'. Round, leather-covered
butt with engraved steel mounts. Dates probably from
last quarter of the 18th century.

Firearms Curiosa

Gunmakers were great innovators and also great adaptors. From the introduction of gunpowder and the firing mechanism they had used their skills to make a number of devious and often amusing weapons. Many of these were dual purpose weapons as, particularly in the days of single-shot guns, there was a great feeling of insecurity and vulnerability in the event of the marksman missing with his first shot.

The most vulnerable moment for the musketeer was when he had fired and was reloading. This problem was alleviated by the addition of the bayonet. At the same time, many weapons were designed where the firearm was fitted to a sword, knife or dagger. There had been wheellock pistol swords but these were not common and hence it was the introduction of the more simple and reliable flintlock which increased the popularity of such arms. Many pistol swords were made for hunters as they were a useful combination, firstly to maim and then finish off the prey. This was not their exclusive use, as some were attached to military swords and were used in combat situations. With the introduction of percussion the length of the blade seemed to decrease and knife pistols were much more common, looking very like a normal penknife.

Towards the end of the 19th century, knuckle duster guns were in great demand. The most famous of these guns was probably 'My Friend'. This was a pepperbox pistol and was operated by a hole in the butt for the little finger. In contrast to this was the much smaller squeezer pistol or palm pistol. Squeezers were intended as a concealed weapon of personal defence which were to be hidden in the hand and fired by clenching the fist.

A close relative of the Squeezer was the Protector revolver which was fired by the same mechanism and was patented in 1888. Perhaps the most deadly of this group was the Apache pistol. This was by far the most versatile weapon of its time and was basically three-in-one; a pistol, a knuckle duster and a knife. It reputedly got its name, not from the Indian tribe, but from an infamous band of Paris criminals known as the Apaches, and quite as deadly as their namesakes.

Many firearms curiosa were designed to conceal the fact in some way that the owner was in fact carrying a weapon, such as the walking stick, the percussion key pistol or the baton pistol.

However, 'curiosa' does not only cover weapons as firing mechanisms could be adapted to various domestic purposes; for example the large numbers of flintlock tinder lighters made throughout the 17th and 18th centuries. Another member of the family was the powder-tester or eprouvette. This was extremely necessary as gunpowder was a mixture of three compounds; saltpetre, charcoal and sulphur and there were numerous variable mixtures which differed in explosive quality. The eprouvette had a small chamber into which was placed a small quantity of powder. When ignited, a lid held by a spring was forced open and held by an arm. This arm was calibrated and the reading could be checked against subsequent firings.

Firearms curiosa is an interesting collectors' field in which many real treasures can still be found and individual eccentricities explored.

WELL MADE FLINTLOCK KEY PISTOL in the French style of circa 1640, 11in. Barrel 6¼in from vent. Boxlock-action, sidecock double pierced, unbridled frizzen. Frame lightly floral and linear engraved. Small baluster on ring and 'barrel'.

WELL MADE PERCUSSION KEY PISTOL, circa 1850 in style, 7½in. Turn-off barrel 4in. Boxlock-action, scroll engraved frame and ring box, baluster turned at breech.

FUSE PISTOL

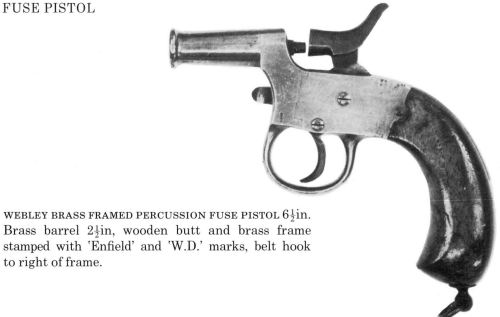

WEBLEY BRASS FRAMED PERCUSSION FUSE PISTOL $6\frac{1}{2}$in. Brass barrel $2\frac{1}{2}$in, wooden butt and brass frame stamped with 'Enfield' and 'W.D.' marks, belt hook to right of frame.

BOOTLEG PISTOL

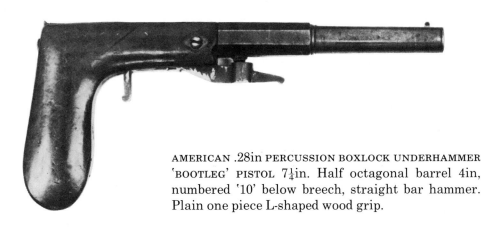

AMERICAN .28in PERCUSSION BOXLOCK UNDERHAMMER 'BOOTLEG' PISTOL $7\frac{1}{4}$in. Half octagonal barrel 4in, numbered '10' below breech, straight bar hammer. Plain one piece L-shaped wood grip.

KNIFE AND DAGGER PISTOLS

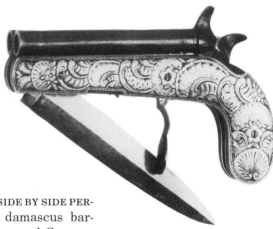

BELGIAN 90-BORE DOUBLE BARRELLED SIDE BY SIDE PER-
CUSSION KNIFE PISTOL 6in. Round damascus barrels 4in, with Liege proofs, finely engraved German
silver sideplates decorated with rocailles, flowers,
shells, etc, and with toothed borders. Folding triggers on each side of the 5in double edge knife blade.

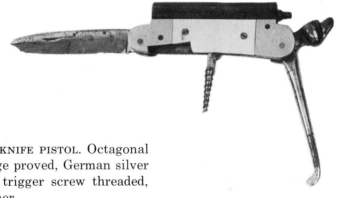

'HORSEMAN'S' PERCUSSION KNIFE PISTOL. Octagonal
damascus barrel 2¾in, Liege proved, German silver
mounts, horn panels, the trigger screw threaded,
single blade cup type hammer.

DOUBLE BARRELLED 80-BORE SIDE BY SIDE BOXLOCK
CONTINENTAL PERCUSSION KNIFE PISTOL 14½in. Single
fullered double edge blade 10in, barrels 3¼in, hammers formed as part of cross piece, with milled spurs
or terminals. Folding trigger, engraved white metal
backstrap, two piece chequered wooden grips with
swollen butt.

GERMAN FLINTLOCK DOMESTIC KNIFE PISTOL, circa 1730. Blade 4½in, deeply impressed with cutler's mark (a clay pipe), the scroll and foliate engraved brass hilt containing a 1¾in barrel of .20in calibre. Small pipe and groove on underside for ramrod, external mechanism including pierced and engraved brass bridle.

DOUBLE BARRELLED 28-BORE OVER AND UNDER PERCUSSION DAGGER PISTOL 16½in. Barrels 10¾in, Liege proved. Swivel breech drum with two nipples firing either barrel in alternate position. Side belt hook, profusely scrolled and engraved white metal birds head handle, concealed butt trap, small button releases dagger.

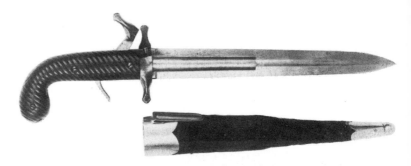

DOUBLE BARRELLED 80-BORE PERCUSSION DAGGER PISTOL. Barrels 3½in. The double edged spear pointed blade 8in, centrally fullered to facilitate loading, and stamped 'Dumouthier Brevet Dun', the two hammers being formed by the double quillons, and released by the concealed single trigger, which will release one hammer on the first pressure, and the remaining hammer on a second pressure. Horn pistol type fluted grips.

SPANISH COMBINATION PERCUSSION CUTLASS PISTOL 14½in. Heavy Bowie type clipped back blade 10in, scroll brass inlaid. 32-bore barrel 5½in with its original muzzle plug incorporating ramrod. The slab trigger and slab hammer together form the cross piece, heavy brass re-inforce at cross piece, chequered slab horn grip containing a pricker and a pair of tweezers.

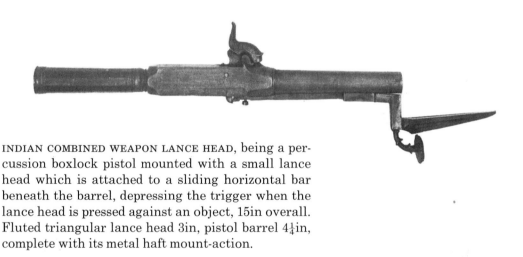

INDIAN COMBINED WEAPON LANCE HEAD, being a percussion boxlock pistol mounted with a small lance head which is attached to a sliding horizontal bar beneath the barrel, depressing the trigger when the lance head is pressed against an object, 15in overall. Fluted triangular lance head 3in, pistol barrel 4¼in, complete with its metal haft mount-action.

AXE PISTOL

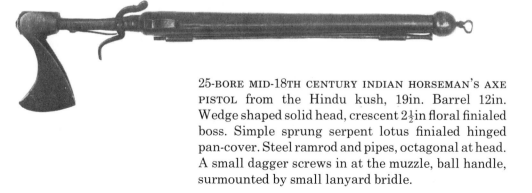

25-BORE MID-18TH CENTURY INDIAN HORSEMAN'S AXE PISTOL from the Hindu kush, 19in. Barrel 12in. Wedge shaped solid head, crescent 2½in floral finialed boss. Simple sprung serpent lotus finialed hinged pan-cover. Steel ramrod and pipes, octagonal at head. A small dagger screws in at the muzzle, ball handle, surmounted by small lanyard bridle.

BATON AND CANE PISTOLS

20-BORE UNDERHAMMER DAY'S PATENT PERCUSSION WALKING-STICK GUN 38in. Turn-off twist barrel 18½in, Birmingham proved, slight scroll engraved around breech, chequered butt. White metal escutcheon and plates.

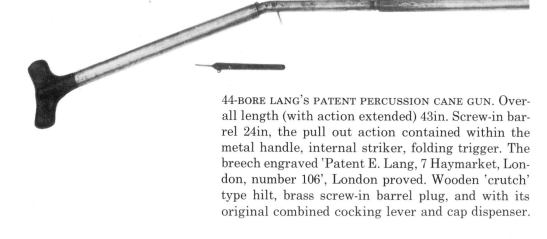

44-BORE LANG'S PATENT PERCUSSION CANE GUN. Overall length (with action extended) 43in. Screw-in barrel 24in, the pull out action contained within the metal handle, internal striker, folding trigger. The breech engraved 'Patent E. Lang, 7 Haymarket, London, number 106', London proved. Wooden 'crutch' type hilt, brass screw-in barrel plug, and with its original combined cocking lever and cap dispenser.

HARMONICA PISTOL

88-BORE SINGLE-ACTION 10-SHOT PINFIRE HARMONICA PISTOL by Jarre and Co, 10in. Smooth boresighted barrel 4¼in, octagonal breech engraved 'Ion Jarre a Paris', stamped 'Jarre and Cte Btes S.G.D.G.' around a lion couchant within an oval. This stamp recurs on the magazine. Both pistols and magazine are numbered 198. Deeply foliate engraved overall incorporating vine fruit clusters and tendrils. The magazine 5½in slides transversely through the frame and has a locked hinged plate across it to secure the pins. Two piece ebony grips.

MISCELLANIA – INCLUDING
EPROUVETTES AND TINDERLIGHTERS

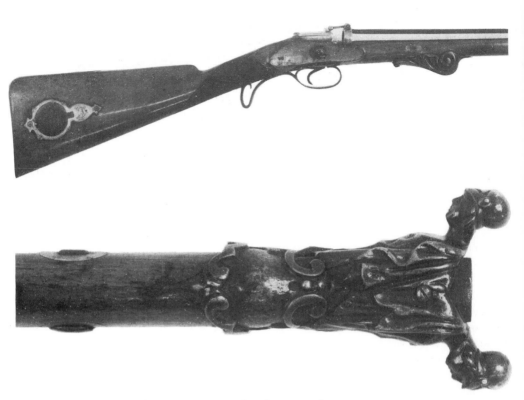

HODGE'S PATENT (1849) ELASTIC GUN 48in. Octagonal barrel slide 30in, engraved 'R. E. Hodges Patentee, Southampton Row, Russell Square, London', scroll engraved German silver sear-cover, brass classical heads at muzzle for securing elastic, engraved steel mounts including scrolled trigger guard, hinged trap in butt.

SEARLES PATENT FLINTLOCK ALARM GUN. A good quality flintlock lock attached to a wooden base, containing a 12-bore barrel 7½in, brass mounted at breech and muzzle. Bar attached to sear runs parallel to the barrel suspended by an iron hoop. The cock and sear stamped twice with crown and ' Patent Searles'. A most interesting weapon, possibly intended to be suspended from ceiling in imitation of an oil lamp, but when the cord is tripped, the barrel swings parallel to the intruder, discharging a charge at him.

INTERESTING AND STRONGLY MADE PERCUSSION ALARM by Wallis of Hull, 10in. Open-action, hammer cocked by double edged trip bar, cap fires bronze pot with heavy iron lid.

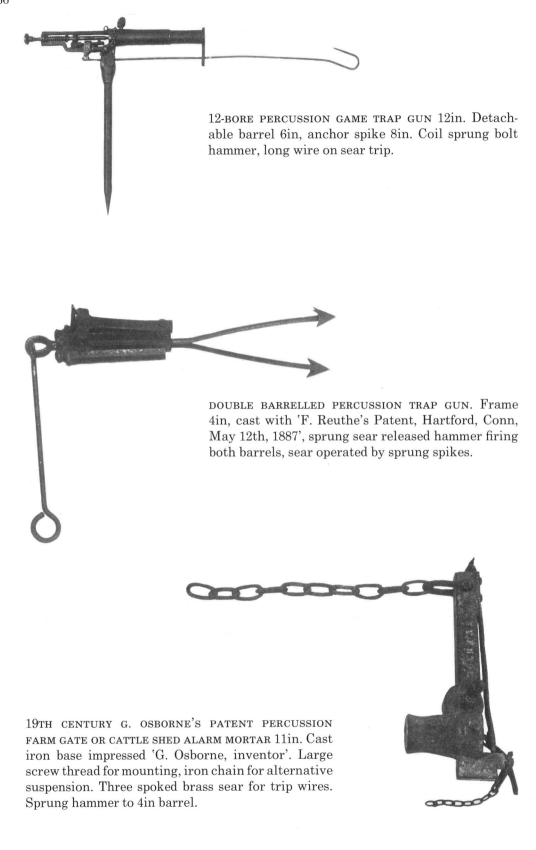

12-BORE PERCUSSION GAME TRAP GUN 12in. Detachable barrel 6in, anchor spike 8in. Coil sprung bolt hammer, long wire on sear trip.

DOUBLE BARRELLED PERCUSSION TRAP GUN. Frame 4in, cast with 'F. Reuthe's Patent, Hartford, Conn, May 12th, 1887', sprung sear released hammer firing both barrels, sear operated by sprung spikes.

19TH CENTURY G. OSBORNE'S PATENT PERCUSSION FARM GATE OR CATTLE SHED ALARM MORTAR 11in. Cast iron base impressed 'G. Osborne, inventor'. Large screw thread for mounting, iron chain for alternative suspension. Three spoked brass sear for trip wires. Sprung hammer to 4in barrel.

GEORGIAN MILITARY FLINTLOCK BOXLOCK CANNON
IGNITER $22\frac{1}{4}$in. Brass frame engraved with crowned
'GR' cypher and stamped with an ordnance
inspector's stamp. Brass pan with high fence on left,
hole on bottom right of pan for ignition, sunken frizzen spring, long lower frame spur integral with trigger guard. Rounded wooden stock flattened at grip.

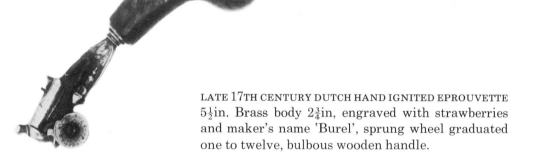

LATE 17TH CENTURY DUTCH HAND IGNITED EPROUVETTE
$5\frac{1}{2}$in. Brass body $2\frac{3}{4}$in, engraved with strawberries
and maker's name 'Burel', sprung wheel graduated
one to twelve, bulbous wooden handle.

HAND IGNITED EPROUVETTE $7\frac{1}{4}$in. The barrel $1\frac{1}{2}$in, by
G. and J. W. Hawksley, of lacquered brass with steel
wheel and turned ebonised handle. Probably late
19th century for use with cartridge re-loading equipment.

EARLY EPROUVETTE 7in. Hand ignited brass frame and numbered wheel, bulbous wooden handle.

EARLY WROUGHT IRON 18TH CENTURY POWDER TESTER 8in. Pierced open work toothed wheel spring controlled, with arm attached, with small pan-cover attached, the pan hand ignited, simple line gradings on wheel, on metal base with stylised bird's head terminal.

FLINTLOCK COTTAGE TINDERLIGHTER 7in. Brass box stamped 'T. Lee' (maker), simple cross hatch engraved top plate, side door, iron candle holder and support, slight incised wooden butt.

MID-18TH CENTURY FLINTLOCK COTTAGE TINDER-LIGHTER 7in. Brass frame and box with door, stamped 'Hinde', side candle holder, T-shaped rest, slab wooden butt.

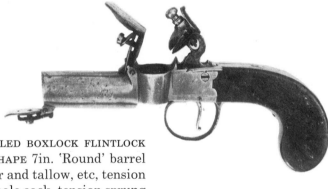

BRASS FRAMED AND BARRELLED BOXLOCK FLINTLOCK TINDERLIGHTER OF PISTOL SHAPE 7in. 'Round' barrel 2in, for holding flints, tinder and tallow, etc, tension sprung muzzle cap. Throat hole cock, tension sprung frizzen to avoid tinderbox. Slab walnut butt.

LATE 17TH OR EARLY 18TH CENTURY ENGLISH COTTAGE FLINTLOCK TINDERLIGHTER $5\frac{1}{2}$in. Enclosed box-lock action, side cock, rounded frizzen with round base on tub-shaped tinderbox. Rounded frame, frizzen spring fits beneath action. Rounded swollen walnut butt with carved perimeter.

MID-18TH CENTURY COTTAGE FLINTLOCK TINDER-
LIGHTER 7in. Rectangular brass frame by I. Savage,
external mechanism, brass candle holder, curved
wood butt.

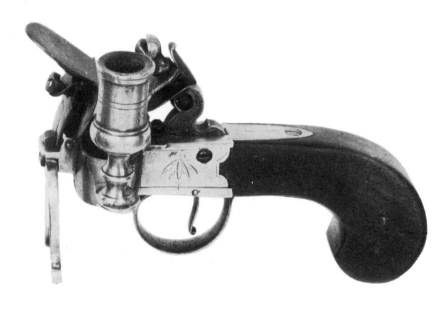

LATE 18TH CENTURY BRASS FRAMED FLINTLOCK BOX-
LOCK TINDERLIGHTER 5in, by Lewis and Jones. With
brass candle holder, stand, etc, slab sided wooden
butt.

RUSSIAN COMBINATION BOXLOCK FLINTLOCK PISTOL
AND TINDERLIGHTER 8in. Barrel $3\frac{1}{4}$in. Linear engraved
grip with foliate and floral engraving. Throat hole
cock, shovel over pan for tinder. Removes to reveal
breech vent. Linear engraved boxes with floral motif
to lids (en suite with butt) marked 'MYNA 1794',
boxes having slight engraved toes to feet. Boxes
removable by sliding scroll engraved trigger guard.

WEBLEY MK II SAFETY FUSE PISTOL, 1880 model, 7in.
Barrel $3\frac{1}{4}$in to hinged breech block, the frame and
screw-off barrel of bronze with short steel belt hook
on left side. Plain one piece butt with lanyard ring.
See also another example on p.258.

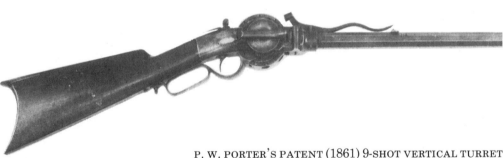

P. W. PORTER'S PATENT (1861) 9-SHOT VERTICAL TURRET
PILL LOCK REPEATING RIFLE 45in. Octagonal 34-bore
rifled barrel 26in to turret stamped 'Address P. W.
Porter, New York. P. W. Porter's Patent, 1861'.
Sights offset for side sighting, sprung top lever, rammer, side gate opening, under lever trigger guard
with sliding retaining catch, iron buttcap wood butt.

Powder Horns, Flasks and Cap Dispensers

To every musketeer his most important accessory, after his trusted weapon, was his powder flask. One of the simplest ways devised to carry powder was the bandolier. This was a belt which crossed over the musketeer's shoulder and had suspended along its length various wood or horn containers which held a meticulously measured amount of powder. This was an extremely simple solution to the loading problem, as all the musketeer had to do was pull off one container and tip the charge down the barrel. This system, however, had two major disadvantages. One was that it was very simple to set off the Roman Candle effect; one spark starting a chain reaction and, secondly, the bandolier was not suited to a surprise attack as the containers tended to get in the way.

This led some musketeers to prefer powder horns. The treated cowhorn was blocked at the wide end by a piece of wood and had an extremely clever measuring nozzle at the narrow end. This measuring device was spring-operated and measured the amount of powder required. Powder horns tended to be rather crudely decorated with hunting scenes. The horns were usually joined to a string which could be tied round the waist or worn as a bandolier over the shoulder, although a few had belt hooks and were carried dangling from the musketeer's belt. Many musketeers also carried a small horn in which they carried their priming powder.

With the introduction of the wheellock, flasks became much more richly decorated. Wheellocks were expensive weapons and the rich who patronised the gunmakers insisted on a much higher level of craftsmanship, both on the guns themselves and the accessories. Flasks were made in a variety of shapes and forms and using many materials but perhaps the most common was those using the Y section of an antler. The same spring-operated device was used to measure the powder and the two ends were blocked off with metal or wood.

The decoration on some of these flasks is quite exquisite. They are frequently carved with an elaborate hunting scene on a polished smooth surface. There were also intricate classical carvings and some inlay of high quality.

There was a gradual change to paper cartridges in the 17th century but this was mainly in the military sphere. In sporting circles the flask retained its popularity as it was felt necessary and 'right' to measure out each charge for an accurate shot. It was part of the tradition of the sport. Many flasks of this period were copper formed in a pear shape and often embossed with hunting scenes.

BRASS PERCUSSION CAP DISPENSER OF CIRCULAR FORM $2\frac{3}{4}$in. Knurled sunken borders, sprung dispensing with ratchet type internal coil, swivel suspension ring.

COPPER PERCUSSION CAP DISPENSER OF TEARDROP FORM $3\frac{3}{4}$in. Revolving boss embossed with cow and bull heads between shells, the inside stamped 'J. S. Bovy, Geneve'. One suspension ring, gravity dispensing.

BRASS CAP DISPENSER OF CIRCULAR FORM $3\frac{1}{2}$in. Stamped 'Ersebach 40', sunken ring borders, intercepting disc cover latch, coil sprung dispensing. Swivel suspension ring.

BRASS PERCUSSION CAP DISPENSER OF CIRCULAR FORM
2½in. Knurled borders, frontplate stamped 'Amorcoir
A L'y Garanti A Paris', sprung dispensing with numbered wheel indicating caps left, through pierced
window.

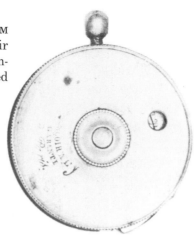

COPPER PERCUSSION CAP DISPENSER OF TEARDROP
FORM 3¾in. Revolving boss embossed with game ani-
mals and hunting trophies, the inside stamped 'J. S.
Bovy, Geneve', gravity dispensing.

WHITE METAL CAP DISPENSER OF TRUNCATED COMMON
FORM 3½in. The lid stamped 'Registered April 20, 1846
by James Dixon and Sons, Sheffield L.L.', gravity
dispensing with button release, swivel suspension
ring.

PLATED BRASS CAP DISPENSER OF BOAT FORM $3\frac{3}{4}$in. Hinged lid stamped 'Amorcoir A L'y Garanti a Paris', lid retaining hook stamped 'Number 3', gravity dispensing with button release, swivel suspension ring.

FLASKS

BAG-SHAPED COPPER POWDER FLASK of the type cased with percussion sporting guns, by G. and J. W. Hawksley, $6\frac{1}{2}$in.

CARVED COCONUT FLASK the surface decorated with medallions bearing hunting trophies, dead game, etc. The silver charger issuing from the mouth of a grotesque mask with inset ivory eyes.

PLATED POWDER FLASK 'MEDALLION'. Gilt panel with scene, by Dixon and Sons.

CONICAL TRANSLUCENT HORN POWDER FLASK. Brass charger unit, brass base with small crown 'GR' stamp.

COPPER BODIED POWDER FLASK. Embossed with hanging game in medallion, patent brass top.

EMBOSSED COPPER POWDER FLASK OF 'GUNSTOCK' FORM 5in. Embossed with acanthus borders and chequered Dixon patent top.

VERY LARGE BRASS POWDER FLASK embossed with buffalo hunter, buffalo and trophy of arms reverse. Patent brass top stamped 'G. and J. W. Hawksley, Sheffield'.

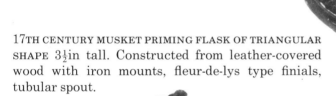

17TH CENTURY MUSKET PRIMING FLASK OF TRIANGULAR SHAPE $3\frac{1}{2}$in tall. Constructed from leather-covered wood with iron mounts, fleur-de-lys type finials, tubular spout.

GERMAN 17TH CENTURY CIRCULAR POWDER FLASK. Surface covered with circular inlaid bone patterns contained within metal inlaid borders and heightened with bone studded decoration. Diameter $4\frac{1}{4}$in central hole, two iron hanging rings, bone nozzle.

LEATHER-COVERED POWDER FLASK FROM A CASED RIFLE $8\frac{1}{2}$in. The patent top stamped 'Sykes Patent'. Sliding graduated charger (from 76–106 grains) with separate lever cut off.

17TH CENTURY COMBINATION WHEELLOCK SPANNER
AND POWDER FLASK OF FLATTENED FORM 14in. Staghorn base plug, wooden stopper with foliate mounted
triple spanner.

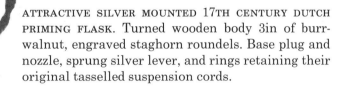

ATTRACTIVE SILVER MOUNTED 17TH CENTURY DUTCH
PRIMING FLASK. Turned wooden body 3in of burr-
walnut, engraved staghorn roundels. Base plug and
nozzle, sprung silver lever, and rings retaining their
original tasselled suspension cords.

LARGE 18TH CENTURY LEATHER POWDER FLASK 11in.
Flattened back, swollen belly, stitched seam with
suspension loops, well made brass screw top with
hinged locking lever.

FRENCH COPPER POWDER FLASK fitted with Boche Patent charger. Body decorated overall with star pattern, four hanging rings, marked at neck 'B.A. Paris'. Brass charger unit with glass side panels and horn nozzle slide.

NIELLOED SILVER MOUNTED CAUCASIAN PRIMING FLASK 5½in. Horn body, border nielloed silver mounts with gilt 'flower head' decoration, long bar charger.

THREE WAY COPPER POWDER FLASK OF OVAL SECTION from a cased pair of flintlock duelling pistols, circa 1790, 5in. Common charger, shell embossed hinged lid to ball compartment, swivel lid to flint compartment on base.

PERSIAN SHELL POWDER FLASK. Made from a large, curled mother of pearl shell extended by means of a band of nine flat shells supported by a framework of mother of pearl, the flat top covered with mother of pearl plaques in the form of a flower and with domed centre, original holding the charger. Two metal loops for attachment to belt.

UNUSUAL EARLY 17TH CENTURY COMBINED WHEELLOCK
PRIMING FLASK $7\frac{1}{4}$in. Mounted with two spanner keys
made from a chamois horn, brass mount with turned
charger, the keys with scrolled iron mounts.

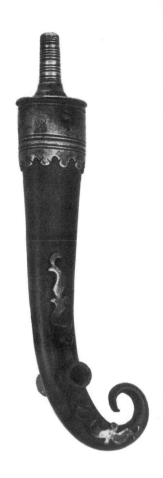

SILVER ARAB PRIMING FLASK with silver cut off.

LARGE 17TH CENTURY EUROPEAN TRIANGULAR MUSKET-EERS POWDER FLASK. Red velvet covered wooden body with steel sideplate decorated with two hounds and a mask, with belt hook.

EMBOSSED COPPER GUN FLASK. 'Dead Game' by Hawksley, Sheffield, German silver top with charger to three drams, with four hanging rings and carrying cords.

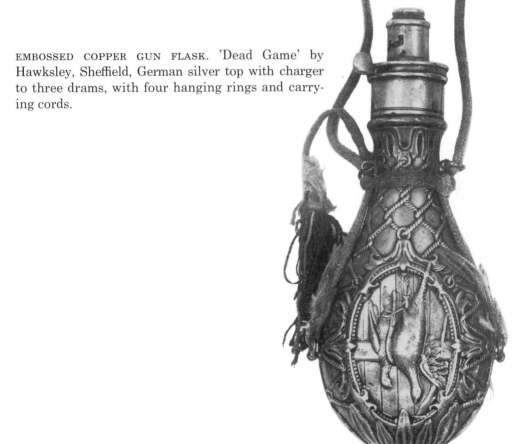

EMBOSSED COPPER GUN FLASK depicting hunter and animals descending from hill.

EMBOSSED COPPER GUN FLASK depicting dogs, oak leaves, stag and foxes heads.

EMBOSSED COPPER GUN FLASK depicting shell.

EMBOSSED BRASS GUN FLASK depicting entwined dolphins.

EMBOSSED COPPER GUN FLASK depicting game birds.

EMBOSSED FIDDLE PATTERN COPPER FLASK depicting game amid foliage.

EMBOSSED COPPER GUN FLASK depicting grapevines.

EMBOSSED COPPER GUN FLASK depicting flutes.

EMBOSSED COPPER GUN FLASK depicting dead game hanging.

EMBOSSED COPPER GUN FLASK depicting shell.

EMBOSSED SLIM COPPER GUN FLASK depicting laurel leaf borders.

EMBOSSED COPPER GUN FLASK depicting hobnail pattern and acanthus.

289

EMBOSSED COPPER GUN FLASK depicting scrolled trellising.

EMBOSSED COPPER GUN FLASK by P. Powell and Son, 'Cincinnatio' with beads, flutes and acanthus.

EMBOSSED COPPER GUN FLASK fluted sides.

EMBOSSED COPPER GUN FLASK depicting Greek classical scene.

FOLIATE EMBOSSED COPPER GUN FLASK.

EMBOSSED COPPER GUN FLASK depicting dog and dead game.

EMBOSSED COPPER GUN FLASK depicting flutes and acanthus.

EMBOSSED COPPER GUN FLASK depicting basket weave and acanthus.

EMBOSSED COPPER GUN FLASK depicting flowers and foliage.

EMBOSSED COPPER GUN FLASK depicting dog and hunter.

EMBOSSED COPPER GUN FLASK depicting stars, dots and acanthus.

EMBOSSED COPPER GUN FLASK depicting flutes and acanthus.

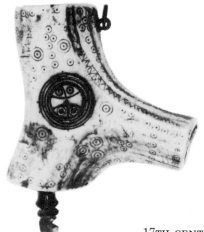

17TH CENTURY SCANDINAVIAN ANTLER FORK POWDER HORN. Surface engraved in circular geometric patterns, and crude animals, horn stopper.

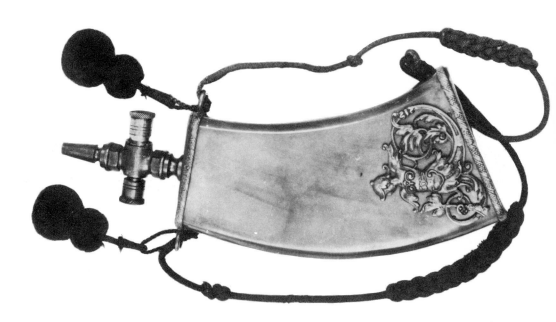

FRENCH MID-18TH CENTURY TRANSLUCENT HORN POWDER FLASK 13in, of flattened form. Elaborate turn-off copper charger unit, mounted with pierced design of a classical figure within scrolled foliage. Beaded brass mounts to base and top.

EARLY 19TH CENTURY CONTINENTAL POWDER HORN
with gilt metal mounts. Spring loaded plunger charger unit, turned baseplate with hanging ring 8½in.

FRENCH LATE 18TH CENTURY TRANSLUCENT CURVED
HORN POWDER FLASK fitted with Boche Patent
charger. Brass mounts, spring loaded, horn tipped
charger with grades on circular charger unit, four
hanging rings.

294

EARLY 19TH CENTURY ROYAL REGIMENT OF ARTILLERY
GUNNER'S PRIMING HORN 8in. Brass charger with
spring cut off. The brass base engraved 'R.R.A.
7B. 43' with two brass hanging loops and ribbon sus-
pender.

ENGRAVED STAGHORN POWDER FLASK probably for a
wheellock, 11in. Decorated with entwined dolphins,
stallions, stylised deep and geo-foliate borders, single
suspension loop, turned nozzle.

LATE 17TH CENTURY FLATTENED HORN POWDER FLASK
8½in, for a wheellock, with baluster charger and plain
wooden base. The centre of the body pierced with
rectangular key for spanning the wheellock, supported on each side by an engraved brass rosette.

EARLY 19TH CENTURY ENGRAVED POWDER HORN 15in,
with well executed contemporary scenes of fortress,
naval men-of-war, mounted officer, double headed
bird, town scenes, etc, and 'Wilm Bencley 3rd Gds'.
Most of scenes within circular borders.

Bibliography

General

BLACKMORE, H. 'Hunting Weapons'. London 1971.
  'Guns and Rifles of the World' London and New York 1965
BLAIR, C. 'European and American Arms'. London and New York 1962
  'Pistols of the World' London 1969
BOOTHROYD, G. 'The Handgun' London 1970
DOWELL, W. C. 'The Webley Story' Leeds 1962
DUNLAP, J. 'American, British and Continental Pepperbox Firearms' Palo Alto 1967
HAYWARD, J. F. 'Art of the Gunmaker' 2 vols. London, rev. ed. London 1964
HELD, R. 'The Age of Firearms' London 1959
HOGG, I. V. 'German Pistols and Revolvers' 1871–1945' London 1971
LENK, T. 'The Flintlock' ed. by J. T. Hayward. New York 1965
NEAL, W. K. and BACK, D. H. L. 'The Mantons, Gunmakers' New York and London 1967
SMITH, W. H. B. 'The Book of Rifles, London 1972
  'The Book of Pistols and Revolvers' London 1972
TAYLERSON, A. 'Revolving Arms' London 1967
  'The Revolver 1818–1865, 1865–1888, 1889–1914' 3 vols. London 1966–1970
WESLEY, L. 'Air-guns and Air-pistols' London 1955
WINANT, K. 'Early Percussion Firearms' London and New York 1961
WILKINSON, F. 'Antique Firearms' London 1969
  'British and American Flintlocks' London 1971
  'Flintlock Guns and Rifles' London 1971

British

BAILEY, D. W. 'British Military Longarms 1775–1815'. London 1971
  'British Military Longarms 1815–1865'. London 1972.
BLACKMORE, H. 'British Military Firearms 1650–1850' London and New York 1961
CAREY, A. M. 'English, Irish and Scottish Firearms Makers' New York 1967
ROADS, C. H. 'The British Soldier's Firearms, 1850–1864' London and New York 1964.

Glossary

Arquebus	an early musket, with a match-lock mechanism. Spelling variants – hagbut, harquebus or hackbut.
Blunderbuss	a weapon devised to scatter a large amount of shot at close range. It was a heavy, short weapon mainly used for self-defence.
Bombard	an extremely primitive form of cumbersome cannon used to propel stone-shot. It was an extremely large mortar which was made from long iron staves hooped around in the form of a barrel.
Bore	the internal diameter of the barrel of any firearm.
Break	the action of 'breaking' a shot-gun (breech-loading) into its three components for casing and also cleaning.
Caliver	a hand-gun, a short, useful early musket, with a matchlock mechanism.
Carbine	a musket used by the cavalry carrying the same ammunition and with the same bore as its infantry equivalent but due to the lack of bayonet much shorter.
Carbine bore	about .65in, hence slightly smaller than the classic musket bore.
Carbine-thimble	a stiff leather socket, secured to a D-ring on the off-side of the saddle by a strap and buckle, to receive the muzzle of the horseman's carbine.
Cartridge	a case of paper, flannel, parchment or metal, fitting the bore of a firearm and containing an exact charge of powder. It is called a ball cartridge when a projectile is used and a blank when there is none.
Chamber	the part of the bore of a firearm in which the charge lies. It is usually constructed slightly larger in diameter than the rest of the bore. In the earliest firearms this was detachable.
Chasing	the portion of the gun forward of the trunnions to the swell of the muzzle. In more modern firearms the swell is suppressed and the chase extends to the muzzle.
Chasing	a method of decorating metal, particularly popular on the ornate wheellocks.
Cock	an arm which in early firearms held the pyrites or flint between two jaws.

Corned Powder	this is purely the grinding down of gunpowder to suit its purpose; for cannon one required very coarse powder whereas for priming a hand gun one needed very fine powder. Corning of gunpowder started in the 16th century.
Damascus barrels	frequently called 'twist barrels' due to the spiral tapes of Damascus iron which bedecked the barrel.
Frizzen	the striking plate of a flintlock – it was a movable plate placed vertically above the pan of a gun-lock which combined with the opening of the pan-cover received the blow.
Full-cock	the term which denotes that the firearm is ready to fire with just pressure on the trigger.
Fulminate	mercuric fulminate – it explodes sharply on being struck, one kilogram of mercury will make fulminate sufficient for 40,000 caps. There are also fulminates of silver and gold but for obvious reasons they are seldom used! Fulminate of mercury is the basis of all percussion caps and the detonators of cartridges.
Guard	a part of a firearm which is solely there as a safety factor. There are many such 'guards' on firearms, i. the trigger guard ii. a safety lock of a fowling piece to prevent the accidental dropping of the hammer. iii. a nipple-shield which protects the tube which receives the percussion cap.
Gunpowder	Gunpowder had been known in China and India from a remote period of antiquity as an agent for blasting rock, but the powder referred to in this volume is an explosive mixture of saltpetre, sulphur and charcoal. Proportion 75–15–10. This powder is essential for old firearms and under no circumstances should Cordite (used from 1880) be used. The earlier powder is usually called black powder.
Half-cock	a slightly-raised position from which the cock cannot be released and accidental discharge was when a gun went off at half-cock.
Hammer	the arm which strikes the firing pin in hammer guns. This term is often erroneously used for the cock. In a snaphaunce mechanism the hammer was the striking plate.
Inlay	ornate materials placed into parts of the weapon for decoration; this took various forms at different times. Ivory was a great favourite in the stocks of 16th and 17th century firearms whereas in the fine quality pistols of the 19th century gold and platinum were used for touch-holes and aiming lines.
Lands	the projections inside a rifled barrel which are so designed to grip the bullet to rotate it as it is propelled up the barrel.

Lock	the firing apparatus of a gun – this is the actual mechanism which attached to the stock fires the charge. The lock was, in the early days of firearms, made by a specialist.
Mainspring	the powerful spring which operated the cock or hammer.
Match	in early firearms this was the means of ignition – it was a cord soaked in saltpetre and dried. When lit it was extremely difficult to put out and smouldered rather than burned.
Musket	the firearm of the infantry soldier for centuries. A smooth-bore, extremely heavy shoulder piece it was frequently laid across a staff or rest before firing. It was fired by match, wheel or flint being adapted to each new mechanism – it started life as a weapon of 5ft in length but by the end of the 18th century had been reduced to just over 3ft. The bore was a calibre of about .75in.
Nitro-proof	having NP stamped on the barrel, indicating that the firearm has 'stood proof' with cordite. Would be so marked by a proving officer with either a crown or crossed keys above. Cordite cannot be used in weapons which do not have this mark, as the explosion caused by cordite is much in excess of that of black powder.
Pan	basically the receptical for the priming powder. It could be either the powder cavity for the flintlock weapon or purely a slight indentation on top of the barrel directly above the touch hole on early weapons.
Priming	the combustible powder, which is of a finer grain than the main charge, which communicates fire to the main charge.
Proof	connected with nitro-proof above – this refers to tests done on a firearm where it was subjected to much heavier load of both powder and shot than it would have in actual use. This proofing of the firearm was done at the Tower of London.
Pull	the pressure required to cause the trigger to fire, this can be accurately assessed by a spring balance.
Pyrites	an isometric mineral occurring frequently crystallised – it strikes fire when struck with a hammer. Frequently called 'Fools Gold' it was used in the firing mechanism of wheellocks.

Rifling   the spiral grooving inside the barrel which makes the bullet have a rotatory motion. The rifling may be polygrooved as in the Armstrong, with only two grooves as in some early weapons, with the two grooves with the angles rounded away so as to produce an oval and yet twisted bore as in the Lancaster guns, or with three or more grooves as in more modern weapons. The grooves are of varying size, form or width and of different degrees of twist.

Sear   the pawl or pin that is pivoted in the gun-lock and enters the notches of the tumbler to hold the hammer at full or half-cock and is released by pulling the trigger in the act of firing. The half-cock notch is made so deep that the sear cannot be withdrawn by the trigger.

Sear spring   the spring which causes the sear to catch in the notch of the tumbler – to hold the sear in position and determine the weight of the 'pull' required to release it.

Spanner   the winding key which was used in the mechanism of the wheellock.

Stock   the part of a firearm to which the barrel and lock are attached – the wooden part of the weapon. (The Butt is the part of the stock behind the lock.)

Tang   a projection of metal which is there for fixing purposes – literally a tongue of metal.

Touch-hole   the priming hole or vent of a firearm which connects the priming with the main charge. So called as in early weapons the hole was touched with hot metal.

Trajectory   the path taken by a projectile after firing – in the case of a bullet a parabola. Usually applied to its maximum rise over a given distance.

Tumbler   the wheel in the interior of the lock by which the mainspring acts on the hammer causing it to fall and explode the cap. It also accommodated the sear at half or full-cock.

Turn-off Pistol   also called the screw pistol and more commonly the Queen Anne pistol – the barrel was made to screw off for loading.

Twist   the spiral in the bore of a rifle. It is spoken of as a $\frac{3}{4}$ twist etc as it completes that much, more or less, of a revolution in the length of the barrel. A rifle is also said to have a right-hand or a left-hand twist depending on whether the rifling is clockwise or anticlockwise.

Twist-over   a type of revolver which had an action of 'twisting-over' one barrel to bring the next one up to the lock. Two or more barrels could in this way be pivoted to the lock.

View/View mark   to examine a firearm very closely to determine any defect prior to going to proof. If the weapon passes the viewer he would stamp it with the View Stamp, normally a 'V' with the crown or crossed keys above.

List of Abbreviations

(commonly used in sale catalogue descriptions)

ASSTD	Assorted
BIRM	Birmingham
BL	Blade
BP	Black Powder
BRL	Barrel
BXLK	Boxlock
CAV	Cavalry
CENT	Century
CF	Centre Fire
CHEQD	Chequered
CHPD	Chipped
CIRC	Circular
CLRD	Coloured
CTGS	Cartridges
CYL	Cylinder
DA	Double Action
DAMAS	Damascus
DB	Double Barrelled
DE	Double Edge(d)
DIAM	Diameter
EIC	East India Company
FLK	Flintlock
FS	Field Service
GD	Guard
GEO	Georgian
GS	German Silver
HM	Hall Marked
INF	Infantry
JAP	Japanese
LACQ	Lacquer
LON	London
LR	Long Rifle
MAG	Magazine
MECH	Mechanism
MIL	Military
MIQ	Miquelet
MLK	Matchlock
MOP	Mother of Pearl
MSG	Missing
MTD	Mounted
MTS	Mounts

NP	Nitro Proved
OCT	Octagonal
ORIG	Original
O.R.'s	Other Ranks
O & U	Over and Under
OV	Overall
PERC	Percussion
PF	Pinfire
PG	Pistol Grip
PKT	Pocket
PTG	Pitting
PVD	Proved
REGTL	Regimental
REV	Revolver
RF	Rimfire
SA	Single Action
SB	Single Barrelled
S BY S	Side by Side
SCBD	Scabbard
SP	Sporting
STKD	Stocked
S & W	Smith & Wesson
TRAV	Travelling
TRIG	Trigger
VIC	Victoria
VOL	Volunteer
WM	White Metal
WT	Weight
WWI &	
WWII	World War I and II
YEO	Yeomanry